The Politics of
Constructionism

The Politics of Constructionism

edited by

Irving Velody and Robin Williams

SAGE Publications
London · Thousand Oaks · New Delhi

First published 1998

 SAGE Publications Ltd
6 Bonhill Street
London EC2A 4PU

SAGE Publications Inc.
2455 Teller Road
Thousand Oaks, California 91320

SAGE Publications India Pvt Ltd
32, M-Block Market
Greater Kailash - I
New Delhi 110 048

British Library Cataloguing in Publication Data
A catalogue record for this book is available from the British
Library

ISBN 0 7619 5041 9
ISBN 0 7619 5042 7 (pbk)

Library of Congress catalog card number 98–060207

Typeset by Type Study, Scarborough
Printed in Great Britain by Biddles Ltd, Guildford, Surrey

Contents

Part IV   The Politics of Constructionism

Notes on Contributors

Ian Burkitt lectures in sociology and social psychology in the Department of Social and Economic Studies, University of Bradford, UK. His research interests centre on social theory and the self, and he is author of *Social Selves: Theories of the Social Formation of Personality* (1991).

Wil Coleman is lecturing in sociology at the University of Manchester, UK. Prior to that he held temporary appointments in Manchester while completing his PhD which reflects his central interest in the philosophy of social science and social theory, with particular focus upon the topic of language.

Mitchell Dean is Associate Professor in Sociology at Macquarie University, Sydney, Australia. He is the author of *The Constitution of Poverty: Towards a Genealogy of Liberal Governance* (1991), *Critical and Effective Histories: Foucault's Methods and Historical Sociology* (1994) and *Governmentality* (forthcoming). He is co-editor of *Governing Australia* (with Barry Hindess, 1998).

Steve Fuller is Professor of Sociology at the University of Durham, UK. He is the founding editor of the journal *Social Epistemology*, and is the author of four books, the latest of which is *Science* (1997). He is completing a book-length study on the origins and impacts of Thomas Kuhn's *The Structure of Scientific Revolutions*.

Kenneth J. Gergen is Mustin Professor of Psychology, Swarthmore College, USA and the author of *Toward Transformation in Social Knowledge* (1994), *The Saturated Self* (1991), and *Realities and Relationships* (1994).

Ian Hacking teaches philosophy at the University of Toronto, Canada. His most recent books are *Rewriting the Soul* (1995), *Mad Travelers* (1998) and *The Social Construction of What?* (forthcoming).

Erica Haimes is Senior Lecturer in sociology in the Department of Social Policy at the University of Newcastle upon Tyne, UK. Her research interests are in the sociology of assisted conception and the sociology of identity. She is co-author of *Adoption, Identity and Social Policy* (with Noel Timm, 1985), co-editor (with Ken Daniels, 1998) of *International Social*

Science Perspectives on Donor Insemination and is working on the provisionally titled *Families and Identities*.

Pat Lovie is Senior Lecturer in Statistics at Keele University, UK. She is editor of the *British Journal of Mathematical and Statistical Psychology*, an associate editor of *Statistics and Computing* and a consulting editor to *History of Psychology*. Her publications are mainly in subjective judgement, decision-making and history of statistics.

Sandy Lovie is Senior Lecturer in Psychology at Liverpool University, UK. He is a former editor of the *British Journal of Mathematical and Statistical Psychology*, and now serves on the editorial board. His publications are mainly in the history of psychology and the psychology of science; he is the author of *Context and Commitment: A Psychology of Science* (1992).

Michael Lynch is Professor in the Department of Human Sciences, Brunel University, UK. Among his publications are *Scientific Practice and Ordinary Action: Ethnomethodology and Social Studies of Science* (1993) and *The Spectacle of History: Speech, Text and Memory at the Iran–Contra Hearings* (with D. Bogen, 1996).

Craig Mackenzie is visiting fellow at the Department of Psychology at Bath University, UK, where he was recently awarded a doctorate. He is responsible for developing ethical investment practice at Friends Provident, and seeks to implement pragmatist and neo-Aristotelian ethical theory in concrete business settings.

Philip Manning is an Associate Professor in the Department of Sociology at Cleveland State University, USA. He is the author of *Erving Goffman and Modern Sociology* (1992).

Thomas Osborne is lecturer in the Department of Sociology, University of Bristol, UK. He is the author of *Aspects of Enlightenment: Social Theory and the Ethics of Truth* (1988).

Paul A. Roth is a professor in the Department of Philosophy at the University of Missouri-St Louis, USA. He is the author of *Meaning and Method in the Social Sciences: A Case for Methodological Pluralism* (1987) and is working on a book on narrative as a form of explanation in history, anthropology and psychoanalysis.

Tom Shakespeare is a Research Fellow in the Department of Social Policy and Sociology at the University of Leeds, UK. He is an active member of the disability movement, co-author of *The Sexual Politics of Disability* (1996), and editor of *The Disability Reader* (1998).

Wes Sharrock, Professor of Sociology at Manchester University, UK, has published numerous studies on ethnomethodology and philosophy of social science, including *The Ethnomethodologists* (1986, with Bob Anderson).

Stephen Turner is Distinguished Research Professor of Philosophy at the University of South Florida, USA. His most recent books are *The Social Theory of Practices* (1994) and *Max Weber: The Lawyer as Social Thinker* (1994, with Regis Factor).

Irving Velody is editor of *History of the Human Sciences* and teaches in the Faculty of Economics and Social Science at the University of the West of England, UK. He has published widely on Weber, Foucault and political theory.

Robin Williams, Senior Lecturer in the Department of Sociology and Social Policy at the University of Durham, UK, has been review editor of *History of the Human Sciences* since its inception. He has contributed numerous papers on sociological theory and is currently completing a book-length study on the sociology of identity.

Introduction

Irving Velody and Robin Williams

A characteristic feature of the human sciences is their eager responsiveness to conceptual and linguistic innovation. New terminologies and their underlying theoretical presuppositions are in constant movement across both time and disciplinary boundaries. The life of some of these innovations has been fleeting, attracting few users and securing only local influence. Others have had longer periods of popularity, gaining a sufficiently strong hold to last for more than a decade or so and attracting scholarly interest from a variety of differing human science enterprises. The more successful have provided a vocabulary for more than a single generation of prac-titioners, appearing regularly in book and paper titles as well as course and textbook section headings that guide how students are taught the develop-ing elements of a disciplinary culture. Perhaps the pinnacle of such successes – reserved for the especially attractive – has been the creation of a newly minted currency accepted as a token of exchange in the wider intellectual economy outside the confines of the specialized academic communities responsible for its initial design.

Some of these innovations have been predominantly terminological: they permit a characterization of a type – or a classification of several types – of society, culture, social process or social action (modernity, capitalism, globalization, rationality). Others provide something broader than this – a 'theoretical stance' or 'style of work' for one or several human science disciplines or sub-disciplines (structuralism, historicism). Both innovatory types, however, involve more basic presuppositions concerning the nature of the objects under examination as well as appropriate practices of investigation, description, interpretation and explanation in one or several realms of the social. The richest – and therefore most contested – of such innovations have both established an object of inquiry and asserted the limits of inquiry itself. 'Postmodernity' is a good example of this latter kind.

Needless to say, the rise and fall of such innovations can be explained both logically and ideologically and there are social and political impli-cations as well as cognitive ones in their acceptance and use.[1] Exploration of the origins, possibilities and limits of such conceptual developments is part of the stock-in-trade of reflexive human science practitioners and such an exploration is the aim of this volume. In this case the conceptual innovation is represented by the rather awkward neologism 'social constructionism'. The popularity of this term has grown remarkably over the last decade, and there are no signs that its growth is set to diminish. Exactly what the term signifies, however, remains an open question, and a clear and uncontested formulation of its lineage and usages remains to be written.[2] While many self-described social constructionist studies cite the work of Berger and Luckmann (1967) as seminal, the phenomenological character of their particular perspective is rarely sustained, and there are many more such studies in which the work of Kuhn (1962), Foucault (e.g. 1977) or Garfinkel (1967) are declared to be of greater genealogical significance.

This introduction will not attempt to provide a definitive history of social constructionism. We very much doubt whether such an account could ever be written, but it is certainly too early to attempt it now. We will, however, offer an opening definition of the term and indicate what seem to us to have been the major issues and arguments surrounding its deployment.

Agreeing with Lynch (this volume), we see social constructionism as 'a useful term to collect together studies with eclectic surface affinities'. While the degree of agreement below this surface level is somewhat contested, it may be useful to begin with a version of constructionism which is optimistic in its perception of existing agreement and future potential. The following definition has been provided by one of the foremost and confident adherents of the position, Kenneth Gergen:

> Drawing importantly from emerging developments most prominently in the history of science, the sociology of knowledge, ethnomethodology, rhetorical studies of science, symbolic anthropology, feminist theory and post-structuralist literary theory, social constructionism is not so much a foundational theory of knowledge as an anti-foundational dialogue. Primary emphases of this dialogue are based on: the social-discursive matrix from which knowledge claims emerge and from which their justification is derived; the values/ideology implicit within knowledge posits; the modes of informal and institutional life sustained and replenished by ontological and epistemological commitments; and the distribution of power and privilege favoured by disciplinary beliefs. Much attention is also given to the creation and transformation of cultural constructions: the adjustment of competing belief/value systems: and the generation of new modes of pedagogy, scholarly expression and disciplinary relations. (Gergen, 1995a: 20)

A number of features of Gergen's definition are taken up by the contributors to this volume and we will discuss them later, but it is worth noting now the most significant assertion he makes: that constructionism is 'not another foundational theory of knowledge but an anti-foundational dialogue'. This goes to the heart of any attempt to situate and evaluate the contribution of this approach within the human sciences. The chapters in this volume contribute to such a dialogue not by an easy commendation or condemnation of the project(s) of constructionism but by considering its nature and promise from a number of differing positions. Some supporters – and critics – do indeed commend the constructionist impulse as anti-foundational in the way that Gergen suggests; others are sceptical about the nature or the implications of its claim to an anti-foundationalist stance; a third group asserts that such a commitment is an unnecessary feature of construction-ism in the first place and that the merits of the approach rest on a different basis altogether. There are difficulties in coming to an agreed position on this, like most of the other matters covered in Gergen's definition, since not all of those who claim an allegiance to constructionism hold the same views on its logic or relevance. In addition there are a number of important critical positions external to constructionism itself which merit consider-ation. This collection contains a wide range of such views; some contribu-tors are more optimistic in their evaluations than others, but whatever the particular arguments advanced, all are united in the view that a consider-ation of the strengths and weaknesses of this loose assemblage will add colour and depth to our ability to think about the subject matter and methods of the human sciences.

Constructionism and Epistemological Critique

The apparent commitment of (some) constructionists to relativism and ontological scepticism has done much to generate an air of irritable suspicion amongst many outside and some within the 'movement' (to use Fuller's chosen collective noun). For Bhaskar (1993), for example, con-structionism offers a conceptual reduction: 'existence' becomes 'human knowledge',[3] and assertions of the blindness or ambivalence of construc-tionism to extra-cognitive features of the social have been made by others. In some ways these attacks are puzzling since two of the writers most often thought to be relevant to constructionist writing – Foucault and Kuhn – have provided important resources for helping us in the analysis of 'thought as a non-subjective domain' (Foucault) and in the analysis of the non-cognitive factors in the growth of scientific knowledge. Be that as it may, there remain suspicions concerning the degree of epistemological scepti-cism amongst the broad range of constructionists. Critiques advanced by Roth, Turner, Lynch and Coleman and Sharrock (this volume) also target this weakness in some constructionist writings. Roth and Turner castigate constructionists for the relativist pretensions of their approach, while at the same time pointing to the way in which inconsistently non-relativist conclusions are arrived at within the majority of such studies. Both Roth and Turner also argue that constructionist stories can be translated into simpler languages of narrative and historical accounting without serious loss and that therefore constructionism is characterized by its tendency to unnecessary conceptual inflation. For the latter three writers, however, the argument is very different from that of Bhaskar, Roth or Turner. Lynch argues that the anti-objectivist stance of some constructionist writers embodied in their accounts of a 'semblance of reality' continues to be underpinned by a referential view of language and that this has resulted in the simple substitution of one shaky version of what makes things 'seem' real for another ('practices' simply replace 'thoughts'). Coleman and

Sharrock's position is that the phenomenological foundations of constructionism exemplified by Berger and Luckmann's work have been misappro-
priated or misunderstood by some of those who seek to stand on them.
What Berger and Luckmann proposed was not an epistemological
corrective to scientism or to scientific realism, but a type of analysis which
would   like all phenomenological analysis – 'leave everything as it is'. The
point of phenomenology (at least the phenomenology of Schutz and his
followers) is not to produce a sceptical view of reality but rather to establish
the grounds on which we claim certainty for our knowledge of reality.[4] If
the invitation to correct is resisted, the sociological potential of constructionism may more effectively be realized. Lynch is similarly concerned to
point out that little in the text licenses the 'epistemic, reflexive or political
uses' of more recent constructionist writing and speculates on the decision
of Berger and Luckmann to jettison the more conventional phenomenological term 'constitution' in favour of the term which will preoccupy most
of the contributors to this volume.

The main location for working out these disputes has been the study of
scientific practice. While a number of chapters focus on this important
strain of constructionist work, we have sought to consider disputes and
claims concerning the application of constructionism in other disciplinary
contexts. Writings that we think of as sympathetic to constructionism
exemplify a range of positions concerning the question of epistemology.
For some in this volume (e.g. Lynch, Coleman and Sharrock), care needs to
be exercised in distinguishing the work of 'professional epistemologists'
whose declarations concerning the status of knowledge may well be naturalized or 'respecified' from the work of 'lay epistemologists' whose practices
constitute what may be known of human intersubjectivity. For others (e.g.
Dean, Haimes and Williams), constructionism is neither an epistemology
nor a sociological substitute for epistemology but a technique or mode of
analysis. Fuller on the other hand appeals to constructionists to 'allow the
realist conception of knowledge to devolve openly' in their work even if
scientifically generated knowledge is granted the status of 'justified true
belief'. This appeal, however, seems to be based on non-epistemological
grounds since his notion of 'simulated realism' is offered as necessary
largely to advance the highly politicized constructionism that he, along
with Shotter, Gergen and Shakespeare, wants further to promulgate.

Realist Residua

A number of the contributors are concerned with the question of what, if
anything, is conceded to remain 'unconstructed', outside the domain of
constructionism proper. For many of those discussed or who have written
the chapters in this collection, the question of the 'residually real' has come
to replace the search for ghostly yet transcendental causal presences behind
the appearances of the social. In the chapter by Lovie and Lovie, the

seemingly technical issue of the treatment of 'outliers' in statistics can best be understood as an attempt by those who present and analyse statistical data to 'ward off serious challenges to their power as experts at dealing with (or even transcending) uncertainty. This type of assertion is a fairly standard one within constructionist studies of science – characteristically, argues Lynch, the 'accent of reality' is removed from the operation of the 'constructors' but 'retained for the analyst's stand towards the disputes themselves'. This latter, as he points out, are treated as real social events which are to form the objects of the interpretation offered. But whether this residuum consists of 'actors', 'communication', 'dialogue', 'power', 'practices' or 'relationships' many – if not all – constructionists remain tied to a predicative sociological programme of one kind or another. Such predications are of course necessary for the conduct of inquiry but what is not necessary, according to some contributors to this collection, is their deployment in a general theory or explanation of reality – either social or natural.[5] This issue is raised in a number of different ways, for example, Burkitt and Shakespeare are concerned with the role of the 'material' in constructionist thought. The former seeks to supplement 'linguistic constructionalism' by incorporating arguments from Ilyenkov and Latour in which increased attention is given to the creation and deployment of material artefacts in social life as well as to the material contexts within which social action is necessarily located. Shakespeare also argues for the necessity of dealing with the material world within social constructionism, arguing the necessity to theorize the nature of the biological as part of the necessary and limiting material context of possible constructions. Both of these differ from the view of Haimes and Williams that the division between the social and the natural is a shifting and unstable one. They are thus concerned with the idea of the residuum as such as well as with the permeability of the boundary between unconstructed nature and the constructed social. Their own solution to this issue promotes a kind of 'respecification' of the distinction as one which is capable of empirical examination in particular historical contexts. Likewise, Hacking's concerns with the logic of the metaphor of constructionism forces him to argue that we need to think hard both about the idea of the raw materials from which constructions are assembled and about the assembly processes themselves. This is something best done through the study of particular events or constructions rather than in any generalized theoretical way.

The Accent of Constructionism

Coleman and Sharrock offer an important distinction for those who want to evaluate the claims and achievements of constructionism. They are concerned with the difference between a causal answer and a conceptual answer to the question, 'What makes something knowledge?' The latter answer – the answer they seek to pursue in their own work – directs attention away from the issue of veridicality and speaks in a constitutive accent, being concerned to 'give an account of what we are saying about something when for example we say that we know it'. This Wittgensteinian emphasis seems to us to signal an important sub-version of the constructionist stance and it is at odds with a good deal of the science studies tradition that has provided the highest profile of all variants of constructionism in the past decade. Manning contrasts two kinds of social constructionist writing: 'procedural', which generates detailed descriptions of naturally occurring events and which seeks to produce an account of the underlying orderliness of such events; and 'reflexive', in which explicit attention is paid to the process of analysis itself. The dependence of the latter kind on the accent of literary studies stands in marked contrast to what they see to be the realist (if fictional) ambitions of the 'proceduralists'.

For some of our contributors constructivism in either of these two basically interpretative modes is incomplete. Fuller, looking back to the history of the tradition of hermeneutic scholarship in the human sciences, argues that 'whenever interpretation is promoted as a field of study it is typically done in order to foster a sense of ambiguity or scepticism amongst those who would otherwise act in a decisive but presumably coarse manner'. Referring to interpretation as 'a temporizing gesture', he is impatient for constructionist studies of science to be brought into play in a public debate on the status and role of scientific knowledge and intervention in the contemporary world (see also Fuller, 1992; 1993; 1994). Gergen is similarly of the view that constructionism has passed through its 'critical moment' and is ready to take on a 'generative' role in 'offering an orientation towards creating new futures, an impetus to social transformation' (Gergen, 1995b).

Constructionism and Politics

The title of this collection announces our interest in what we have called 'the politics of constructionism'. We use this phrase to draw attention both to the politically informed nature of the growth of interest in constructionist thought and also to the repercussions of constructionist themes on the understanding and practice of politics itself.[6]

Both Shakespeare and Gergen offer accounts of the relevance of political movements and political attractions of constructionism. Both see the potential of constructionism as critique which can be utilized by a variety of political groups and, indeed, is influenced by them. Certainly, there were common influences on constructionist thought in its more expansive mode and on the social movements of the 1960s and 1970s: these were later to come into closer alignment with constructionism. This link is especially noticeable in the field of science studies and in studies in the construction of self and identity. In contrast, Osborne's chapter advocates the analysis of the construction of 'expertise' as such, especially expertise in the human sciences. He seeks to do this as part of a Foucault-like concern with how humans are 'subject to authority' whether or not the authority in question is constitutive of our being. Some constructivists – including some contributing to this volume – argue that constructionism invites the possibility of a positive and active political stance and are eager to initiate the possibility of a restoration of the public sphere. Most notable in this respect is Kenneth Gergen who, in an earlier discussion, has argued for a reconstitution of 'identity politics' based on a 'relational turn in social constructionism'. Here Gergen seeks to re-found politics on the basis of a 'relational' theory of the formation of human subjects (Gergen, 1995b). Shakespeare also contrasts the traditional uses of essentialist difference arguments to justify subordination with the subordination with the potential for constructionist arguments for a more egalitarian and progressive democratic structure. Political theorists are likely to see little novelty in the recognition of the primordially social nature of the individual self (and therefore a politics based on such a view). After all, the axis of the contemporary debate between liberals and communitarians turns largely on differing images of the human subject.[7] One element of such images has to do with the proposed nature of human competences and the necessity for framing political arrangements in the light of those capacities. Burkitt's argument takes one of the clear positions within that debate, arguing for a parallel between a 'relational and communicative view of the world' and a 'broadly based polity where there is democratic access to debate and government'. Mackenzie's chapter also takes up the liberal–communitarian distinction arguing that, while the 'interpretative' turn in political theory permits its advance from abstract and timeless assertions concerning the nature of individual and collective human kind, it continues to lack the 'local, empirical, social constructionist historicism' that Hacking has recommended. Fuller's contribution to this volume also emphasizes the political possibilities inherent in constructionism while criticizing the relative absence of the realization of these possibilities in constructionist studies of science to date. His chapter urges us to consider the possibility of the 'emergence of social inquiry as a social movement', a deeply ambitious project in which this particular 'discourse field' would generate sufficient resources to enable it to participate directly in large-scale cultural change. No other contributor to this volume would seek to vault so high.

The Politics of Constructionism

While a persistent theme in the history of the human sciences has been the search for a unified epistemological field of operation in which social and political disciplinary trajectories could work in harmony – at one time celebrated by positivist and neo-positivist sociology on the one hand and by the 'behavioural revolution' in political science on the other – a countervailing theme has been the impossibility, perhaps danger, of the pursuit of such a project.

The difficulty of the attempt to bring together political and social accounting practices can be shown in the disjunctions displayed in the following passages. Contrast:

> There are three pure types of legitimate authority. The validity of their claims may be based on 1. rational grounds. 2. traditional grounds. 3. charismatic grounds. . . . The fact that none of these pure types is usually found in historical cases in 'pure' form, is naturally not a valid objection to attempting their conceptual formulation in the sharpest possible form. (Weber, 1964: 328–9)

with:

> Surely, politics is made with the head, but not with the head alone in this the proponents of an ethic of ultimate ends are right. One cannot prescribe to anyone whether he should follow an ethic of absolute ends or an ethic of responsibility. . . . Politics . . . takes both passion and perspective. (Gerth and Mills, 1993: 127–8)

As is now generally recognized, Weber saw both of these realms, the political and the social, as matters of vital interest to an understanding of the direction and possibilities of Western society.

In Weber's research innovation – a methodological procedure which has been called the only one developed for sociology, the application of ideal types to the understanding of social processes – we can see that the essential nominalism of this practice is but a verion of what is here called social constructionism. But how is this kind of practice related to questions of ethical and political choice and practice? Does constructionism offer a contribution to any of the currently available programmes seeking to unify epistemology and politics?

Some clearly believe that it can. As Chantal Mouffe writes:

> for we feminists committed to a political project whose aim is to struggle against the forms of political subordination that exist in many social relations and not only in those linked to gender, an approach that permits us to discuss how the subject is constructed through different discourse and subject positions is certainly more adequate than one that reduces our identity to one position – be it class, race or gender. (1993: 88)

A popular resource for such a project has been Foucault's work. As he says: 'It is a matter of shaking this false self-evidence, of demonstrating its precariousness, of making visible not its arbitrariness, but its complex interconnection with a multiplicity of historical processes, many of them of recent date' (1991: 75). His strategy of uncovering the conventional beneath the natural offers a useful political as well as explanatory resource.

While Foucault adopts a stance which avoids, perhaps evades, the ghostly and ontological question of what ultimately is there (is there really madness?), the work of many of his epigones has moved rapidly toward the re-establishment of concepts like ideology under the guise of exposing the limits of humanism through textual and discursive analysis. Of course the notion, if not the word itself, of *Ideologiekritik* is quite central to these covert operations aimed at discerning conspiratorial causal mechanisms.

However, while constructionism seems available for some kinds of political service, its own corrosive tendencies mean that it will be an unreliable element in any attempt to underpin conventional political interventions. Hacking's work offers fruitful suggestions for thinking about the relationship between the epistemological and the political from within constructionism. He links the realms of the political to other social science projects in a way quite different to those strategies that previously led to the subordination of one or other of the undertakings.

Hacking is concerned to distinguish between the relevance and application of different kinds of constructivist practice. His chapter argues that one such type undertakes to extend our knowledge of inanimate nature; as a practice this involves a kind of unmasking which as Hacking notes has metaphysical aims, and is not untypical of much of the sociology of scientific knowledge (or, to use the standard abbreviation, SSK) style of work. However, a second type focuses on ideas about people, knowledge of people. It is through an examination of those practices which involve the interaction of people that constructivism has a political point to make: to show how categories of knowledge are indeed used in power relations.

In spite of the apparent micro-issues with which his studies are concerned (e.g. 1988; 1992; 1995), Hacking is continuously able to relate his investigations to large-scale, indeed political, questions. Further, he is enabled to do this by an adroit but cunningly limited application of constructivist strategies able to examine on text and the discourse of experts, clients and other participants in the scenes described.

Key examples of this strategy can be found in his analysis of False Memory Syndrome and in the papers relating to the phenomenon of child sexual abuse (Hacking, 1991; 1994). In developing this account there are two significant points to observe. First we must register, and take note of, the constructed nature of social themes: child sexual abuse has a history and indeed a beginning. Its appearance can be perceived in the medical literature of the 1970s and its rapid growth observed and noted in legal, psychiatric and further medicalization procedures. But is it really there? This is the question parallel to the aggressive natural scientist questioning of SSK work on science: 'But is science only a social construct?'

Before even attempting to sketch a candidate answer to this type of question it is necessary to take a second step with Hacking. For his investigations go on to raise questions about the adequacy of the claims in their own terms (i.e. the terms of the debate of the Western tradition of rational exchange and accounting) which are used in substantiating such warrant to memory and recall.[8] In this way Hacking (like Foucault) is laying claim to matters of legitimation and truth-telling in the world. For although sociologists are not psychiatrists they are quite prepared to express statements that effectively subvert some claims that might be made by the medico-psychiatric professions.

Hacking and researchers like him are in a pivotal position to affect the kinds of claims and counter-claims that may be made in the public and professional domains concerned with the character of child sexual abuse. For the counter-versions (repressed memory; the chemical impact of molecular structures on social process) can be seen to have direct links to professional training and practice concerned with these matters. Just as the literature of social causation has played a central role in offering explanations – and solutions – for social issues ranging from crime to homelessness, so it must be recognized that new kinds of perspectives – say those stemming from Foucault's vision and the constructionist undertaking more generally – will have consequences in the training and appropriation of techniques for new generations of social workers, teachers, reformers, political activists and others with a pragmatic concern with the social. Here, terms like 'training', 'practice' and 'appropriation of techniques' do not require some further occult machinery to give sense to either these particular expressions or to Hacking's work as a whole.

Perhaps then there is room for dispute about Gergen's claim that '[a]s a metatheoretical outlook, constructionism is deeply pluralistic. There are no foundational grounds for discrediting any form of discourse'. For the dissolution of foundations does not necessarily entail the fearful chaos of 'anything goes'. Nor does it legitimize the claim – again Gergen's – that every voice needs to be heard. Let us recall our comment earlier, that Hacking's discussion takes place within 'the terms of the debate of the Western tradition of rational exchange and accounting'. To put it otherwise: while the empirical conduct of research, analysis and publication may bear but a distant relation to formal claims about these matters and the outcome of such investigations may not necessarily conform to pre-judged formulations of the way of the world, nevertheless this is but to note that there is a multitude of powers and forces which deny the possibility of a sheer contingency of knowledge production.

It is worth noting the convergence of some forms of constructionist undertaking with Lyotard's classic formulation of postmodernism as 'scepticism towards grand narratives'. Hacking's detective work on the sudden appearance of the term 'child sexual abuse' in the textbooks and the disappearance of 'child cruelty' are indicative of the politics of narrative constructions – and reconstructions. Similarly Mitchell Dean notes in his chapter that 'Foucault is concerned with the way in which the mechanisms, rituals, and techniques of truth (and falsity) vary historically'. That is, there is both a diachronic and a synchronic aspect to such constructionist goals. It is then no accident that the chapters in this collection are discursive in style. If we use the earlier examples from Weber's writing as a guide, the writing in this collection can be expected to resemble more the essay form in 'Politics as a Vocation' than the formalism of *The Theory of Social and Economic Organization*. Is there then a further set of political issues to consider: the politics of inscription? We leave this question to the reader. . . .

Conclusion

We have suggested that there are serious questions concerning the overall shape and consistency of 'social constructionism'. None of those who have contributed to this collection are confident that there is one single stance or position that can exemplify the work of those that it seems reasonable to include under this umbrella heading, and this is not seen as a simple problem of perspectival difference. We began with Gergen's attempt at an inclusive definition. It may be useful to conclude with Lynch's more limited observation:

> the word construction therefore is a pivotal term because it provides an initial hook that captivates adherents, encouraging them to invest their theoretical, methodological and political hopes in an academic approach or movement. But it can be confusing when adherents try to replace the eclectic surface affinity which facilitated the success of constructionism in the first place with something deeper and more coherent. (Lynch, this volume: 29)

Notes

1 An example of a recent text on social theory which is concerned to explain changes in this domain by reference to both logical and ideological factors is Alexander (1996).

2 The whole question of writing the history of constructionism remains a vexed question. See Lynch's chapter in this volume for an interesting attempt to deal with this.

3 See Burkitt (this volume) and Shotter (1993) for a discussion of Bhaskar's views.

4 See Sharrock and Anderson (1991) for a fuller discussion of this point.

5 Here perhaps Foucault and Garfinkel may be in agreement.

6 In addition to several chapters in this volume, there are interesting contributions to the collection edited by Calhoun (1994). These can be read for general treatments of this topic.

7 There are many collections of essays on this theme, but see Strong (1992) for one of the most useful.

8 Similar issues are taken up in his paper on multiple personality disorder (Hacking, 1991).

References

Alexander, Jeffrey C. (1996) *Fin de Siècle Social Theory: Relativism, Reduction and the Problem of Reason*. London: Verso.

Berger, Peter and Luckmann, Thomas (1967) *The Social Construction of Reality*. London: Allen Lane.

Bhaskar, Roy (1993) 'Afterword', in John Shotter, *Conversational Realities: Constructing Social Life through Language*. London: Sage.

Calhoun, Craig (ed.) (1994) *Social Theory and the Politics of Identity*. Oxford: Blackwell.

Foucault, Michel (1977) *Discipline and Punish*. London: Allen Lane.

Foucault, Michel (1991) 'Questions of method', in G. Burchell, C. Gordon and P. Miller (eds), *The Foucault Effect: Studies in Governmentality*. Hemel Hempstead: Harvester Wheatsheaf.

Fuller, Steve (1992) *Social Epistemology*. Bloomington, IN: Indiana University Press.

Fuller, Steve (1993) 'Social constructivism teaching itself a lesson: science studies as a social movement', *Danish Yearbook of Philosophy*, 28: 47–60.

Fuller, Steve (1994) 'The reflexive politics of constructivism', *History of the Human Sciences*, 7: 87–93.

Garfinkel, Harold (1967) *Studies in Ethnomethodology*. Englewood Cliffs, NJ: Prentice-Hall.

Gergen, Kenneth J. (1995a) 'Metaphor and monophony in the 20th-century psychology of emotions', *History of the Human Sciences*, 8 (2): 1–23.

Gergen, Kenneth J. (1995b) 'Social construction and the transformation of identity politics', htpp://www.swarthmore.edu/SocSci/kgergen1/text8.html.

Gerth, H. and Mills, C.W. (eds) (1993) *From Max Weber: Essays in Sociology*. London: Routledge & Kegan Paul.

Hacking, Ian (1988) 'The sociology of knowledge about child abuse', *Nous*, 22: 53–63.

Hacking, Ian (1991) 'The making and moulding of child abuse', *Critical Inquiry*, 17: 253–88.

Hacking, Ian (1992) 'Multiple personality disorder and its hosts', *History of the Human Sciences*, 5: 3–31.

Hacking, Ian (1994) 'Memoro-politics, trauma and the soul', *History of the Human Sciences*, 7: 1–32.

Hacking, Ian (1995) *Rewriting the Soul: Multiple Personality and the Sciences of Memory*. Princeton, NJ: Princeton University Press.

Kuhn, Thomas (1962) *The Structure of Scientific Revolutions*. Chicago: University of Chicago Press.

Mouffe, Chantal (1993) *The Return of the Political*. London: Verso.

Sharrock, Wes and Anderson, Bob (1991) 'Epistemology: professional scepticism', in Graham Button (ed.), *Ethnomethodology and the Human Sciences*. Cambridge: Cambridge University Press. pp. 51–76.

Shotter, John (1993) *Conversational Realities: Constructing Life through Language*. London: Sage.

Strong, Tracy B. (ed.) (1992) *The Self and the Political Order*. Oxford: Blackwell.

Weber, Max (1964) *The Theory of Social and Economic Organization*. New York: Free Press.

PART I
FORMULATING CONSTRUCTIONISM

1
Towards a Constructivist Genealogy of Social Constructivism

Michael Lynch

Genealogies of academic fields typically take the form of disciplinary histories. They specify legacies of ancestors, founders and followers linked together by ideas and scholastic connections. Disciplines (or schools, literatures, perspectives, approaches, epistemic communities, movements, etc.) are thus defined predominantly in terms of individual cognitive achievements. Although it is always possible to outline a genealogy of constructivism along such lines, to do so is incommensurable with the emphasis on social practice and cognitive disunity that is so prominent in constructivist accounts. Constructivists openly espouse multivocality and anti-foundationalism; they defend subjugated knowledges against unitary notions of progress. In a word, they are incredulous toward master narratives (Lyotard, 1984). In the spirit of such incredulity, this chapter explores some of the alternatives to conventional histories of constructivism. Although it does not entirely disregard intellectual matters, it focuses more on the immediate, circumstantially specific movement through which writers with diverse intellectual and practical agendas hitch on to the constructivist bandwagon.

Constructivism in the Social Sciences

There is no getting around the resurgence of constructivism in the social sciences. Special issues of journals, theme conferences and many lively debates all testify to current interests in the subject. It is virtually impossible to remain indifferent to constructivism, as colleagues, students and more distant critics all challenge us to take up positions in the debates about it.

This is similar to the situation a few years earlier when postmodernism became lively even in the most far-flung reaches of the academy. It was then common to ask 'What the hell is it?' and 'Are you for it or against it?'. The unsettling thing about such questions is that constructivism and post-modernism often are associated with the claim that there is no 'it': no essence, no centre, no foundation, no overarching definition, no universal method and certainly no literary canon. Understood in its own terms, the constructivist movement might best be described as a fragile coalition of marginal, nomadic academic bands. The knowledge produced by these bands is stitched together less by adherence to a body of dogma, technical protocols, master narratives or clear-cut ideologies than by a tolerance of diverse 'voices'. Now, of course, constructivists do have their opponents. Various practical and philosophical positivists, absolutists, realists, rational-ists, logocentrists and phallocentrists staff the opposition. Often these opponents are made of straw, but sometimes they rise up and denounce constructivists and their kindred spirits for being enemies of free inquiry. The funny thing about such denunciations is that they refuse to counten-ance the marginality and tolerance of diversity claimed by constructivists, and the denouncers argue instead that relativistic, radical and deconstruc-tivist tendencies are today dominant, powerful and conventional in a large segment of the academic world.[1]

Astute readers may already have noticed that I have conflated construc-tivism with a panoply of avant-garde radical intellectual movements: relativism, radical feminism, cultural studies, deconstructionism, post-modernism and so forth. I am not alone in this, as such conflation is itself a feature of the field. Persons affiliated with these various movements (or are they schools, positions or philosophies?) freely overstep and disregard epistemic boundaries, and even celebrate the transgression of such bound-aries. In addition to voluntarily meeting in hybrid academic groupings, members sometimes find themselves lumped together by their vociferous opponents.

It is thus difficult to impute particular intellectual contents and political implications to constructivism, and no less difficult to take stock of the alleged membership in the constructivist community. Many of those who are presumed to be in the constructivist movement opt out of it, wholly or partially. For example, when asked, 'Do you consider yourself a construc-tivist?', a colleague who is widely identified with the movement answered, 'It depends on the audience.' This of course is a perfectly good constructiv-ist answer. Nothing could be more definitive of constructivism than the thesis that social identities depend on audience ascriptions. At the same time, the answer sets up a paradox for any effort to specify an academic genealogy, if by this is meant a narrative line that identifies a scholarly community with a set of ideas and methodological precepts and traces the roots of those ideas back through lines of intellectual ancestry. One could perhaps specify what various audiences make of constructivism, but such a project would run into a parallel problem of identifying the relevant audiences and defining the contents of their attributions (these too may depend on the audience).

Nevertheless, it is possible to construct an ideal-typical disciplinary history of constructivism or, as I shall shortly attempt, of a more specific constructivist development in social studies of science. It is possible to do this because many examples of such genealogies are available in the literature. These genealogies are rehashed at academic conferences, in university seminars, over electronic mail networks and in casual shop talk. They are commonplace in the constructivist literature, especially in review articles and in the introductory sections of books and papers. But are they *constructivist* genealogies?[2] I believe it should be obvious that they are not. It is less obvious what a constructivist genealogy of constructivism should look like. In what follows, I will start out by demonstrating what a constructivist genealogy definitely should *not* look like, and then proceed to discuss some of the problems raised by the task of constructing more exemplary alternatives.

Conventional Histories[3]

Following Kuhn (1970 [1962]), it is well established among the groups of historians, philosophers and sociologists of science who (sometimes) call themselves constructivists that conventional histories of science tend to be unduly heroic. A concise example of such a conventional history is found in *The World Almanac and Book of Facts*. Proponents of constructivist lines of research in the sociology of science have often given ironic descriptions of such whiggish histories. As Table 1.1 shows, however, a genealogy of the new (constructivist) sociology of science can be written along the lines of the *Book of Facts*. To a startling extent this recovers a familiar style of recital that appears in review articles, introductory sections of research papers, and in other summary accounts of developments in the field.

Heroic genealogies like these emphasize the importance of key discoveries and theoretical advances. They lay out a lineage of heroes and their monumental works to describe a progressive development and expansion as more recent innovations overcome previous limitations and diffuse into new fields. Note the way the most important names are highlighted in bold type. The names are associated with achievements, which are marked with dates (dates of birth and death for the scientific revolution; dates of key publications for the constructivists). Sometimes in museums (or even in places like the Kendall Square subway station near MIT in Cambridge, Massachusetts), one finds a time-line inscribed along a wall which gives a capsule summary of the landmark achievements in science and engineering. (Thus far, I have not seen the parallel for constructivism.)[4]

Characteristic features show up in conventional histories. The historian makes an effort to link the present to the past by tracing back a historic line of work through a canonical tradition. Starting in the present and speaking

16   *The politics of constructionism*

Table 1.1   *Heroic Genealogies*

Scientific revolution	Constructivist revolution
The late nominalist thinkers (Ockham, *c.*1300–49) of Paris and Oxford challenged Aristotelian orthodoxy, allowing for a freer scientific approach. But metaphysical values, such as the Neoplatonic faith in an orderly, mathematical cosmos, still motivated and directed subsequent inquiry.	The neo-Kantian thinkers (Mannheim, 1936; Merton, 1942) of Germany and America challenged Marxist orthodoxy, allowing for a freer and more general approach to the sociology of knowledge. But metaphysical values, such as Mannheim's Neoplatonic faith in mathematical reality and Merton's belief in the scientific ethos, still motivated and directed subsequent inquiry.
Copernicus (1473–1545) promoted the heliocentric theory, which was confirmed when Kepler (1571–1630) discovered the mathematical laws describing the orbits of the planets. The Christian-Aristotelian belief that heavens and earth were fundamentally different collapsed when **Galileo** (1564–1643) discovered moving sunspots, irregular moon topography, and moons around Jupiter. He and Newton (1642–1727) developed a mechanics that unified cosmic and earthly phenomena. To meet the needs of the new physics, Newton and Leibnitz (1646–1716) invented calculus. Descartes (1596–1650) invented analytic geometry.	**Barnes** (1974) promoted the sociocentric theory, which was confirmed when Bloor (1976) discovered the symmetry principle for describing the origins of knowledge production. The logical-empiricist belief that society and nature were fundamentally different collapsed when **Latour** (1987) discovered immutable mobiles, heterogeneous network topography, and the insides of black boxes. He and Callon (1981) developed a model that unified human and non-human phenomena. To meet the needs of the new constructivism, Gilbert and Mulkay (1984) imported discourse analysis. Collins (1985) invented empirical relativism.
An explosion of observational science included the discovery of blood circulation (Harvey, 1578–1657) and microscopic life (Leeuwenhoek, 1632–1723), and advances in anatomy (Vesalius, 1514–64, dissected corpses) and chemistry (Boyle, 1627–91). Scientific research institutes were founded: Florence, 1657; London (Royal Society), 1660: Paris, 1666. Inventions proliferated (Savery's steam engine, 1696).	An explosion of observational studies included the discovery of the circulation of credit (Latour and Woolgar, 1979) and the microsociology of the lab (Knorr-Cetina, 1981), and analyses of anatomists (Lynch, 1985, dissected scientists dissecting rats) and chemistry (Shapin and Schaffer, 1985 deconstructed Boyle). STS research institutes were founded: Cornell; London (CRICT); Paris (CSI). Studies of inventions proliferated (Law's heterogeneous engineering, 1986).

From Hoffman, 1992: 500.

in a corporate voice, the disciplinary historian draws linkages between a set of landmark authors and key texts. Despite the many variations and idiosyncrasies, I believe it is safe to say that such histories assume a conventional form partly because they borrow liberally from one another and are reiterated in numerous presentations and courses of instruction. It becomes possible to recite the conventional history – giving a standard line or two for each of the landmark works and authors – without reading the constituent texts.

These histories can be more or less elaborate. Lévi-Strauss (1966: 258–62) underlines this point with his distinction between 'hot' and 'cold' chronologies. This distinction marks the relative intensity of notations and commentaries along a time-line which endows history with variable degrees of eventfulness and vividness. Chronologies also can follow a series of stages reminiscent of folk tales and mythologies. For example, a more elaborate version of the genealogy of constructivist science studies can follow a ritual progression through a series of stages, not unlike those identified for myths and ritual dramas (Turner, 1974):

(1)   Prehistory: This begins with a characterization of 'positivism', some-times going into a brief account about the Vienna Circle and the unity of science movement in twentieth-century philosophy of science. Rules of method, demarcation criteria, fact–value separations and falsificationism are all part of this picture. Invariably, mention is made of the idealized version of natural science featured in Mertonian sociology of science: the ideas of the autonomy of science, and of the norms of universalism, disinterestedness, communalism and organized scepticism. It is obligatory to mention that Karl Mannheim, who helped develop the sociology of knowledge early in the twentieth century, excluded mathematics and natural science from his programme of explanation. He did so out of a conviction that, once established, scientific laws and mathematical verities become independent of history and culture.

(2)   Crisis: Invariably, this includes an account of the rupture in 1960s philosophy of science associated with 'Kuhnian' ideas about revolutions, paradigms and incommensurability, together with other sceptical problems about the underdetermination of theories by facts and the theory-ladenness of observation.

(3)   Schism and resolution: This is a narrative about the origins of a 'new' sociology of scientific knowledge, associated with the Edinburgh School Strong Programme and related developments. Disciplinary histories most often reiterate the Strong Programme's proposal that social explanations apply across the board to the technical contents in all branches of science and maths, and that such explanations should be 'symmetrical' or 'impartial' as to the (alleged) truth or falsity of the 'beliefs' in question.

(4)   Development: An account of the line(s) of empirical studies linked to the recent, (relatively) relativistic programmes in science studies. Often, the results of ethnographic 'laboratory studies' published in the late 1970s and early 1980s are mentioned as strong demonstrations that 'actual' scientific practices differ profoundly from the honorific versions promulgated by positive philosophy and the pop-science media, and that even the most detailed laboratory facts and discourses are subject to 'social construction'.

(5)   Diffusion and dissipation: In an up-to-date account, mention is made of how the new programmes have worked their way into neighbouring fields such as technology studies, social problems research and cultural studies. This is one sense of the 'diffusion' of innovation.

Another, vernacular sense of 'diffusion' describes the fractious rivalries, ambiguities and uncertainties that begin to become evident at this point. As interest in this 'field' diffuses into, hybridizes with and develops independently from pre-existing lines of scholarship in the social sciences, philosophy and history, and literary and cultural studies, a somewhat dissonant chorus of complaints begins to be heard. One commonly mentioned complaint is that lab studies and historical case studies tend not to develop explanations that focus 'beyond the laboratory walls'. Another is that too often the avowed relativists fail to take normative or politically committed positions. And still another is that the alleged 'relativists' unreflexively assume empiricist stances toward their subjects. A complaint coming from a different quarter is that the sociology of scientific knowledge has 'gone too far' in a relativist direction, and that it ought to seek a more 'reasonable' position with respect to scientific realism.

(6)   Rebirth and 'post' history: Hybrid constructivisms proliferate, avow-edly (re)radicalizing selected initiatives from the sociology of scien-tific knowledge and integrating them with radical feminist, neo-Marxist, postmodernist, cultural, cognitivist, literary-theoretic and other contemporary academic movements and developments. A loose consensus emerges to the effect that science has been shown to be 'heterogeneous' and disunified; that 'practice' is the heart of the matter; that 'boundaries' between science and non-science, and between science and technology, are temporal and rhetorical con-structs; that scientific knowledge is 'gendered' and suffused with the particularistic vantage point of the early-modern European gentry; and that science and technology are indissociable from a 'seamless web' of knowledge/power.

This (re)construction is intended to represent the vantage point of someone who situates their own work in phase 6, and who looks back with mixed sympathies toward the earlier phases.[5]

The above are examples of 'grand narratives'. In actual instances, authors frequently build 'petit narratives'. These also include canonical histories of notable authors and great works, but they are more localized in organiz-ation. Such chronologies and lists tend to be deployed around an argument or scholastic position, and they mobilize categorical distinctions and chronological references in a way that supports or accentuates the author's position. Like ordinary storytellers, authors of published papers often place themselves in a central position in the narrative field.[6] The author's centrality is indicated by, among other things, a trail of citations to their own and close colleagues' publications (including references to unpublished writings by the author). I do not mean to imply that such auto-citational narratives are products of individual self-promotion, as they often involve collective efforts to promote a nascent 'school' or (in Garfinkel's termin-ology) a 'company' or 'gang'. This does, however, create difficulty for an attempt to reconstruct a genealogy of constructivism. A great deal of confusion and angst can attend the question of where to begin the genealogy, which works (or 'schools') to include in it and exclude from it, and how to rank or order the list. Much of this confusion arises from the fact that the most authoritative scholarly genealogies tend to be constructed by those who have (or aspire to have) a prominent place in them.[7]

Conventional histories are not always heroic. A genealogy specified by someone who is (or thinks s/he is) hostile to constructivism is likely to differ significantly from more heroic versions. Such a hostile genealogy tends to resemble a history of a pathological condition, identifying detours and focusing on individual frailties (ignorance, irrationality, susceptibility to negative influences) which lead afflicted individuals away from a more natural contact with reality. Such tendentious ways of framing a genealogy exhibit the author's positional relation to the narrative without necessarily mentioning or referencing the author directly. Lewis Wolpert (1992: 109) draws an historical contrast between '[t]he more traditional sociologists of science, as represented by the work of Robert K. Merton', and the more recent 'Strong Programme'. Wolpert (1992: 110) adds that, whereas the Mertonians attempted to *understand* social processes in science without threatening the self-understanding of scientists, adherents to the 'strong' approach make no distinction between 'good and successful science and what most scientists would regard as second- and third-rate work'. Contrary to its claims, he argues, the Strong Programme's view of science is based largely on the analysis of weak sciences like phrenology, and not, for example, the incontestable knowledge of DNA in molecular genetics. The very idea that such knowledge could be a mere social construction 'could only appear to be so to someone ignorant of the complex science involved' (Wolpert, 1992: 115). Here we can see that the account is not a genealogy so much as an argument (or, more accurately, a series of assertions). Like the heroic genealogy presented in Table 1.1, this one places Merton in a 'traditional' or preliminary position, only in this case Merton does not represent a precursor whose limitations were overcome by the Strong Programme. Instead, Merton represents a reasonable sociological approach that the later 'relativists' left behind when they went off in a mistaken direction. In the end, this degenerative (and not progressive) turn in the sociology of scientific knowledge is diagnosed as the result of sheer ignorance of 'complex science'. In a more sweeping indictment of the 'academic left' (which includes what they call 'cultural constructivism'), Gross and Levitt (1994: 43ff.) also draw a contrast between a benign 'weak form' of cultural constructivism which describes particular contextual influences upon historical sciences without undermining the credibility of the entire enterprise, and a more ambitious 'strong form' which challenges the objectivity of science and disputes the very notions of scientific and technological progress. Like Wolpert, Gross and Levitt 'explain' the ascendancy of this 'strong form' as a matter of technical ignorance, but they go a step further by ascribing it to a deep resentment of the successful sciences by frustrated remnants of the New Left who have taken refuge in university humanities and social science departments.

There is nothing intrinsically wrong with writing conventional histories, whether heroic or denunciatory. However, the 'construction' of intellectual genealogies such as those I have just sketched does seem incongruous with the analytic perspective of constructivism. Even though one often finds such disciplinary histories in avowedly constructivist writings, they tend to play an instrumental or rhetorical role by setting up (or discounting) claims about recent advances in understandings about science, and by situating a given study (the study in which the history appears) as an authoritative review of, and often the latest addition to, a coherent line of literature.[8] In brief, although they provide genealogies of constructivism, they are *constructed* but not *constructivist* genealogies.

Constructivist Genealogies

So what would a constructivist genealogy of constructivism look like? There seem to be different ways to go, depending upon what one supposes the 'construction' of a disciplinary history to entail. 'Construction' for many writers implies the possibility of reconstruction in accordance with values or purposes that are held to be more desirable than those that are grounded in tradition and bolstered by naturalistic interpretations. Understood in a non-radical way, however, such a reconstructive orientation would simply reproduce commonplace scholastic tendencies. Scholarly writings often begin by noting that a certain canonical version of the history of ideas has been taken for granted. Then a revision is suggested. In science studies, for example, Ludwik Fleck's *Genesis and Development of a Scientific Fact* (1979 [1935]), one of the few sources cited in Kuhn's *Structure of Scientific Revolutions* (1970 [1962]), was 'rediscovered' and translated into English well after Kuhn's essay became popular. More recently, Boris Hessen, Edgar Zilsel and other early social historians of science have been reinserted into the canon, after having been forgotten by recent generations. Such restoration efforts do more than keep the historical record straight; they tendentiously exhibit a line on history that promotes or demotes certain present-day conceptions of progress. Other efforts have been made to reconfigure the canonical division between Mertonian and post-Mertonian sociology of science (see Merton, 1976: 59–60, for an especially interesting example). Still others have tried to set the record straight by showing that Mannheim did not simply exclude the natural sciences from the purview of his programme, and that his work in fact was far more subtle than his latter-day 'strengtheners' supposed (Hekman, 1986; Pels, 1996). Such moves are the stock-in-trade of academic scholarship, and they do not radically disrupt the frame of conventional disciplinary history.

A radical reconstruction might take this a step further. Let's say one wanted to construct more edifying disciplinary histories in order to empower a broader range of 'voices'. So, for example, instead of citing a canonical line of key writers and major works, one might try to cite lesser-known contributors and lesser-known works. An individual effort to do this would not be radical enough, however, as it would merely reproduce the bourgeois tendency to make conspicuous displays of learning by calling attention to the author's command of the more arcane sectors of a literature. To take it in a truly radical direction, we would need to prescribe new conventions for an entire community's practices. Imagine, for example, the possibility of institutionalizing support for the citationally challenged. To this end we could formulate a principle of citational charity: 'When given a choice always cite the least known relevant author other than yourself.' Or imagine if quotas were set on how often particular authors or categories of author could be cited. Such simple modifications of existing practice, together with appropriate enforcement mechanisms, would radically change the moral economy of academic writing. The resulting changes in conventional usage would, in turn, modify the terrain upon which intellectual histories are written. It would become more difficult to assign discoveries to persons, or to identify the biggest names in a field, because the routine recording of credit would continually shift away from prior sites of accumulation. Although perhaps revolutionary, this also would give writers headaches, because many short cuts would no longer be available when reviewing a literature.

Perhaps this still is not radical enough. Constructivism is sometimes believed to require deconstructive efforts to transgress and disrupt, in order to reveal taken-for-granted assumptions and/or constitutive practices that remain hidden by conventional methods of naturalized description. Although my fanciful suggestions of how conventional citational practice might be modified point in the direction of a radical difference between the usual way of writing intellectual histories and a constructivist alternative, they do not take the project beyond a serious engagement in a system for distributing individual credit for 'good works'. We are still taking far too much for granted. To get an appreciation of an alternative, consider examples of truly radical constructivism which are found in the arts. Just to cite a conspicuous (if vulgar) example, a 'constructivist garden' was exhibited at the 1994 Chelsea Flower Show, an annual event held in London. A newspaper article described the garden as

> a confection of stainless steel, concrete and rubber. Its [spray-painted] black grass and mildly erotic decorations did not impress the judges who decided, in a rare move, not to recommend it for any award.
> Mr. Colin Elliot, the garden's landscaper, accused them of being 'extremely humourless' but admitted: 'I only found out what constructivist meant when I looked it up in the dictionary this morning.'[9]

Mr Colin Elliot's professed ignorance of the meaning of the word 'constructivist' was directly contradicted by the slick brochure he and other staff distributed at the flower show. (Such contradiction should of course be no embarrassment to a 'true' constructivist.) According to the brochure, the garden design was 'inspired by the art and design of the Constructivist Movement of the 1920s and 1930s'. It went on to say that a characteristic feature of that movement was an ironic use of geometric forms and modern materials. Accordingly, the garden's constructivism was expressed through a garish arrangement of artificial materials adhering strictly to a set of mathematical forms and ratios.

Although associated with a particular artistic style, the garden's constructivism was also a function of perspective by incongruity, a displacement of expectancies that cast into relief the constructed nature of the normal garden. The cheeky humour of the constructivist garden was set off against the traditional aesthetics of the many other garden exhibits surrounding it, which tended to include contrived emblems of antiquity, aristocracy and naturalism. Like other artistic disruptions, it created perplexity for viewers and judges as to whether it was simply an ugly mockery of a garden or a profound revolutionary statement.

For my purposes, the most radical aspect of this example is the statement by Mr Colin Elliot in the above quotation: 'I only found out what constructivist meant when I looked it up in the dictionary this morning.' Although we do not know whether to believe him, his statement suggests that the modifier 'constructivist' was attached to the installation with no more (or less) care for established convention than were the wooden fish placed on sticks amongst the plants, the lumps of coal sprinkled on the ground as ornamental gravel, or the garish chromium fountain bedecked with blinking coloured lights. Like the found-materials and ready-mades from which the garden was assembled, the name 'constructivist' and the slick brochure's impressive description of the theory behind it were likely to have been thrown together as part of the installation rather than as a description of it. 'Constructivist' is not simply a name for a tradition. It is an emblem for a bandwagon to be joined by whomever might find a place in it (Fujimura, 1988). 'Constructivism' thus becomes a *proper* name for a large, extended and expanding family of dubiously related members: a family of bastards.[10] Moreover, the intellectual linkages are forged retrospectively through a kind of bastardization of selected themes from prior works to make them suitable for the current instantiation. Even if there are no deep genetic criteria uniting the members of this family, a variety of cross-cutting rationales for membership may be specified after the fact.

So, where do we go from here? Inspired by the constructivist garden, we can imagine the possibility of playful, truly bizarre, almost unrecognizable, constructivist genealogies. There are endless possibilities, and a few exemplary publications that suggest experiments along these lines: articles employing 'new literary forms', or rather old literary forms like plays, imaginary dialogues, performances and poems, inscribed in scholarly collections and journals that didn't previously accept such stuff (see Ashmore, 1989; Woolgar, 1988). One could perhaps write an epic, or an ode set to music; one could experiment with the odd geometric matrices (vortices, spirals, fractals) for setting up chronologies. Such experiments might be amusing, and even revealing, but in the remainder of this chapter I intend to take a different tack. I intend to construct a genealogy that construes constructivism as a play on the word 'construction'. This approach is inspired by the example of Mr Colin Elliot, who (according to his doubtful story, quoted in a doubtful source) joined the constructivist movement prior to looking up the word and finding out what it meant.

Plain Translation

A constructivist genealogy, as I envision it, would describe a progression of acts through which participants join a named group. They may do so for different reasons or for no reason at all. Innumerable anarchistic acts would thus generate the direction the movement takes, much in the way participants in a political celebration or protest march may join in for good political reasons and/or bad personal reasons, or because they just happen to be around when it sweeps by. Any explanation (including this one) of why they all happen to be together is constructed in the wake of the movement. This is a way of speaking about a 'history of the present', but it is more than a history that makes sense of the present in terms of the past (it does that as well). It is a developing history whose construction is subject to the vicissitudes of present circumstances and vantage points. This may seem to trivialize the field, or to support hostile versions that reduce it to intellectual fashion, but it would be better understood as an account of a more general phenomenon that is made perspicuous and transparent when one is reflexively engaged in the field described by the genealogy.[11]

I believe the word *construction*, and its scholastic variants 'constructivism' and 'constructionism',[12] are centrally important to the growth and success of the movement. While it may be impossible to define what adherents to the various constructivist approaches hold in common, at least they have the word 'construction'. It is a word that appears often, and increasingly, in titles of scholarly writings and theme conferences. It is one of several philosophical 'isms' that tend to be juxtaposed (as well as opposed) in critical discussions and debates. The realist–constructivist debate is perhaps the most familiar of these. The importance of focusing on the word 'construction' also follows from the nominalist tendency often (if not invariably) associated with constructivism. For example, the labelling theory of deviance and various other semiotic and symbolic interactionist approaches in sociology emphasize the constitutive importance of names, labels, inscriptions, signifiers and representations for defining situations, establishing social identities and demarcating moral communities.

Things quickly get complicated, however, when we recognize that the word 'construction' is an indexical expression, the meaning of which depends upon the context of use (Garfinkel and Sacks, 1970). If we assume that this word should be associated with a singular, self-consistent referent, we may be led astray. As indicated earlier, it seems clear that programmes and movements that have espoused constructivism are diverse and tenuously connected. Even when approached within a more restricted field of study, constructivists seem to be linked together more by an affiliation with the name, and perhaps a few slogans, than by a set of original ideas or a foundational theory or methodology.

This conception of the matter problematizes our usual ways of specifying intellectual lineages. For example, in sociology an explicit orientation to the 'social construction of reality' was first announced by Berger and Luckmann (1966). As innumerable references to this work indicate, it proved to be an influential treatment, and one might be tempted to assign to Berger and Luckmann's text a foundational status for latter-day social constructivist approaches. However, if what is wanted is a genealogy, and not an illusory chronology of titles and authors, we should not assume that Berger and Luckmann's text was the unique source of a theory or set of key ideas that gave rise to a sustained intellectual development. As I reconstruct the matter, *The Social Construction of Reality* remains important mainly as a landmark *title* in a conventional history. Very little intellectually has been preserved from the book in contemporary constructivist writings in the sociology of knowledge other than the title, author and date of publication. Such minimal citation is enough to preserve the original proposition that 'reality is socially constructed' (whatever that means). Read with hindsight, Berger and Luckmann's text espoused a not very radical version of social construction, in any of the epistemic, reflexive or political senses of the term used today (Turner, 1991). Indeed, their treatment was far less radical than the approaches taken by many of their contemporaries in the late 1960s who did not happen to use the words 'social construction' in their titles. In the social sciences, a diverse, overlapping array of semiotic, ethnomethodological, symbolic interactionist, radical feminist, cultural-Marxist, literary-theoretic and discourse-analytic approaches coincided with Berger and Luckmann's treatment and turned out to be more influential for various collectives of latter-day constructivists. However, while the content of Berger and Luckmann's theory may have had little subsequent influence, their literary practice was exemplary. They succeeded in developing a plainly written account that integrated Schutz's (1964) social phenomenology with more mainstream lines of social theory. The word 'construction' was pivotally important for introducing the concept of phenomenological 'constitution' to a large social science readership that was, and remains, more familiar with causal and instrumental idioms. Understood in terms of Schutz's phenomenological project, 'constitution' does not imply a causal or instrumental relation between acts and their products, nor does it suggest a mutual influence between subjective activities and objective social institutions. The convention of representing such relations as unidirectional or bi-directional arrows connecting separate domains simply does not apply, nor does a means–ends scheme of action effectively frame the matter. Schutz goes to great length to establish that his writings are *explications* of the natural attitude of an ideal-typical member of a society or group (or, in the case of his essay on the stranger, a non-member). His writings did not develop an explanation, and certainly not a causal theory, and in many respects his phenomenological treatment was alien to the explanatory schemes prevalent in American sociology at the time. It can fairly be said that Schutz's American contemporaries (most notably Talcott Parsons) did not see the point of his project. His writings did not contribute to the building of an American sociology modelled on a generalized image of natural science, nor did they provide a basis for predictions and policy recommendations.

Not all North American sociologists disregarded Schutz. Garfinkel's (1963; 1967) ethnomethodological essays on trust and rationality were heavily indebted to Schutz. Those essays expanded upon and substantiated some of Schutz's conceptual themes, such as the retrospective–prospective sense of temporal occurrence, the reciprocity of perspectives, and the difference between the attitude of scientific theorizing and the natural attitude of daily life. Garfinkel's and other ethnomethodologists' writings diverged from Schutz's tendency to develop his explications of the social world from a first-person vantage point. In line with Wittgenstein's (1958a) recommendation that many emblematic features of first-person 'subjective' usage can be recovered without loss in descriptions from the third-person vantage point, ethnomethodologists located constitutive acts within public environments in which the intersubjective recognizability, relevant and interplay of actions become thematically significant. Again, however, the difficult prose in Garfinkel's *Studies in Ethnomethodology* (1967) did not support an effort to construct causal hypotheses, testable propositions, structural models or theories of structuration, and many readers were troubled by the strangeness of the project.

Berger and Luckmann did not capitulate to the demands of positivist sociology, but they did successfully integrate Schutz's teachings with a Weberian programme of value-free interpretative sociology. Schutz took some steps in that direction himself, though he insistently distinguished his phenomenological descriptions of interpretative understandings embedded in the constitution of the ordinary society from Weber's more restricted attention to the requirements of a professional social science method. Both Weber and Schutz recognized that 'subjective understanding' was a constitutive property in the social world that had profound implications for any description of it, but unlike Weber, Schutz assigned priority to the task of recovering a pre-theoretical interpretative sociology which, he argued, was fundamental to the ordinary member's life-world. In contrast, mainstream sociologists, partly encouraged by Parsons's translations of Weber, assigned priority to an ideal observer's detached overview of the social and historical processes through which social aggregates progressively objectify, and then internalize, social institutions. Some of the more prominent sociologists mistook Schutz's and Garfinkel's abandonment of a transcendental observer's view of society-as-a-whole for a methodological orientation to 'subjective', 'micro', and even 'trivial' matters. What such criticisms missed was that this de-transcendence was designed to bring into relief how *anybody*, whether a prominent social theorist or nobody in particular, manages to take account of an intersubjective order while acting constitutively within it.

A descriptivist programme of research may seem to give rise to disappointing insights, especially when understood in terms of the more ambitious social science and philosophical projects, but a different valuation of 'mere description' can arise when we turn away from the 'craving for generality' implied by such ambitions (Wittgenstein, 1958b: 18). As soon as one becomes indifferent to the victories of the natural sciences, and as soon as one abandons all hope that the social sciences might some day rise above common sense to attain victories of their own, a whole array of practical, locally organized, linguistically expressed ways of making ordinary judgements about matters of fact, truth, credibility and reality become available for description. No longer are they cast as dim, distorted or degraded versions of an idealized science. The injunction to describe such practices as phenomena in their own right recognizes the incredible diversity of epistemic procedures which are unlikely to fit into any general theory of knowledge.

The writings by Schutz, Garfinkel, Wittgenstein and others who took descriptivist approaches to language use and practical action almost seem designed to frustrate the many philosophers and social scientists who insist upon progressive, normatively guided programmes. This is where the work of plain translation has proved to be so crucial for developing mainstream programmes from more obscure sources. For example, in the sociology of deviance Scheff (1963) formulated a series of testable propositions that summarized a labelling (or societal reactionist) approach to mental illness, and Becker (1963: 20) managed to use a plain fourfold table to schematize the interaction between deviance and deviance attribution. These schemas, with their causal propositions and graphic formats, became emblematic of an approach that assimilated a more diffuse set of arguments and examples from histories of madness, ethnographic descriptions of asylum life and anti-psychiatric polemics. Similarly, in the sociology of scientific knowledge, Bloor (1983) turned Wittgenstein into a social theorist of knowledge, allying his investigations of language use to a programme of causal explanation. Bloor chose to disregard Wittgenstein's explicit disavowals of science and causal explanation, and his version was quite effective for provoking widespread interest among social scientists. Interestingly, in both the sociology of deviance and the sociology of science the plain translation not only provided concise, readily understood accounts; their clearly stated propositions and causal claims became magnets for criticism.[13]

Plain translation is the stock-in-trade of academic teaching and writing, and none of us can claim to be exempted from its demands, rewards and compromises. I mention it here because I believe it is a crucial aspect of the genealogy of constructivism. This genealogy should not be conceived as a time-line linking a series of seminal theorists through the medium of their ideas. Instead, it is a more of a contingent annexation of ways of working and writing. The word 'construction' is pivotal to such annexation, because it bridges a gap between obscure descriptive explications of constitutive practices and a more plain interest in general aspects of knowledge-making. By the same token, constructivist research becomes enmeshed in linguistic ambiguities that are both intractable and productive. When understood in familiar contexts of discussion in the natural and social sciences, 'construction' suggests an unnatural order of things, and 'deconstruction' is understood as a way of revealing the illusionist tricks hidden by naturalistic description or representation. This sense of unmasking is consistent with the language commonly found in research literatures, law courts and many other discursive settings where particular facts, allegations, evidences and interpretations are sceptically examined. For example, a fact stated in a molecular biology publication may be said to be 'deconstructed' by a critic who argues that the fact is really an artefact of unmentioned (and perhaps at the time unknown) contingencies of the investigative procedure (Latour and Woolgar, 1986 [1979]). Similarly, an expert witness's claim about the reliability of a forensic technique and its general acceptance in relevant scientific fields may be said to be 'deconstructed' under cross-examination by a well-informed attorney who calls expert witnesses to testify about dubious technical and interpretative procedures (Jasanoff, 1991).

Vernacular uses of 'construction' and affiliated terms (artefact, invention, fabrication, manufacture) often have evaluative connotations. They suggest that something has been 'made up', as opposed to being naturally available.[14] It is a serious charge among molecular biologists to say that a researcher 'fabricated' her data, or 'deleted' relevant features of her experiments from her lab notebooks. Such terms suggest that she could, and should, have known better and done otherwise. Other terms like 'artefact' and 'construction' do not always imply wrongdoing; instead, they connote material phenomena – sometimes produced by unwitting interventions in the organization of the field under analysis – misrecognized as thematic things and properties (Lynch, 1985).

While an ordinary sense of the word can imply an intentional effort to manufacture or manipulate a product or outcome, a more general, theoretical sense of construction can apply to any mode of practical action, whether honestly or dishonestly motivated, and whether defensible or indefensible in terms of local standards of judgement and competence (Fish, 1989: 226). In social studies of science, medicine and law one often finds 'construction' and 'deconstruction' used in second order descriptions. The analyst tries not to endorse a position internal to the arguments studied, and develops an *account of others' accounts and disputes about what is or is not constructed*. Although the analyst retains a focus on particular facts, artefacts and disputes which (internally) presume unconstructed alternatives, she or he endeavours *not* to presume a stable ontological contrast between the particular constructions in question and what is, or should have been, known to be real. In many case studies, the accent of reality is withheld by the analyst when describing what participants in a controversy avow or presume to be true, but this does not apply to the analyst's stance toward the disputes themselves. The disputes, and their relevant social contexts, are treated as actual social events to be described (and sometimes explained) with all due empirical care (cf. Collins, 1985).

Much of the confusion and debate about constructivism has to do with how the word 'construction' (as well as many of the terms and themes associated with it) suggests a particular evaluative or critical stance toward the object of analysis even when this is denied explicitly by the analyst (Coulter, 1989: 32ff.). Although, in principle, constructivist sociologists of science neither credit nor discredit the substantive claims of the scientists they study, critics like Cole (1992) argue that their generalized position implies a rejection of such well-established matters as the double-helical model of DNA and gauge theory in particle physics. He fails to recognize that a global substitution of constructivist for naturalistic descriptions no longer should carry the evaluative implications of an assertion made within a particular positive science that 'this feature is an artefact, not a natural phenomenon'. This can get confusing when, for example, constructivists like Pickering (1984) argue that currently accepted theories in particle physics do not provide the only possible account of the phenomena investigated in the relevant experiments. It seems but a small step to assume that he is implying that the physicists *should* have taken better account of alternative theories, but then this would reiterate exactly the sort of complaint one group of physicists might make about another. To make such a complaint is to provoke an argument in experimental physics, needless to say a difficult type of argument for a sociologist to pursue.

Similar confusions about 'construction' come into play in explicitly politicized versions of literary, legal, social and cultural studies. Boosted by the theoretical confidence that even the most obdurate of 'objective' matters are socially constructed, the analyst attempts to show that a particular fact or theory only *seems* to be objective, but in fact originates in unacknowledged contexts of production and interpretation. This opens the door for critical readings and reformist proposals. Such criticisms can be made effectively or ineffectively, but they can just as easily be made (as they have been for years) in terms of realistic idioms that contrast an illusory or distorted 'reality' to a real reality. The tendency nowadays is to run such criticisms under the banner of constructivism (or its left-handed twin, deconstructionism). This testifies to the widespread appeal of the approach – while helping to make it even more widespread – but it has little to do with the efficacy of the general idea of social construction. If there is no getting outside the constructed universe, then what counts as objective in such a universe does not just *seem* to be real, it is real in just that way.

It is important to keep in mind that 'construction' is an ordinary word. It was not invented for a specific analytic purpose, and it does not circulate only among highly specialized initiates. It would be possible to invent or adopt another word for a specialized use in social constructivist writings, so that whenever speaking in a special theoretical way about the social construction of something, a neologism like 'consustentation' or a hyphenated phrase (concerted-production-and-temporal-development) might be used. Perhaps this would lend precision (or at least a sense of precision) to our discussions, but it would begin to complicate plain English usage. The account would also lose the hook provided by the word 'construction'. For the very reason that the social construction of reality suggests something amazing, even bizarre, to readers unacquainted with the theoretically generalized sense of the term 'constructed', a phrase like 'the concerted production and temporal development of stable intersubjective orders' comes across as leaden, arcane and uninteresting.

Conclusion

My genealogy comes down to a simple 'model' of diverse constituencies latching on to the word 'construction' for different reasons. I also noted that the word 'construction', which is often associated with particularistic criticisms, is a pivotal term because of the productive confusion its use tends to engender. It is productive because it provides an initial hook that captivates adherents, encouraging them to invest their theoretical, methodological and political hopes in an academic approach or movement. But it can be confusing when adherents try to replace the eclectic surface affinity, which fostered the success of constructivism in the first place, with something deeper and more coherent.

If this conclusion seems disappointing, readers should take heart from the fact that with a little effort they should be able to replace my 'constructivist' genealogy with a more palatable alternative (this is because of the flexibility inherent in the situation). My argument might also be construed as a *reductio ad absurdum* of constructivism, thus motivating a rejection of the entire approach. My own preference is to conclude that constructivism is benign enough, but that it provides no guarantee of originality, correctness or deep metaphysical understanding. By virtue of its current popularity, constructivism provides a useful handle for presenting and legitimizing academic work, but this handle can become slippery indeed when employed as a lever to effect radical epistemological reform (cf. Sharrock and Anderson, 1991).

Notes

1 See, for example, Gross and Levitt (1994).
2 I ask this question not out of a knee-jerk reflexivity which would presume that it is always relevant to apply a method or practice to its own production. If one were to write history of

calligraphy, it would be odd to figure that such a history should be written calligraphically (particular specimens might be included as examples). (See Wittgenstein (1958a: §121) for a related example.) In this case, however, I am arguing that there is an incongruity between conventional ways of writing disciplinary histories and a constructivist alternative.

3 See Lynch and Bogen (1996: Ch. 2) for a discussion of conventional histories.

4 Although I know of no heroic time-lines, Flynn (1991) uses a genealogical scheme in his history of ethnomethodology that takes the form of a family tree or kinship network.

5 This is not my vantage point. For my version, see Lynch (1993: Chs 2–3).

6 See Sacks (1992: 483) on the phenomenological positioning of an ordinary storyteller as a main character, often the 'hero', in his or her own stories.

7 See Bowker (1994: 119) for a discussion of interpretative difficulties when 'the only material a historian has to hand is archives that have been written with the official history in mind'. Also see Bogen and Lynch (1989) for an account of a case in which the 'archival' records were designed strategically to mislead later investigators.

8 See Woolgar and Pawluch (1985) for a critical discussion of instrumental conceptions of the construction of social problems.

9 Dan Conagham and Kathy Marks, 'Bought-in plants no bar to gold-medal', *Daily Telegraph*, 25 May 1994: 10.

10 The term 'bastard' can be an endearing term in this context. Harold Garfinkel once remarked that the ethnomethodological 'company' of which he is the 'founding father' is 'a company of bastards'.

11 Sensitivity to charges of intellectual fashion is especially evident in discussions of postmodernism. For example, Featherstone (1988: 195) begins an introductory essay by saying that '[a]ny reference to the term "postmodern" immediately exposes one to the risk of being accused of jumping on a bandwagon, of perpetuating a rather shallow and meaningless intellectual fad'. Also see Knorr-Cetina (1994: 1). Someone who has thoroughly assimilated the 'postmodern attitude' should be happy to accept such accusations without embarrassment, since the complaint against such a bandwagon presumes the possibility of avoiding the ubiquitous 'postmodern condition' of incessant, meaningless and shallow cultural production; a possibility denied by the theory that goes under that name.

12 For my purposes, 'constructionism' and 'constructivism' are synonymous terms, and 'deconstructionism' defines an associated (anti)analytic orientation.

13 See, for example, Gove's (1970) criticisms of Scheff's labelling theory, Pollner's (1974) critique of Becker, and Laudan's (1981) criticisms of Bloor and the Strong Programme.

14 Arthur Fine (1996) plays on the vulgar sense of 'construction' when he uses the title 'science made up' to refer sarcastically to the claims made by constructivist sociologists of science.

References

Ashmore, Malcolm (1989) *The Reflexive Thesis: Wrighting the Sociology of Scientific Knowledge*. Chicago: University of Chicago Press.

Barnes, S.B. (1974) *Scientific Knowledge and Sociological Theory*. London: Routledge & Kegan Paul.

Becker, Howard (1963) *Outsiders: Studies in the Sociology of Deviance*. New York: Free Press.

Berger, Peter and Luckmann, Thomas (1966) *The Social Construction of Reality*. New York: Anchor Books.

Bloor, David (1976) *Knowledge and Social Imagery*. London: Routledge & Kegan Paul.

Bloor, David (1983) *Wittgenstein: A Social Theory of Knowledge*. New York: Columbia University Press.

Bogen, David and Lynch, Michael (1989) 'Taking account of the hostile native: plausible deniability and the production of conventional history in the Iran-contra hearings', *Social Problems*, 36(3): 197–224.

Bowker, Geof (1994) *Science on the Run: Information Management and Industrial Geophysics at Schlumberger, 1920–1940*. Cambridge, MA: MIT Press.

Callon, Michel and Latour, Bruno (1981) 'Unscrewing the big Leviathan: how actors macro-structure reality and how sociologists help them to do so', in Karin Knorr-Cetina and Aaron Cicourel (eds), *Advances in Social Theory and Methodology: Toward an Integration of Micro- and Macro-Sociologies*. London: Routledge & Kegan Paul.

Cole, Steven (1992) *Making Science: Between Nature and Scoiety*. Cambridge, MA: Harvard University Press.

Collins, H.M. (1985) *Changing Order: Replication and Induction in Scientific Practice*. London and Beverly Hills, CA: Sage.

Coulter, Jeff (1989) *Mind in Action*. Cambridge: Polity Press.

Featherstone, Mike (1988) 'In pursuit of the postmodern: an introduction', *Theory, Culture & Society*, 5: 195–215.

Fine, Arthur (1996) 'Science made up: constructivist sociology of knowledge', in Peter Galison and David Stump (eds), *The Disunity of Science: Boundaries, Contexts, and Power*. Stanford, CA: Stanford University Press.

Fish, Stanley (1989) *Doing What Comes Naturally: Change, Rhetoric, and the Practice of Theory in Literary and Legal Studies*. Durham, NC: Duke University Press.

Fleck, Ludwik (1979 [1935]) *Genesis and Development of a Scientific Fact*. Chicago: University of Chicago Press.

Flynn, Pierce (1991) *The Ethnomethodological Movement*. Berlin: Mouton de Gruyter.

Fujimura, Joan (1988) 'The molecular biological bandwagon in cancer research: where social worlds meet', *Social Problems*, 35: 261–83.

Garfinkel, Harold (1963) 'A conception of, and experiments with, "trust" as a condition of stable concerted actions', in O.J.Harvey (ed.), *Motivation and Social Interaction*. New York: Ronald Press. pp. 187–238.

Garfinkel, Harold (1967) *Studies in Ethnomethodology*. Englewood Cliffs, NJ: Prentice-Hall.

Garfinkel, Harold and Sacks, Harvey (1970) 'On formal structures of practical actions', in J.C. McKinney and E.A. Tiryakian (eds), *Theoretical Sociology: Perspectives and Development*. New York: Appleton-Century-Crofts. pp. 337–66.

Gilbert, G. Nigel, and Mulkay, Michael (1984) *Opening Pandora's Box: An Analysis of Scientists' Discourse*. Cambridge: Cambridge University Press.

Gove, Walter (1970) 'Societal reaction as an explanation of mental illness: an evaluation', *American Sociological Review*, 35: 873–84.

Gross, Paul and Levitt, Norman (1994) *Higher Superstition: The Academic Left and its Quarrels with Science*. Baltimore, MD: Johns Hopkins University Press.

Hekman, Susan (1986) *Hermeneutics and the Sociology of Knowledge*. Notre Dame, IN: University of Notre Dame Press.

Hoffman, Mark (ed.) (1992) *The World Almanac and Book of Facts 1993*. New York: Pharos Books.

Jasanoff, Sheila (1991) 'Judicial construction of new scientific evidence', in Paul Durbin (ed.), *Critical Perspectives in Nonacademic Science and Engineering*. Bethlehem, PA: Lehigh University Press. pp. 215–38.

Knorr-Cetina, Karin (1981) *The Manufacture of Knowledge: An Essay on the Constructivist and Contextual Nature of Science*. Oxford: Pergamon Press.

Knorr-Cetina, Karin (1994) 'Primitive classification and postmodernity: towards a sociological notion of fiction', *Theory, Culture & Society*, 11: 1–22.

Kuhn, Thomas S. (1970 [1962]) *The Structure of Scientific Revolutions*, revised edn. Chicago: University of Chicago Press.

Latour, Bruno (1987) *Science in Action: How to Follow Scientists and Engineers through Society*. Cambridge, MA: Harvard University Press.

Latour, Bruno and Woolgar, Steve (1986 [1979]) *Laboratory Life: The Social Construction of Scientific Facts*. London: Sage, 1979; revised edn, Princeton, NJ: Princeton University Press.

Laudan, Larry (1981) 'The pseudo-science of science?', *Philosophy of the Social Sciences*, 11: 173–98.

Law, John (1986) 'On the methods of long-distance control: vessels, navigation and the Portuguese route to India', in John Law (ed.), *Power, Action and Belief*. London: Routledge & Kegan Paul. pp. 231–60.

Lévi-Strauss, Claude (1966) *The Savage Mind*. Chicago: University of Chicago Press.

Lynch, Michael (1985) *Art and Artifact in Laboratory Science*. London: Routledge & Kegan Paul.

Lynch, Michael (1993) *Scientific Practice and Ordinary Action: Ethnomethodology and Social Studies of Science*. New York: Cambridge University Press.

Lynch, Michael and Bogen, David (1996) *The Spectacle of History: Speech, Text & Memory at the Iran-Contra Hearings*. Durham, NC: Duke University Press.

Lyotard, Jean-François (1984) *The Postmodern Condition: A Report on Knowledge*, trans. G. Bennington and B. Massumi. Minneapolis, MN: University of Minnesota Press.

Mannheim, Karl (1936) *Ideology and Utopia*. New York: Harvest Books.

Merton, Robert K. (1942) 'Science and technology in a democratic order', *Journal of Legal and Political Science*, 1: 115–26.

Merton, Robert K. (1976) *Sociological Ambivalence and Other Essays*. New York: Free Press.

Pels, Dick (1996) 'Karl Mannheim and the sociology of scientific knowledge: toward a new agenda?', *Sociological Theory*, 14: 30–48.

Pickering, Andrew (1984) *Constructing Quarks: A Sociological History of Particle Physics*. Chicago: University of Chicago Press.

Pollner, Melvin (1974) 'Sociological and common-sense models of the labelling process', in Roy Turner (ed.), *Ethnomethodology*. Harmondsworth: Penguin.

Sacks, Harvey (1992) *Lectures on Conversation*, Vol. 2, ed. G. Jefferson. Oxford: Basil Blackwell.

Scheff, Thomas (1963) 'The role of the mentally ill and the dynamics of mental disorder: a research framework', *Sociometry*, 26: 436–53.

Schutz, Alfred (1964) *Collected Papers*, 3 vols. The Hague: Martinus Nijhoff.

Shapin, Steven and Schaffer, Simon (1985) *Leviathan and the Air Pump*. Princeton, NJ: Princeton University Press.

Sharrock, Wes and Anderson, Bob (1991) 'Epistemology: professional scepticism', in Graham Button (ed.), *Ethnomethodology and the Human Sciences*. Cambridge: Cambridge University Press. pp. 51–76.

Turner, Stephen (1991) 'Social constructionism and social theory', *Sociological Theory*, 9(1): 22–33.

Turner, Victor (1974) *Dramas, Fields and Metaphors: Symbolic Action in Human Society*. Ithaca, NY: Cornell University Press.

Wittgenstein, Ludwig (1958a) *Philosophical Investigations*, trans. G.E.M. Anscombe. Oxford: Basil Blackwell.

Wittgenstein, Ludwig (1958b) *The Blue and Brown Books: Preliminary Studies for the 'Philosophical Investigations'*. New York: Harper & Row.

Wolpert, Lewis (1992) *The Unnatural Nature of Science*. Cambridge, MA: Harvard University Press.

Woolgar, Steve (ed.) (1988) *Knowledge and Reflexivity: New Frontiers in the Sociology of Knowledge*. London: Sage.

Woolgar, Steve and Pawluch, Dorothy (1985) 'Ontological gerrymandering: the anatomy of social problems explanations', *Social Problems*, 32: 214–27.

2
Constructionist Dialogues and the Vicissitudes of the Political

Kenneth J. Gergen

Active dialogues devoted to the social construction of self and world are now everywhere apparent. Constructionist writings currently span the full range of human sciences; they have generated active exchange between these sciences and wide-ranging inquiry in the humanities (most notably, literary theory, romance languages, philosophy, and rhetoric); they have fostered important new ranges of scholarship in traditional sciences such as biology and geography; and they have played an essential role in a variety of newly developing areas of study (for example women's studies, cultural studies and media studies). Further, constructionist conceptions are now making their way into a variety of practical settings (especially therapy, counselling, social work and organizational development). Although there is not always full agreement on what is entailed or implied by constructionist dialogues, there is little doubt concerning their impact on contemporary scholarly and practical affairs.[1]

Contemporary debates are certainly prefigured in works of earlier times (from Vico to Nietzsche), and within the present century constructionist ideas have long been extant in the academy (most notably in sociology). However, the present dialogues are scarcely a recapitulation of these earlier lines of argument. Significant new elements have made their way into the arena, and it is to these that the current watershed can most significantly be traced. Notably, these entries began to make their way into prominence in the late 1960s, a time of enormous political unrest. The present volume invites special attention to the political ramifications of the emerging dialogue. In what senses, then, did the political climate give rise to the academic transformation; what internal harmonies and discords can be discerned; and what now are the political implications of constructionist dialogues? Although such questions are without bounded answer, the present effort is an attempt to open discussion on the political lodgement and implications of the developing discourses.

The Weakness of the Word: Cradle of Constructionism

There is a pervasive tendency to view current constructionist inquiry as a unified front, with broad antipathy for the various forms of essentialism, realism, foundationalism and structuralism that have served to rationalize and sustain traditional claims to truth beyond perspective, transcendent rationality, universal morality, cultural superiority and progress without limit. Or, in a broad sense, social constructionism is congenially identified as a constituent of a *postmodern* as opposed to a *modern* cultural perspective. The more judicious view, however, is that there is no unified or canonical constructionist position, but a range of variegated and overlapping conversations and practices that draw from various resources and with varying emphases and combinations. Further, in many of these conversations there remain distinct commitments to one or another form of all the above elements of modernism. Nothing is legislated and nothing is fixed – including the meaning of constructionism itself.

However, if we are to strive for historical intelligibility, and a means for understanding current affinities and tensions, it is useful to draw several broad distinctions. In particular, we may distinguish three major movements of recent decades, each formed within differing contexts and each with differing political sensibilities. These movements can be roughly identified in terms of their choice of explanatory fulcrum: *ideological, literary-rhetorical* and *social*. Each now contributes substantially to, and in certain respects virtually circumscribes, the current range of constructionist conversation. In an important sense these movements also gain their primary affinity through their critical impulse. I am not pointing here only to a mode of intellectual and political comportment; critique itself would scarcely serve to distinguish this particular confluence of movements. Rather, what is most significant and unifying about this critique is its selected site of vulnerability. Each, in its own way, has brought into critical focus a central assumption within longstanding intellectual (and political) institutions.

This principal point of vulnerability concerns the function of language. Regardless of the modernist aspiration – essentialist, realist, foundationalist, structuralist – or the site of application – science, education, business organization, governance – there has been a broadly shared belief in the capacity of language to represent or depict the world in an accurate and objective manner. For scientists in particular, the assumption is of no small moment, for as philosophers of science have long been aware, it is primarily in the degree to which there is correspondence between theoretical language and real-world events that scientific theory acquires value in the marketplace of prediction. If scientific language bears no determinate relationship to events external to the language itself, not only does its contribution to prediction become problematic, but hope that knowledge may be advanced through continued, systematic observation proves futile. More generally, one may question the fundamental grounds for authority – scientific and otherwise. The claim to objectivity has furnished a chief basis for authority – in the academy, policy-making circles, business and elsewhere. With the truth-bearing capacity of words thrown into question, so is authority in the modernist state.

In one way or another, each of the constructionist movements grows out of a reconsideration of the representational duties traditionally assigned to language. The potential for such critique was already well in place earlier in the century, when logical empiricist philosophers were keen to establish a close relationship between language and observation. At the heart of the positivist movement, for example, lay the 'verifiability principle of meaning' (in revised form called 'meaning realism'), to wit, the meaning of a proposition rests on its capacity for verification through observation. Propositions not open to corroboration or emendation through observation are unworthy of further dispute. The problem was, however, to account for the connection between propositions and observations. Schlick (1925) proposed that the meaning of single words within propositions must be established through ostensive ('pointing to') means. In his early work, Carnap (1928) proposed that thing predicates represented 'primitive ideas', thus reducing scientific propositions to reports of private experience. For Neurath (1933), propositions were to be verified through 'protocol sentences', which were themselves linked to the biological processes of perception. Russell (1924) proposed that objective knowledge could be reduced to sets of 'atomic propositions', the truth of which would rest on isolated and distinguishable facts. In the end, none of these proposals proved viable, leaving the philosophy of science open first to the attacks of Popper (1935) on the lack of an inductive base for scientific description, and then Quine (1960) on the impossibility of pure, ostensive definition of scientific terms.

Convergencies of Critique

With the Achilles heel of the modernist promise of truth in language laid bare – along with the rationalization of authority – the way was open for the marginalized, dispossessed and politically active scholar to generate ferment. It was in this context that constructionist inquiry found an eager audience. In a certain sense, each of the constructionist critiques can be traced to a political base. However, in my view, the way in which these movements was political was dramatically different. Let us consider then the emergence of ideological critique, in which motivational unmasking is the dominant means of undermining the authority of language, and scholarship was most purposefully political; literary-rhetorical critique in which authority is reduced through linguistic reductionism and the primary battles were internecine; and social critique, in which authority is converted to communal expression and the implicit commitment was to democratic liberalism.

Ideological Critique and Political Commitment

For the better part of the century a strong attempt has been made to cut the modernist institution away from moral debate. Whether it be in science, education, public policy formation or national planning, the hope was to escape ideological and religious influences, and to reach decisions through objective and rational means. The institution of science served as a prominent icon. The task of the sciences, as commonly put, is to furnish objectively accurate accounts of 'what is the case'; matters of 'what ought to be' are not principally matters of scientific concern. When theoretical description and explanation are suffused with values, it is said, they are untrustworthy or prejudicial; they distort the truth.

However, during the 1960s–1970s the fallacy of the fact–value dualism became excruciatingly apparent. In particular, the moral outrage of the Vietnam war raised significant questions concerning the many complicit institutions (business, the university, science, etc.). The claims to scientific neutrality seemed, at best, to be a cheap means of escaping political deliberation; at worst, neutrality was just another word for legitimizing unjust and exploitative policies. Not only was there nothing about the scientific outlook that gave reason to reject the imperious brutality of the West, but the scientific establishment often lent its efforts to enhancing the technologies of aggression. The impulse to refurbish and revitalize the language of 'ought' gained further impetus from other political enclaves. Marxist critique of capitalist institutions was well in place in the academic sphere, and gained striking new momentum in critical and dialectic movements of the period. Class-based critique formed an active if not symbiotic relationship with civil rights and early feminist activism.

In order to achieve these various goals – peace, justice, equality and the like – it was essential to locate a means of discrediting the authority of the major institutions. The weakness of 'the word' served as a chief lever. Given the lack of philosophical justification for claiming 'truth through language', the ideological critic focused primarily on the motives underlying language. The ideological critic removes the authority of the truth claim by shifting the focus from the claim itself to the ideological or motivational basis from which it derives. By giving an intelligible account of the motives of the truth-teller to suppress, to gain power, to accumulate wealth, to sustain his/her culture above all others and so on, the suasive power of truth claims is destroyed. In effect, the language of description and explanation is reconstituted as motive language; claims to neutrality are viewed as 'mystifying', and factual talk is indexed as 'manipulation'. In this way the authority's claims to language as truth bearing are reduced to mere propaganda.

In important respects, the grounds for this form of critique were already well in place. The 1930s writings of the so-called Frankfurt School – Horkheimer, Adorno, Marcuse, Benjamin and others – were most immediately available. Critical school writings effectively traced a broad spectrum of social and individual ills to the Enlightenment quest for a historically and culturally transcendent rationality. The commitments to positivist philosophy of science, capitalism and bourgeois liberalism – contemporary manifestations of the Enlightenment vision – lent themselves to such evils as the erosion of community, the deterioration of moral values, the establishment of dominance relationships, the renunciation of pleasure, and the mutilation of nature. In this respect the neo-Marxist writings of the 1960s–1970s – borrowing from the critical tradition – furnished a model for many other scholars whose political interests were not in themselves Marxist. The process of motivational unmasking could be employed for sundry political purposes. Emblematic is R.D. Laing's *Politics of Experience*, a volume that is not itself Marxist, but employs the device of demystification for broader political ends. Laing's charge that, 'The choice of syntax and vocabulary is a political act that defines and circumscribes the manner in which "facts" are to be experienced. Indeed, in a sense it goes further and even creates the facts that are studied' (1983: 39) is without a bounded target. Additional expansions of the boundaries of political critique, employing much the same logic, include Gouldner (1960), Apfelbaum and Lubek (1976), Sampson (1978) and much of the writing in the anti-psychiatry movement.

Deconstruction through motivational unmasking has now become widespread. In terms of its extensiveness, sophistication and intensity it reaches its zenith in the feminist movement. It is represented in a host of recent works that extend the range of targets to include the authoritative voices of biological science (Martin, 1987), empiricist philosophy (Harding, 1986) and the natural sciences more generally (Keller, 1984). This same form of critical analysis now flourishes across the humanities and sciences. It is used by Afro-Americans, for example, to discredit implicit racism in its myriad forms, by gays to reveal homophobic attitudes within common representations of the world, by area specialists concerned with the subtle imperialism of Western ethnography. In effect, the form of critique calls attention to the constructed character of authoritative discourse, and does so for explicit political purposes.

Literary-Rhetorical Critique and the Politics of the Academy

Let us contrast motivational unmasking with a second threat to the mirroring capacity of language. If statements about the world are not derived from essential differences in the world itself, as traditional wisdom would have it, then how are we to account for our modes of description and explanation? One possible answer to this question is implied by much continental semiotic theory. If, following Saussure (1983), we view language as a system in itself – connected to the world of signifiers through arbitrary conventions – then we can understand the modes of description and explanation in terms of the demands of the linguistic system more generally. However, to the extent that description and explanation are demanded by the rules of language, the 'object of description' fails to impress itself upon the language. As literary requirements absorb the process of authoritative accounting, so do the objects of such accounts – as independent from the accounts themselves – lose ontological status and authority loses credibility.

In one form or another, this argument serves as the mainstay of much theory of literary criticism and rhetorical theory of recent decades. Unlike ideological criticism, which was (and is) political in its attempts to alter societal structures, the critique of linguistic reductionism was (at least initially) political in a more restricted sense. In my view, such critique served primarily to unsettle existing structures of power within the intellectual sphere. In the case of French 'intellectual politics' in particular, the dominant motif was structuralist. For the structuralist, a major distinction is made between the overt and the covert, the observable and its underlying cause, manifestation and origin, or, as in the case of language, between the word and its underlying meaning. For the structuralist the given – overt and observable – furnishes the rationale for inquiry, the endpoint of which is an elucidation of the underlying cause or origin – typically (though not exclusively) viewed as some form of structure. Structuralist assumptions were essential to most of the major intellectual traditions of the time. Marxist intellectuals were structuralist in their emphasis on material modes of production that underlie conditions of alienation and working-class oppression. The psychoanalytic movement stressed the use of the spoken word ('manifest content') as providing clues to the structure of unconscious desire ('latent content'). Even the dominant explorations of many semioticians presumed structures or organizing principles underlying local formations of language. Similarly, the celebrated work of anthropologist Lévi-Strauss traced various cultural forms and artefacts to an underlying binary logic (see especially Lévi-Strauss, 1963).

Interestingly, for those holding to truth through language, structuralist thought already began to pose a challenge. To the extent that so-called 'objective accounts' are driven not by events as they are but by structured systems – internal systems of meaning, unconscious forces, modes of production, inherent linguistic tendencies and the like – it is difficult to determine in what sense one can lay claim to an objective or accurate analysis. Description and explanation thus seems to be *structure-* rather than *object*-driven. Yet this challenge to the concepts of truth and objectivity was little developed within structuralist circles themselves. Most structuralists were modernists in their claim to a rational or objective basis for their knowledge of structure. Simultaneously, however, they left themselves vulnerable to the reflexive critique: structuralist analysis itself is in thrall to linguistic determination.

This vulnerability provided the opportunity for aspiring intellectuals to wreak havoc with the dominant intellectual movements in the academy. Most fully aspiring in intent and profound in its consequences were the post-structuralist writings of Jacques Derrida and the deconstruction movement. For Derrida (1976; 1978) the structuralist enterprise (and indeed all Western epistemology) was infected with an unfortunate 'metaphysics of presence'. Why, he asked, must we presume that discourse is an outward expression of an inward being (thought, intention, structure or the like)? On what grounds do we presume the presence of an unseen subjectivity behind the words? The unsettling implications of such questions is enhanced by Derrida's analysis of the means by which words acquire meaning. For Derrida, word meaning depends not only on *differences* between the auditory or visual characteristics of words, but on the process of *deferral*. That is, each word depends for its meaning on other words, for example oral and written definitions, formal and informal usages, furnished on various occasions over time. The meaning of each of these words and phrases depends on still other deferrals to other definitions and contexts, traces of uses in countless other settings.

If there is 'nothing outside of text', as such an analysis suggests, then a vast range of semiotic and literary analytic techniques becomes available for the more general discrediting of textual authority. In philosophy, for example, Rorty's (1979) significant attack on traditional philosophy of knowledge was grounded in literary analytics. The entire history of Western epistemology, proposed Rorty, results from the unfortunate metaphor of mind as mirror, a 'glassy essence' reflecting events in the external world. In effect, the longstanding debate between empiricists and rationalists is not about a realm existing outside the texts, but a combat between competing literary traditions. Remove the central metaphors and the debate largely collapses. Resonant with this deconstruction of philosophy were explorations into the literary basis of historical reality, legal rationality (Levinson, 1982), and other intellectual domains.

These internecine pyrotechnics also proved a stimulus for what might be called 'the revenge of rhetoric'. This 2,500-year-old tradition had come upon hard times. Modernist scholars had drawn a sharp distinction between the *content* of a given text (its substance) and its *form* (or mode of presentation). Science and other truth-generating disciplines, it was argued, are concerned with substance – with communicating content as accurately as possible. The form in which it is presented (its 'packaging') is not only of peripheral interest, but to the extent that persuasion depends on it, the scholarly project is subverted. Within this context, rhetorical study was thrust to the margins of the academy. However, as the truth-bearing capacity of language is threatened by post-structural literary theory, the presumption of content – an accurate portrayal of an independent object – gives way. All that was content stands open to critical analysis as persuasive form. In effect, developments in rhetorical study parallel those in literary criticism: both displace attention from the object of representation (the 'facts', the 'point of the argument') to the vehicle of representation.

Reasoning in this manner, rhetorically oriented scholars were furnished ammunition for a full-scale assault on the bastions of authority. Consider the case of 'human evolution', a seeming fact of biological life. As Misia Landau (1991) proposes, accounts of human evolution are not governed by events of the past (and their manifestation in various fossils), but by forms of narrative or storytelling. Major inquiries were also launched to understand the rhetorical basis of economics (McCloskey, 1985), psychology (Bazerman, 1988; Leary, 1990), and the human sciences more generally (Nelson et al., 1987; Simons, 1989, 1990). The authority claimed by traditional academic disciplines is displaced; rhetorical study holds the trumps.

Social Critique and the Liberal Tradition

The force of the ideological and literary-rhetorical assaults on traditional authority is augmented by a third scholarly movement, one of pivotal importance for the emergence of social constructionism. One beginning to this story can be traced to a line of thought emerging in the works of Max Weber, Max Scheler, Karl Mannheim and others occupied with the social genesis of scientific thought. In particular, each was concerned with the cultural context in which various ideas take shape, and the ways in which these ideas, in turn, give form to both scientific and cultural practice. It is perhaps Mannheim's 1929 volume, *Ideology and Utopia*, that contains the clearest outline of the assumptions of reverberating significance. As Mannheim proposed: (1) theoretical commitments may usefully be traced to social, as opposed to empirical or transcendentally rational, origins; (2) social groups are often organized around certain theories; (3) theoretical disagreements are issues of group (or political) conflict; and (4) what we take to be knowledge is culturally and historically contingent. Yet, with the bursting enthusiasm for empiricist foundationalism and its optimistic invitation for a unified science, the revolutionary implications of these views remained largely unexplored.

In certain respects the revitalization of the social view of knowledge can be traced to the same political ferment inciting the range of ideological critique discussed above. However, in this case the effects were, in my opinion, indirect. Japanese landscape designers make abundant use of the concept of 'borrowed scenery'. By this they mean that the particular design in focus may often be enhanced by using attributes of the ambient context – a distant mountain, a neighbouring monument or a nearby stand of trees. In similar fashion, the anti-institutional movements of the 1960s–1970s lent themselves strongly to a critical ethos in which the scientific knowledge industry, allied as it seemed with the 'military-industrial complex', was viewed with scorn. The social analysis of science essentially served a significant political need.

It is interesting to consider the alternative course that history might have taken if Thomas Kuhn had not entitled his 1962 volume, *The Structure of Scientific Revolutions*. The political climate into which this title was injected virtually ensured that its reading would be charged with far more energy than the specifics of the book could warrant. With such a plausible title as *Social Factors in the Copernican Controversy*, or *Paradigms and Progress*, I suspect that neither the social studies of science nor social constructionism would be flourishing as they are. Peter Winch's *The Idea of a Social Science*

(1958) had demonstrated the ways in which social theories are constitutive of the phenomena they purport to represent; Berger and Luckmann's *The Social Construction of Reality* (1966) had effectively replaced scientific objectivity with a conception of socially informed subjectivity; Georges Gurvitch's *The Social Frameworks of Knowledge* (1971) had traced scientific knowledge to communal frameworks of understanding. Yet, by comparison, these works simply lingered in the shadows of the Kuhnian controversy.

This is not to say that the social conception of knowledge was otherwise lacking in political consciousness. There are many ways in which these arguments are consistent with the liberal tradition in the social sciences more generally, a tradition in which primary value is placed on individual expression and well-being, progress by merit and freedom from tyranny. From the seminal contributions of, for example, Herbert Spencer, William Graham Sumner, G. Stanley Hall, William James, John Dewey and Max Weber, to the present, the social sciences have been identified as prominently liberal in posture. This same orientation is reflected in much of the social critique, aimed as it is at removing what seemed the tyrannical yoke of empiricist foundationalism in general and natural science authority in particular, and restoring voice to those otherwise dispossessed by the scientific establishment. The implicit politics is made explicit in Feyerabend's *Science in a Free Society*, where scientific specialists are said to be 'using tax money to destroy the traditions of the taxpayers, to ruin their minds, rape their environment, and . . . turn living human beings into well-trained slaves of their own barren vision of life' (1978: 10). For Feyerabend, as for many socially oriented constructionists, scholarly work should strive to create a 'a free society . . . in which all traditions have equal rights and equal access to the centres of power' (1978: 9). In this sense, the social emphasis in constructionism is politically allied with the middle, or bourgeois, class (see Rorty, 1983); this is in contrast to the ideological critics just discussed, where the needs of the lower or marginalized classes are often paramount.

The flowering of the movements variously indexed as the history of science, the sociology of knowledge and the social studies of science is well documented and needs little elaboration here. Particularly significant for contemporary social constructionism were elaborations of the micro-social processes out of which scientific meaning is produced. It is in this vein that sociologists have explored the social processes essential for creating 'facts' within the laboratory (Latour and Woolgar, 1979), the discursive practices of scientific communities, scientific knowledge claims as forms of symbolic capital (Bourdieu, 1977), the social practices underlying inductive inference (Collins, 1985), group influences on the way data are interpreted (Collins and Pinch, 1982) and the locally situated and contingent character of scientific description (Knorr-Cetina, 1981). Such work has also proved highly congenial to the simultaneously developing field of ethnomethodology. For Harold Garfinkel (1967) and his colleagues, the essential defeasibility of descriptive terms was demonstrated in studies of what counts as a psychiatric problem, suicide, juvenile crime, gender, states of mind, alcoholism, mental illness, or other putative constituents of the taken-for-granted world (see Atkinson, 1977; Cicourel, 1968; Coulter, 1979; Garfinkel, 1967; Scheff, 1966). In all cases there is a sense of liberation from the grip of the institutional taken-for-granted.

After the Deluge: Scintillating Schisms

We find, then, three major sources of contemporary construction, all sharing a critique of traditional views of language and authority, but differing in their mode of critique and their political investments. Together these lines of argument lay the basis for a profound shift in the academic temper, and resulting visions of knowledge, scholarship, pedagogy and, indeed, the shape of society. For many of those engaged in these efforts, there is no return to traditional scholarly life. At the same time, because of their disparate roots, these otherwise converging lines of argument harbour substantial tensions. Of particular concern to us here are the political dynamics set in motion by their interpenetration. Let us attend, then, to problems growing out of the incipient fear of falling away from tradition, issues stemming from mutual appropriation of discourses and, finally, emerging doubts concerning the very possibility of politics.

Tradition in Jeopardy   At the outset, while many scholars were drawn to certain constructionist arguments, they were also deeply unsettled by the political uses – both academic and societal – to which constructionist dialogues were put. They wished to contribute to the flow of ideas, but scorned the 'abuses' of the movement by otherwise like-minded colleagues. Or, more broadly, they were committed to various causes or traditions that were placed in severe jeopardy by extensions of constructionist thought. Constructionist critique might be embraced for its challenge to empiricist determinism, for example, but chastised for its deconstruction of humanist assumptions of subjectivity and human agency; it could be lauded for its undermining of social science authority but dismissed for its challenge to the natural sciences. Two politically significant polarities deserve special attention.

   One of the most prevalent conflicts in constructionist writings centres around the status of individual psychological processes (subjectivity, cognition, agency, the emotions). Many constructionists remain committed to individual process as the primary site of construction. Such commitments boast a strong lineage, including Berger and Luckmann's (1966) grounding of constructionism in phenomenology, Kuhn's (1970 [1962]: 111) tracing of paradigm shifts to Gestalt shifts in perception, and Hanson's (1958) arguments for the observer-determined basis of scientific realities. This lingering commitment is politically conservative in at least two important ways. On the one hand, it allies constructionist inquiry with longstanding traditions in the academy. Most of the social sciences are lodged in individualist forms of explanation; a psychologically based constructionism would form a felicitous extension of these traditions. In addition, however, an individually based constructionism is also congenial to central political and moral traditions of Western culture, lodged as they are in the belief in individuals as the originary sources of their own actions. Included here, for example, would be the institution of democracy, claims to human rights and the judicial system. At the same time, for many other constructionists such individualist tendencies are to be strongly resisted. Not only would constructionism fail to do any significant work within the academy – simply supporting the status quo – but it would sustain a deeply flawed tradition of self-contained individualism (see Sampson, 1978; 1988). On this side, many constructionists favour an emphasis on community (interdependence, negotiation, dialogue) over the individual as the site of moral and political action (see, for example, Gergen, 1994a; Shotter, 1993).

A second site of political tension derives from constructionist leanings toward relativism. Much constructionist writing lends itself to some form of relativism – in both the ontological and the moral realm. Once entering the critical corridors, it is very difficult to accept any particular reality posits, truth claims or moral principles as transparent, foundational or beyond construction. In this sense, constructionist thinking tends to remove the grounds for any strong claims to the real and the good. For many who participate in constructionist dialogues, such implications are nihilistic if not societally disastrous in consequence. The work of Rom Harré is illustrative, as it indicates the existence of strong competing tendencies even within the same individual. While Harré has been a vital contributor to constructionist conversations (for example, Harré, 1986), there is also a strongly conserving stance in much of his work. He fears, as he puts it, the 'slide into relativism' (Harré, 1992). Thus, Harré resists abandoning commitments to rational foundations of science (Harré, 1988), essentialist statements about human functioning (Harré and Gillett, 1994) and liberal tenets of moral action (Harré, 1992). More broadly, then, we detect a political split between those favouring retention of certain traditions – both academically and societally – and those advocating more radical change.

Appropriation for Political Purposes   Contributing to these conflicts is a second scholarly development stimulated by early constructionist critique. As participants in these various movements became increasingly aware of their affinities, so they also began to appropriate the neighbouring forms of argument. In particular, scholars committed to various political causes, and relying primarily on a strategy of ideological unmasking, rapidly became aware of the assets offered by the literary-rhetorical and social critiques. Not only could the prevailing powers be challenged on grounds of ideological subterfuge, but it became possible to demonstrate the linguistic and rhetorical artifice with which the dominant ideologies were sustained, and the cultural and historical contingency of their truth claims. In this context, for example, feminist critics demonstrated ways in which andro-centric metaphors guide theory construction in biology (Fausto-Sterling, 1985; Hubbard, 1983), biophysics (Keller, 1984) and anthropology (Sanday, 1988). Psychologists challenged the ideological repercussions of their discipline by probing the field's broad reliance on mechanistic metaphors (Hollis, 1977; Shotter, 1975), along with the socially constructed character of its empirical findings (Kitzinger, 1987; Sarbin, 1986).

Yet it would be shortsighted to view the process of interpolation as travelling in a single direction, with the politically engaged garnering discursive moves from their less committed colleagues. One must also suppose that there was a reciprocal influence, with the broader political implications of constructionist arguments gradually reaching consciousness. Here the pivotal role must be attributed to Foucault's writings – especially *Discipline and Punish* (1979) and *The History of Sexuality, Vol. 1* (1977). For Foucault, there is a close relationship between language (including all forms of text) and social process (conceived in terms of power relations). In particular, as various professions (e.g. the sciences, government, religion, the courts) develop languages that both justify their existence and articulate the social world, and as these languages are used in practice, so individuals come under the sway of such professions. Most pertinently, Foucault's writings single out individual subjectivity as the site where many contem-porary institutions – including the academic professions – insinuate them-selves into ongoing social life and expand their dominion. 'The "mind",' he writes, 'is a surface of inscription for power, with semiology as its tool' (1977: 102). With the broad circulation of these ideas, scholars everywhere were given reflexive pause. If scholarly work is inevitably participation in relations of power, then in what fashion is such power to be used or defused? It is partially in this vein that one may appreciate the increasingly political character of discourse analysis, for example, a movement that has important roots in the social studies of science. One locates strong societal critique in the discourse analytics of Billig et al. (1988; Billig, 1991), Edwards and Potter (1992) and Potter and Wetherell (1989), and in the journal, *Discourse and Society*, more generally.

The Possibilities of the Political   A third dynamic, born of intersecting dialogues from the past, sets an important agenda for the future. In this case, we find that the constructionist inquiry throws the very intelligibility of political action into question. The stage is set for this critical colloquy by the differing political bases of the three forms of critique. Specifically, for those engaged in ideological critique, significant social change is para-mount. 'Emancipation', a term freighted with emotional significance, is the very *raison d'être* of scientific analysis. From this standpoint, scholars engaged in literary and rhetorical deconstruction, or in the social analysis of science, seem politically puerile, if not egregiously blind to (or secretly supportive of) injustice and inequality everywhere apparent. Marxists, feminists, African-Americans and gay activists often scorn those who seem only to play effete literary games, or gain professional stature by producing obscure works on scientific procedures. For many activists, the disclosure of the Nazi sympathies of deconstructionist doyen, Paul de Man, only verified suspicions of political bankruptcy.

Such antipathy has rendered the ideological critic profoundly vulnerable. While engaging in wholesale disparagement of knowledge claims saturated with ideological interests, ideological critics have by necessity clung to some form of realism. Emancipation occurs when one understands the *true* nature of things – class, gender and racial inequality, for example. Yet, for both the literary and social analyst there is little room for a true or objective account of social conditions. All tellings are dominated by textual-rhetorical traditions, in the former instance, and by social process in the latter. In effect, ideological criticism loses any claim to veracity, and seems itself to be the product of ideologically invested and dangerously totalitarian impulses. The intensity of such conflicts is most readily apparent in the feminist movement. Deploying the full range of constructionist critique, many feminists have set out to undermine the empiricist movement in the social sciences and its oppressive effects on women. Those so-called feminist standpoint epistemologists (see Harding, 1986), while decrying empiricism as hopelessly androcentric, claim privileged access to the truth based on their marginal and oppressed position in society. These groups are simultaneously viewed with suspicion by a range of minority feminists – women of colour, lesbians, the poor – who see ideological forces at play in such claims. Further, so-called postmodern feminists (see, for example, Butler, 1990), find the literary-rhetorical and social constructionist arguments compelling, and search for means of justifying politics without ultimate commitment. The result has been profound fragmentation within the movement.

Politics as Relationship by Other Means

Largely owing to the diverse contexts giving rise to social constructionist dialogues, an array of political dynamics have been set in motion. Not only has constructionist thought become increasingly politicized in recent decades, but numerous schisms have developed within the ranks of those who otherwise share a common discursive base. Although some may despair over these tensions, there are also reasons for welcoming such an outcome – even from a constructionist standpoint itself. As a metatheoretical outlook, constructionism is deeply pluralistic. There are no foundational grounds for discrediting any form of discourse, and because discursive practices are embedded within forms of life, to obliterate a language would be to threaten a form of humanity. In effect, there is a place for all entries into intelligibility, even those that would militate against constructionism itself. Thus, in the political domain, any attempt at full amalgamation – the realization of a unified political front – would be reason for suspicion. In this sense, the very existence of political disagreements among constructionists may be viewed as a vital sign.

It is my hope that as constructionist dialogues play out, they will move beyond a contentious politics. As I have suggested, present-day constructionism was nurtured in the soil of conflict; it gained its initial momentum from the dynamics of opposition. Similarly, as tensions have developed among constructionist enclaves, a critical posture has prevailed. We have learned well the skills of deconstructive critique, and as we have come to speak among ourselves (as opposed to the rearguard skirmishes of previous years), we have continued to rely on these skills. However, as I have proposed elsewhere (Gergen, 1994b), there are serious limits to the rhetoric of critique. Most frequently, it serves to breed hostility as opposed to change, encourages a self-satisfied sense of superiority and further fragments and isolates the socius. The problem, then, is not in having political positions; virtually all action is political in implication. The major problem is our inheritance of a tradition of argumentation that favours critique as its major mode of addressing 'the opposition'. In my view, the constructionist dialogues contain the seeds for radical alteration in the mode of politics.

In particular, as we extend the social emphasis of much constructionist writing, 'the word' is removed from the foreground of concern. Rather than focusing on political or rhetorical content, we are drawn to the forms of relationship which bring content and rhetoric to life. This includes the relational implications of critique itself and the possibility that alternative forms of relationship might prove more adequate in determining the collective future. The challenge is to explore the relational frontier for practices that may facilitate the co-habitation of a multiplicity of disparate voices. What forms of dialogue are likely to yield more acceptable outcomes than those produced by argumentation? Attempting to deal with the foibles of identity politics, I have elsewhere outlined the basis for a *relational politics*, that is an orientation to political interchange that emphasizes the interdependent basis of meaning, the defusing and diffusion of blame, and the possibility of collaborative as opposed to agonistic practices. This work serves as but an invitational entry into a more extended discussion of broad potential.

Note

1 For a more complete review of these and related developments, see Gergen (1994a).

References

Apfelbaum, E. and Lubek, I. (1976) 'Resolution vs. revolution? The theory of conflicts in question', in L. Strickland, F. Aboud and K.J. Gergen (eds), *Social Psychology in Transition*. New York: Plenum Press.

Atkinson, J.M. (1977) *Discovering Suicide: Studies in the Social Organization of Sudden Death*. London: Macmillan.

Bazerman, C. (1988) *Shaping Written Knowledge*. Madison, WI: University of Wisconsin Press.

Berger, P. and Luckmann, T. (1966) *The Social Construction of Reality*. New York: Doubleday/ Anchor.

Billig, M. (1991) *Talking of the Royal Family*. London: Routledge.

Billig, M., et al. (1988) *Ideological Dilemmas: A Social Psychology of Everyday Thinking*. London: Sage.

Bourdieu, P. (1977) 'Outline of a theory of practice: consciousness and cognition in the history of psychology', in D. Leary (ed.), *Metaphors in the History of Psychology*. New York: Cambridge University Press.

Butler, J. (1990) *Gender Trouble: Feminism and the Subversion of Identity*. New York: Routledge.

Carnap, R. (1928) *Knowledge, Theory of Ontology*. Berlin: Schlachtensee.

Cicourel, A.V. (1968) *The Social Organization of Juvenile Justice*. New York: Wiley.

Collins, H.M. (1985) *Changing Order*. London: Sage.

Collins, H.M. and Pinch, T.J. (1982) *Frames of Meaning: The Social Construction of Extraordinary Science*. London: Routledge & Kegan Paul.

Coulter, J. (1979) *The Social Construction of the Mind*. New York: Macmillan.

Derrida, J. (1976) *Of Grammatology*. Baltimore, MD: Johns Hopkins University Press.

Derrida, J. (1978) *Writing and Difference*. Chicago: University of Chicago Press.

Edwards, D. and Potter, J. (1992) *Discursive Psychology*. London: Sage.

Fausto-Sterling, A. (1985) *Myths of Gender: Theories about Women and Men*. New York: Basic Books.

Feyerabend, P.K. (1978) *Science in a Free Society*. London: Thetford Press.

Foucault, M. (1977) *The History of Sexuality, Vol. 1: An Introduction*. New York: Pantheon.

Foucault, M. (1979) *Discipline and Punish: The Birth of the Prison*. New York: Random House.

Garfinkel, H. (1967) *Studies in Ethnomethodology*. Englewood Cliffs, NJ: Prentice-Hall.

Gergen, K.J. (1994a) *Realities and Relationships*. Cambridge, MA: Harvard University Press.

Gergen, K.J. (1994b) 'The limits of pure critique', in H. Simons and M. Billig (eds), *After Postmodernism: Reconstructing Ideology Critique*. London: Sage.

Gouldner, A.W. (1960) 'A norm of reciprocity: a preliminary statement', *American Sociological Review*, 25: 161–78.

Gurvitch, G. (1971) *The Social Frameworks of Knowledge*. New York: Harper & Row.

Hanson, N.R. (1958) *Patterns of Discovery*. Cambridge: Cambridge University Press.

Harding, S. (1986) *The Science Question in Feminism*. Ithaca, NY: Cornell University Press.

Harré, R. (1986) 'The social constructionist viewpoint', in R. Harré (ed.), *The Social Construction of Emotion*. Oxford: Blackwell.

Harré, R. (1988) *Varieties of Realism*. Oxford: Oxford University Press.

Harré, R. (1992) 'What is real psychology? A plea for persons', *Theory and Psychology*, 2: 153–8.

Harré, R. and Gillett, G. (1994) *The Discursive Mind*. Thousand Oaks, CA: Sage.

Hollis, M. (1977) *Models of Man*. London: Cambridge University Press.

Hubbard, R. (1983) 'Have only men evolved', in S. Harding and M. Hintikka (eds), *Discovering Reality: Feminist Perspectives on Epistemology, Metaphysics, Methodology, and Philosophy of Science*. Dordrecht: Reidel.

Keller, E.F. (1984) *Reflections on Gender and Science*. New Haven, CT: Yale University Press.

Kitzinger, C. (1987) *The Social Construction of Lesbianism*. London: Sage.

Knorr-Cetina, K.D. (1981) *The Manufacture of Knowledge*. Oxford: Pergamon.

Kuhn, T.S. (1970 [1962]) *The Structure of Scientific Revolution*, 2nd revised edn. Chicago: University of Chicago Press.

Laing, R.D. (1983) *Politics of Experience*. New York: Vintage Books.

Landau, M. (1991) *Narratives of Human Evolution*. New Haven, CT: Yale University Press.

Latour, B. and Woolgar, S. (1979) *Laboratory Life: The Social Construction of Scientific Facts*. Beverly Hills, CA: Sage.

Leary, D. (1990) *Metaphors in the History of Psychology*. Cambridge: Cambridge University Press.

Lévi-Strauss, C. (1963) *The Raw and the Cooked*, trans. D. Weighton. New York: Harper & Row.

Levinson, S. (1982) 'Law as literature', *Texas Law Review*, 60: 388–411.

McCloskey, D.N. (1985) *The Rhetoric of Economics*. Madison, WI: University of Wisconsin Press.

Mannheim, K. (1951 [1929]) *Ideology and Utopia*. New York: Harcourt Brace.

Martin, E. (1987) *Woman in the Body*. Boston, MA: Beacon Press.

Nelson, J.S., Megill, A. and McCloskey, D. (eds) (1987) *The Rhetoric of the Human Sciences*. Madison, WI: University of Wisconsin Press.

Neurath, O. (1933) *Einheitwissenschaft und Psychologie*. Vienna: Gerold.

Popper, K.R. (1935) *Logik der Forschung: Zur Erkenntnistheorie der modernen Naturwissenschaft*. Vienna: J. Springer.

Potter, J. and Wetherell, M. (1989) 'Fragmented ideologies: accounts of educational failure and positive discrimination', *Text*, 9: 175–90.

Quine, W.V.O. (1960) *Word and Object*. Cambridge, MA: MIT Press.

Rorty, R. (1979) *Philosophy and the Mirror of Nature*. Princeton, NJ: Princeton University Press.

Rorty, R. (1983) 'Postmodernist bourgeois liberalism', *Journal of Philosophy*, 80: 585–94.

Russell, B. (1924) 'Logical atomism', in J.H. Muirhead (ed.), *Contemporary British Philosophy*. London: Allen & Unwin.

Sampson, E.E. (1977) 'Psychology and the American ideal', *Journal of Personality and Social Psychology*, 35: 767–82.

Sampson, E.E. (1978) 'Scientific paradigms and social values: wanted – a scientific revolution', *Journal of Personality and Social Psychology*, 36: 1332–43.

Sampson, E.E. (1988) 'The debate on individualism', *American Psychologist*, 43: 15–22.

Sarbin, T.R. (1986) 'Emotion and act: roles and rhetoric', in R. Harré (ed.), *The Social Construction of Emotions*. New York: Basil Blackwell. pp. 83–98.

Saussure, F. de (1983) *Course of General Linguistics*. London: Peter Owen.

Scheff, T.J. (1966) *Being Mentally Ill*. Chicago: Aldine.

Schlick, M. (1925) *General Theory of Knowledge*. New York: Springer-Verlag.

Shotter, J. (1975) *Images of Man in Psychological Research*. London: Methuen.

Shotter, J. (1993) *The Cultural Politics of Everyday Life*. Toronto: University of Toronto Press.

Simons, H. (ed.) (1989) *Rhetoric in the Human Sciences*. London: Sage.

Simons, H.W. (1990) *The Rhetorical Turn*. Chicago: University of Chicago Press.

Winch, P. (1958) *The Idea of Social Science and its Relation to Philosophy*. London: Routledge & Kegan Paul.

3

On Being More Literal about Construction

Ian Hacking

The metaphor of social construction once had excellent shock value, but now it has become tired. Many types of analysis invoke social construction, with the result that distinct objectives have been run together. An all-encompassing social constructionism is rather dull – in both senses of that word, boring and blunted. In an attempt to sharpen, but also to limit, the idea of social construction, six theses are presented:

1   Most items said to be socially constructed could be constructed only socially, if they are constructed at all. Hence the epithet 'social' is usually a tautology which should be used sparingly, and only for emphasis or contrast.
2   There is a wider range of construction ideas than is commonly acknowledged. Logical positivism, usually thought of as the very opposite of constructionism, is also deeply committed to the construction metaphor.
3   We should insist that the metaphor of construction retain one element of its literal meaning, that of building or assembling from parts.
4   Many construction analyses aim at what Karl Mannheim called 'unmasking' an idea or practice, in contrast to refuting that idea or showing that the practice does not well serve its purposes. There are many kinds of unmasking.
5   Analyses that chiefly aim at unmasking are to be distinguished from those that primarily aim at refuting or discrediting, but which also show how what is to be refuted or discredited was constructed in the first place.
6   Construction analyses have been applied primarily (a) to ideas about people, knowledge of people, or practices that involve the interactions of people. They have also been applied to (b) knowledge of inanimate nature. The unmasking aimed at in analyses of type (b) has been essentially different from that in type (a). Type (b) unmasking has metaphysical aims; while type (a) has sociopolitical ones.

*

1   Most items said to be socially constructed could be constructed only
     socially, if they are constructed at all. Hence the epithet 'social' is usually
     a tautology which should be used sparingly, and only for emphasis or
     contrast.

The adjective 'social' itself has, in the context of 'social construction',
become idle except as a reminder. Take for example the assertion that
gender is a social construction. Lorber and Farrell (1991) is a collection of
papers stating the case, under the title, *The Social Construction of Gender*.
Yet no matter what definition of 'gender' is preferred, the word is used for a
distinction grounded in cultural practices. It is contrasted with 'sex', which
denotes physiological attributes. In this usage, it would be significant to
discuss the social construction of sex, which is arguably the intent of
Laqueur (1990), *Making Sex*. But if gender is, by definition, something
essentially social, and if it is constructed, how could its construction be
other than social?

   The emphasis given by the word 'social' becomes useful when we turn to
inanimate objects, phenomena, or facts that are usually thought of as part of
nature, existing independent of human society. Thus Latour and Woolgar
(1979) was subtitled *The Social Construction of Scientific Facts*. The authors
describe the work done in a laboratory whose head shared a Nobel Prize for
Medicine. The laboratory discovered the structure of a certain tripeptide, a
hormone called Thyrotropin Releasing Factor. The prize was won because
this substance was thought to be central to the endocrine system, to
metabolism and to maturation in mammals, especially humans. Another
basis for the prize was the fact that the substance was not analysed, because
it was available only in the most minute quantities. Instead the experimenters synthesized substances until they got the right one. Thus the
scientific facts focal to Latour and Woolgar (1979) are, for example, 'TRF
has chemical structure so-and-so' and 'Such-and-such is the protocol for an
assay to determine concentration of TRF.'

   It was certainly shocking, in 1979, to be told about the social construction
of such impersonal, pre-social, biochemical facts. In their second edition
(Latour and Woolgar, 1986) the authors nevertheless dropped the word
'social' from their subtitle:

> What does it mean to talk about 'social' construction? There is no shame in
> admitting that the term no longer has any meaning. . . . By demonstrating its
> pervasive applicability, the social study of science has rendered 'social' devoid of
> any meaning. (1986: 281)

Now Latour had his own agenda here, increasingly apparent with the
hybrid natural/social actants of Latour (1987) and the parliament of things
in Latour (1993). He holds that the usual distinction between the natural
and the social is a sham, and he would assuredly question or modify thesis
6 above. But one need not agree with his agenda, in urging that we drop
the 'social' except for an occasional emphasis. First think of essentially
social entities, states or conditions – I strive for sufficiently generic and

noncommittal nouns here – such as literacy or lesbianism. These are the topics of two *The Social Construction of Books* (Cook-Gomperz, 1986; Kitzinger, 1987). If literacy or lesbianism is constructed, how other than socially? Think next of non human items, such as quarks (as in *Constructing Quarks*: Pickering, 1986), or the scientific facts about a certain tripeptide. Now if we argue, as do Pickering, Latour and Woolgar, that these items are less discovered than constructed, how else could they be constructed than socially? You might think that the 'social' is needed, for shock value, yet it is Latour and Woolgar themselves who drop the word, and Pickering did not use it. Given that quarks are, in current theory, the fundamental elements of everything, Pickering's title was eye-catching enough – for we think, if there is anything that is not constructed for sure, it must be quarks!

These philosopher-sociologists of the natural sciences were ahead of those who study more humane topics such as lesbianism or literacy. In 1986–87 the students of natural scientists banned, or never used, the adjective 'social' for their titles or their texts. Authors discussing specifically human affairs continued to employ it rather unreflectively. Forgive me for flogging a horse that ought to be dead, but in the very recent thesis files of my own university, one finds such titles as *The Social Construction of a Medicalized Immigrant* and *The Social Construction of Franco-Ontarian Interests towards French Language Schooling*. One fears that many other institutions are generating comparable titles.

Thesis 1 does not state that it is always pointless to use the word 'social' in connection with construction. For example, 'social constructionist' has come to name a quite widespread body of tenets, theories or attitudes. The adjective 'social' is part of the *name* of this body of thought. For example Donna Harraway (1991: 184) wrote that 'recent social studies of science and technology have made available a very strong social constructionist argument for *all* forms of knowledge claims, most certainly and especially scientific ones'. (Here she cites Bijker et al., 1987; Knorr-Cetina and Mulkay, 1983; and 'especially Latour' on Pasteur.) Such sceptical approaches starkly contrast with John Searle's *The Construction of Social Reality* (1995). So set are we in our expectations that in limited experimentation it appears that on first encounter many people, including booksellers, take the title to be 'The Social Construction of Reality', the radical opposite of what Searle meant. Searle describes something social, namely institutions and customs that become objective, create rights and determine obligations. He offers a theory about how they become objective. Their construction arises from social interactions and habits. But in no sense is Searle a social constructionist. There is hardly a moment of empirical sociological observation in the entire book. More importantly Searle is not interested in unmasking institutions and obligations, in the sense of Mannheim described in thesis 4 below. Instead he argues that the very mode of their construction makes them objective. His project hails from Kant. Searle is faithful to the metaphor of construction, because he tells how a hierarchy of social organizations and practices is built upon what are, at the bottom level, physical and biochemical interactions. The project is foundational. It is important to have a name to indicate the bodies of doctrine that Harraway is, and Searle is not, attracted to.

★

2   There is a wider range of construction ideas than is commonly acknow-
     ledged. Logical positivism, usually thought of as the very opposite of
     constructionism, is also deeply committed to the construction metaphor.

Nelson Goodman, a philosopher of both the arts and the sciences, has described his orientation as, among other things, 'constructionalist' (Goodman, 1978: 1). Possibly two meanings are packed into this label. One refers to Goodman's early work. It involves making or exhibiting constructions. This meaning harks back to the era of Bertrand Russell, who had a theory about logical constructions. If X is a term that, grammatically, is used to refer to something, X is a logical construction when sentences in which X appears as a denoting phrase are logically equivalent to sentences in which X does not occur, and no reference is made to the entity that X refers to. Thus although statements using X appear to refer to such entities, and hence to imply or presuppose the existence of those entities, logical analysis obviates the implication. 'Wherever possible,' Russell famously said, in a nominalist mood, 'logical constructions are to be substituted for inferred entities' (Russell, 1918: 155). This early use of the construction idea was thoroughly anti-realist about constructed entities. Statements that so-and-sos exist are true, but when analysed they turn out not to assert the existence of so-and-so at all. But the anti-realism about so-and-sos is not what we might call same-level anti-realism. It does not assert, 'There are no such things as so-and-sos.' That statement is contrary to but at the same level as 'There are such things as so-and-sos.' Instead Russell's analysis shows that the logical form of such existence statements is not what we think. We discover that below the grammatical surface we were never talking about so-and-sos in the first place. Russellian analyses do not debunk inferred entities. They may be taken to show that there is no commitment to the existence of so-and-sos. But on the other hand, they license, or provide a ground for, statements about so-and-sos, precisely because they show that those statements do not have the existential commitments we expect them to have.

Russell's programme was energetically pursued in Rudolf Carnap's *Der logische Aufbau der Welt* (1928). The English translation renders *Aufbau* as 'structure' but *Aufbau* means 'construction' (or in context the gerund 'building'), and that is what Carnap meant. The heir to *Aufbau* was Nelson Goodman's *The Structure of Appearance* (1951), based on Goodman's doctoral dissertation (1990 [1940]). Goodman's early version of constructionalism was an active philosophy which constructed, or showed how to construct abstract objects. It was also a radical critique of *Aufbau*, arguing that 'The World' could be 'constructed' in many ways. Might some ways be 'simpler' than others? No. Goodman is the author of the most trenchant of critiques of the notion that simplicity has any existence outside of the eye of the beholder. Any one world may be made in many ways, and many worlds may be made.

Before turning to a later genre of constructionalism, another of Russell's heirs should be mentioned – from empirical psychology. Hypothetical entities or quantities in psychology came to be called constructs. Familiar examples are IQ or Spearman's controversial *g*, the factor called 'general intelligence'. In the late 1930s logical positivist philosophers of the natural sciences had begun using the word 'construct' for theoretical entities such as electrons (see Beck, 1950 for references). Immediately after World War II this usage was transferred to the philosophy of psychology (e.g. Mac-Corquodale and Meehl, 1948). One problem was how to distinguish constructs that positivists took to be virtuous from those that they took to be suspicious, such as libido. A demarcation problem presented itself: when are hypothetical constructs valid? The most authoritative text on psychological testing states that

> The term 'construct validity' was officially introduced into the psychometrist's lexicon in 1954 in the *Technical Recommendations for Psychological Tests and Diagnostic Techniques*, which constituted the first edition of the 1985 *Testing Standards*. The first detailed exposition of construct validity appeared the following year in an article by Cronbach and Meehl. (Anastasi, 1988: 161)

The logical positivist ancestry of construct validity has been somewhat suppressed in psychology's self-history. In 1955, Lee Cronbach (b. 1916) was rapidly establishing himself as a leading figure in education. Paul Meehl (b. 1920), one of the most sophisticated critics of much experimental and statistical psychology, was a student of Herbert Feigl, the distinguished logical positivist who had emigrated from Berlin to Minnesota. Russell's logical constructions and Carnap's *Aufbau* were very much present at the birth of that cardinal concept of psychological testing, construct validity.

Nelson Goodman became constructionalist in a sense seemingly different from that of Russell and Carnap. His title *Ways of Worldmaking* (1978) means what it says. Goodman contentedly talks of making worlds, and takes for granted that it is we, people, who make them. Moreover, we do so in concert. This sounds social, but Goodman got there in a straight line from Russell and Carnap. Those men might have been troubled by some of the twists of constructionism in recent sociology. Not *too* upset, however. Kuhn is standardly presented as the originator of the modern trend towards social studies of science, but as Peter Galison (1990) has shown, there is a good deal of commonality between Kuhn and Carnap, and both men knew it. The roots of social constructionism are in the very logical positivism that so many of its practitioners profess to detest.

We can help ourselves to a ready-made terminology for distinct attitudes to construction. Goodman has called himself a constructionalist; that is his own made-up word. Let *constructionalism* refer to the philosophical projects of Russell, Carnap, Goodman et al., that aim at exhibiting how, or proving that, various important entities, concepts, worlds or whatever are constructed out of other materials. Constructionalists may hold that constructions are made by people, together, but do not study historical or social events or processes. Their instincts are anti-realist about constructed items, and yet they are not profoundly sceptical about them. They do not say flatly that the items do not exist, or that we cannot have grounds for believing they exist. On the contrary, we have excellent grounds, but our beliefs are not what they seem. Constructionalism is a change in the level of discourse. It can include the Cronbach and Meehl proposals – now so entrenched in experimental psychology of measurement – for legitimizing constructs in psychology which do not derive from direct observation.

By *constructionism* (or social constructionism if we need, on occasion, to emphasize the social) we should mean various sociological, historical and philosophical projects that aim at displaying or analysing actual, historically situated, social interactions or causal routes that led to or were involved in the construction of an entity. Constructionism is far more profoundly sceptical than constructionalism. By chance we are left with a third name, already in use for a third type of emphasis on construction. *Constructivism* is loosely used to include Brouwer's intuitionism and the various types of constructive mathematics (Bishop, 1972). It is the name for the several schools in the foundation of mathematics who maintain that we are entitled to assert the existence of a mathematical object if and only if we are able to, in a certain sense, construct that object. The underlying attitude of constructivism in mathematics is sceptical, because it forbids us to assert the existence of many mathematical objects that most mathematicians take for granted. But construction of a mathematical object is, for these schools, not a way of undermining it but instead is the only proof of authenticity. Thus construction plays an entirely different role, in this minority approach to mathematics, than it does in either (social) constructionism or in (philosophical) constructionalism.

Constructivists, constructionists and constructionalists live in different intellectual milieux. Some constructionists have never heard of constructivism in mathematics. Yet the themes and attitudes that characterize these isms are not so different. From all three we hear that things are not what they seem. All three are iconoclastic, querying the varnished reality of what the general run of people take for real. It is quite easy to delve further into history, and see all three of these isms as emanations from Kant.

Goodman and his fellow constructionalists say almost nothing about actual societies or social processes. This is to some extent a generational effect. Goodman's contemporary, Quine wrote a great deal about translation, but it was all fantasy translation involving fantasy explorers encountering fantasy natives who lived in fantasy jungles which were populated by rabbits. Goodman's world-making has to be social: it is people who do it. Yet his work gives no hint of any actual social process involved in world-making. He has nevertheless been enthusiastic about at least some social studies of construction in the natural sciences. For example his attention was drawn to Latour and Woolgar late in the day by a generally enthusiastic paper about that work (Hacking, 1988). Goodman wrote asking that offprints of that paper be sent to his own immediate circle of constructionalists, because Latour and Woolgar had so brilliantly presented a case of world-making.

It is less often noticed that Kuhn too says little about the social, and that he himself has been an internalist historian of science. His masterpiece, ever fresh, is now well over thirty years old – truly the work of a previous generation. *The Structure of Scientific Revolutions* is rightly honoured, by those who conduct social studies of the sciences, as their pre-eminent predecessor. Yet for all that Kuhn emphasizes a disciplinary matrix of one hundred or so researchers, or the role of exemplars in science teaching, imitation and practice, he has virtually nothing to say about social interaction. Hence in 1979, when Latour and Woolgar published, the word 'social' was doing some work, moving us along from Kuhn. But by 1986 it had lost its bite. We have moved on twelve years from 1986. The word 'construction' itself now seems almost worn out. It has become more of a way of stating whose side you are on than of describing the content of your analysis. But to repeat, there are still occasions when 'social', 'construction' and 'social construction' can do work. For example, we may want to contrast more recent ideas of construction with ones that close readers find in Kant – as in Onora O'Neill's *Constructions of Reason* (1989). Or we may want to contrast ideas of social construction with some notions of constructions of concepts urged in cognitive psychology. But whatever we are doing, we should attend to the building in construction.

*

3   We should insist that the metaphor of construction retain one element of its literal meaning, that of building or assembling from parts.

Here are some more titles from *The Social Construction of* rut, culled from the list of books in a library catalogue: emotion, fertility, homosexual culture, illness, schooling, women refugees, written communication. Titles that begin with *Constructing* include: arithmetical meanings, authorship, brotherhood, childhood, the child-viewer of television, dangerousness, deafness, femininity, homosexuality, inequality – to stop in the first half of the alphabet. (The last entry in the list is *Constructing the Universe*, which happens not to be a social construction book at all.) But of course there is a disjoint set of *Constructing* titles, of which the first in the library catalogue is *Constructing a Five String Banjo*.

In many of these construction/constructing works, nothing like literal construction is presented. Construction has become a dead metaphor. That expression, itself a metaphor, is from Fowler's *Modern English Usage*:

METAPHOR. 1. Live & dead m. In all discussion of m. it must be borne in mind that some metaphors are living, i.e., are offered & accepted with a consciousness of their nature as substitutes for their literal equivalents, while others are dead, i.e., have been so often used that speaker & hearer have ceased to be aware that the words used are not literal; but the line of distinction between the live & the dead is a shifting one, the dead being sometimes liable, under the stimulus of an affinity or a repulsion, to galvanic stirrings indistinguishable from life. (Fowler, 1926: 348–9)

If we are to return 'construction' to life, we should attend to its ordinary meanings, as in constructing a five-string banjo. The core idea, from the Latin to the present, is that of building, of putting together. The fairly new (1992) *American Heritage Dictionary* first offers, 'to form by assembling or combining parts'. Then it gives a dead metaphor, where one does not assemble brick and mortar, or girders and concrete, but 'To create (an argument or a sentence, for example) by systematically arranging ideas or terms'. This metaphor, like the very ancient and very dead geometrical metaphor of constructing with a ruler and compass, retains the sense of systematic arrangement of elements, which become part of a whole (where of course the whole is more than the sum of the parts, because it is a systematic arrangement, a structure). Constructionalists and constructivists are true to the root metaphor of construction as building. Let us now urge constructionists to keep the same faith. Anything worth calling a construction was or is constructed in quite definite stages, where the later stages are built upon, or of, the product of earlier stages. Anything worth calling a construction has a history. But not just any history. It has to be a history of building.

Some who have written metaphorically about construction have been fairly loyal to the literal meaning. Again take Latour and Woolgar for an example. Among the things that make their essay compelling are the specific stages to their story. In some of these stages we find sub-constructions, in which an element essential to the final construction was itself constructed. That resembles the way that construction workers (to use an expression more American than the simpler British word 'builders') install pre-assembled window frames or even windows in the structure that they are erecting. Latour and Woolgar's discussion of the assay for Thyrotropin Releasing Factor is especially useful. The assay for this hormone was not like an assay for gold, a more precise technique for identifying and measuring the concentration of a substance that could already be recognized and identified by other means. The hormone is incredibly rare in nature. Before it was synthesized, the total volume of it that had ever existed in the universe, if collected in a pure state, would have occupied less volume than your hand, perhaps less than your little toe. One of the two successful labs extracted an eyedrop of very dilute TRF from 500 tons of pig-brain soup; the other used 200 tons of sheep-brain stew. The assay for this stuff relied on seeing what it did to the thyrotropin concentration in animals sacrificed after injection, a concentration measured by another assay. The assay for TRF requires standardized protocols (standardized male rats of a certain age reared in constant conditions of sixteen hours of light per day at constant temperature, etc., etc., etc.). Although certain types of bio-assays of the day provided the model, the specific assay for TRH was fought over, and the winning labs won the right to use their assay technique as the standard for TRH. The assay became, to inject a live metaphor, an essential building block in the construction of the facts about TRF. Moreover, it was a very contingent building block. It was not predetermined that a certain assay protocol would become the standard in the field.

Latour and Woolgar could point not only to stages in the assembling of TRF, but also to stages in which certain elements in the final arrangement which also could be thought of as constructed. Latour's later, and very valuable, metaphor of the black box brings life to some talk of constructions. For black boxes are precisely prefabricated ingredients used for making some larger assemblage. Even the assay protocol for TRH became black-boxed. Nowadays you buy what are quite literally black boxes, which you hook up to the grey box of your computer. The black box plus the software does the assay for you.

Latour and Woolgar's *Laboratory Life* is not typical of constructionist work because it is about a natural science, the biochemistry of the endocrine system. The book will be a useful example in arguing for thesis 6, about the difference in objectives between natural and social science applications of constructionism. Danziger's *Constructing the Subject* (1990) is a fine example of how the construction metaphor can be used, fairly literally, when applied to a social rather than a natural science. What is being constructed? As is quite common in *Constructing* books, several categorically distinct kinds of entity are constructed. In Danziger, at least four: a concept, a practice, a body of knowledge and a new kind of person. First an idea or concept was constructed, the idea of the subject to observe or to test in experiments. Danziger is convincing when he urges that this is not a self-evident idea that is definite and well understood as soon as the idea of laboratory-style experimentation on the human mind has come into being. The first subjects of psychological experiments were commonly the experimenters themselves – Gustav Fechner, for example. Or the experimenter and subject were two people who switched roles, the subject becoming the experimenter who subjected the former experimenter to test. This contrasts dramatically with the subsequent notions of an objective psychology, in which the subject is actually thought of as an object who must be scrupulously set apart from the experimenter to avoid contamination.

Secondly, Danziger's book is about constructing a family of practices within which the subject is embedded. The upshot is a laboratory that is expanded to occupy the worlds of business, the military, education, law and pathology, where people are regarded as subjects for testing. In a powerful passage at the end of his book, Danziger writes of 'a fundamental convergence between contexts of investigation and contexts of application'.

the individuals under investigation became the objects for the exercise of a certain kind of social power. This was not a personal, let alone violent, kind of power, but the kind of impersonal power that Foucault has characterized as being based on 'discipline'. It is the kind of power that is involved in the management of persons through the subjection of individual action to an imposed analytic framework and cumulative measures of performance. The quantitative comparison and evaluation of these evoked individual performances then leads to an ordering of individuals under statistical norms. Such procedures are at the same time techniques for disciplining individuals and the basis of methods for producing a certain kind of knowledge. As disciplinary techniques the relevant practices had arisen during the historical transformation of certain social institutions, like schools, hospitals, military institutions, and, one may add, industrial and commercial institutions. . . . This kind of knowledge was essentially administratively useful knowledge required to rationalize techniques of social control in certain institutional contexts. Insofar as it had become devoted to the production of such knowledge, mid-twentieth-century psychology had been transformed into an administrative science. (Danziger, 1990: 170)

Danziger's last chapter is entitled 'The social construction of psychological knowledge'. That is the third category of items constructed: a body of knowledge. Only by implication does Danziger discuss a fourth category, people. We are now trained to answer questionnaires or perform various tasks in order to find out our talents or what ails us. Of course the tests themselves don't settle things. Some readers will wish I had followed the advice given after my vocational aptitude tests early in high school – that I should become a meteorologist. The point is not what the tests say about each of us, but that we are now a kind of person who hardly existed a century and a half ago: fit subject for testing. Without us as common fodder for tests, there could hardly be such a thing as the *Mental Measurements Yearbook* (Mitchell, 1992). This handbook is scrupulous in admitting only very well validated and widely used tests, which may be purchased in standardized printed forms for immediate use. The number of available tests has doubled with each edition over the past decades.

Danziger's book is a paragon of fairly literal constructionism. It presents a history of crafting various parts that are in turn assembled into larger structures. We begin with the physiology laboratory as model. Using that model a new type of investigation is constructed. Certain types of inquiry are pared away from it – Wundt's introspection, for example. A new element is added. Aggregates of subjects become critical as statistical techniques fairly internal to psychology are built up. Concurrently developed statistical procedures from biometrics are incorporated, often in black-box form. The metaphor of construction well fits the chain of events Danziger organizes. This is because there is what is very properly thought of as the building of specific techniques, institutions and problems which are assembled to form a further stage in the production of later techniques, institutions and problems. Notice, incidentally, that although an archaeological investigation (in the sense of Michel Foucault) of empirical psychology would be appropriate, it would be at a far remove from Danziger's constructionism. Danziger has precisely not given an account of an initial sharp cut which sets up the discursive formation of laboratory psychology. On the contrary he presents a sequence that involves building and assembling from elements already built and assembled.

Danziger is an exemplary constructionist. Not every development that jointly produces ideas, practices, knowledge and new kinds of people is helpfully called construction. Since I do not want to criticize individual works by others, allow me an example from my own. I did not think carefully when I chose the title, 'The Making and Molding of Child Abuse', but had the luck to choose one that works (Hacking, 1991). That essay and Hacking (1992) were certainly about an idea (child abuse), practices (including those of publicly funded or charitable organizations that deal with child abuse), new knowledge and newly formulated kinds of people (abusers, abused children). Now child abuse (in the sense of all four categories) was certainly 'made'. It was brought into being, in the sense of these categories, by a very definite event, namely the going public in 1961–2 of a group in Denver, Colorado, headed by the paediatrician, C.H. Kempe. One can say exactly what this group did in order to 'make' child abuse a viable concept with attendant practices and knowledge. But the next twenty years was not an affair of construction, of building or assembling. On the contrary, the concept of child abuse was moulded in various ways, most notably to take on the present connotation of sexual abuse. It is helpful to assign distinct roles to distinct metaphors. Thus moulding makes one think of plasticity, while construction suggests rigidity. The one metaphor fits Danziger's vision of laboratory psychology, the other fits my vision of child abuse. Of course the vision of one or the other of us may be defective. Fairly sharp use of metaphors enables others to identity and challenge a possible error of analysis more expeditiously than does the use of dead-metaphor-as-slogan.

∗

4   Many construction analyses aim at what Karl Mannheim called 'unmasking' an idea or practice, in contrast to refuting that idea or showing that the practice does not well serve its purposes. There are many kinds of unmasking.

Now let us turn to more familiar predecessors of constructionism, from the early days of the sociology of knowledge – exactly contemporary with logical positivism. In his definitive 1925 paper, Karl Mannheim stated the four factors that created a need for the sociology of knowledge:

(1) the self-relativization of thought and knowledge, (2) the appearance of a new form of relativization introduced by the 'unmasking' turn of mind, (3) the emergence of a new system of reference, that of the social sphere, in respect of which thought could be conceived to be relative, and (4) the aspiration to make this relativization total, relating not only thought or idea, but a whole system of ideas, to an underlying social reality. (Mannheim, 1952 [1925]: 144)

There are obvious connections between what Mannheim called unmasking and what Derrida called deconstruction. But the historical order of ideas seems to be: unmasking, construction, deconstruction. 'Unmasking' has been forgotten as a term of art, and so it has a freshness that 'deconstruction' lacks at present. Deconstruction carries a further semantic burden – that of construing. In English, construal was in the first instance a matter of seeing how a sentence was to be understood on the basis of its component parts. But the word quickly acquired the sense of interpretation. In the United States, a strict constructionist is a constitutional expert who argues for a strict construction of the American constitution, going no further than the very words first written. Deconstruction is a verbal art, requiring us to un-construe the established meaning of and relationships between words. Deconstruction works at the level of semantic ascent. Mannheim's unmasking works at the level of institutions and practices. We may re-construe them, but we do not de-construe them. His idea runs parallel to the more recent idea of deconstruction, yet to use Mannheim's old words is to be free of puns that play on construction, deconstruction and construal. (But nothing in language is simple. Two German words translate into English as 'unmasking': *Demaskierung* and *Entlarvung*. Mannheim actually used *Enthüllung*, which could also be translated as 'exposing'.) The 'unmasking turn of mind,' wrote Mannheim, is

> a turn of mind which does not seek to refute, negate, or call in doubt certain ideas, but rather to *disintegrate* them, and that in such a way that the whole world outlook of a social stratum becomes disintegrated at the same time. We must pay attention, at this point, to the phenomenological distinction between 'denying the truth' of an idea, and 'determining the function' it exercises. In denying the truth of an idea, I still presuppose it as 'thesis' and thus put myself upon the same theoretical (and nothing but theoretical) basis as the one on which the idea is constituted. In casting doubt upon the 'idea', I still think within the same categorical pattern as the one in which it has its being. But when I do not even raise the question (or at least when I do not make this question the burden of my argument) whether what the idea asserts is true, but consider it merely in terms of the *extra-theoretical function* it serves, then, and only then, do I achieve an 'unmasking' which in fact represents no theoretical refutation but the destruction of the practical effectiveness of these ideas. (Mannheim, 1952 [1925]: 140)

Mannheim's model was Marxian, and he thought in terms of unmasking entire ideologies. He had, moreover, a sort of functionalism in mind. An ideology would be unmasked by showing the functions and interests that it served. Yet unmasking, in very much the terms used by Mannheim, has broader implications. The Russellian doctrine of logical constructions did not aim at refuting claims to existence, but instead tried to remove extra-theoretical presuppositions of statements about theoretical entities. Mannheim wrote that the hidden history of the unmasking turn of mind 'still calls for more exact investigation' (1952 [1925]: 141). There is lots of not-so-hidden history, featuring such lares and penates as Hegel, Marx and Freud, but an instructive hidden history would take in not only the unmasking of ideologies but the local unmaskings attempted by Bertrand Russell and his admirers. These were also quite literally new ways of construing sentences, because we were to go beneath the grammatical form, of some sentences, to reveal the logical form.

Constructionism today is often a more local sort of unmasking than Mannheim had in mind. Undoubtedly studies of the construction of gender want to unmask an ideology. But let us turn to a more typical example. Here is a set of common beliefs about serial murderers. Serial murders are monstrous – far more crimes thus classified occur in the United States than elsewhere – the number of serial killers has been on the rise in many countries – but serial killers are rare nonetheless – most but not all serial killers are men – these murderers had vile childhoods – their victims are chosen at random from a specific class of hapless people (prostitutes, black homosexuals or whatever) – serial murder involves warped sex – there is a grisly popular fascination with the topic, catered to by the media, films and the police.

Every one of those beliefs is widely held. Each is, in the main, true. They form objective knowledge about a class of crimes, established by experts. Then we come across Philip Jenkins's *Using Murder: The Social Construction of Serial Homicide* (1994). We know what to expect. The author will not strictly refute our beliefs, but he will teach how the classification has been made up. He will show that the categorization of certain crimes as serial homicides functions for the benefit of some elements of law and order enforcement, and he will tell us how a new kind of expertise has come into being.

The effect of this is somewhat unsettling. It is not at all clear what to do, or that anything should be done. To take a true anecdote, a successful freelance businesswoman told me that she will not let a courier with a package into her premises, especially when her young attractive assistant is there. Her office is on the fourth floor of an up-market mixed-use building in central, well-ordered, Toronto. What is a relevant observation? At the level of truths about serial killers – this is not the *modus operandi* of the type? Or at the unmasking level – you have somehow been conned into an irrational fear about a kind of person who was constructed (as a category) in order to serve certain interests, and to gratify certain fantasies? The anecdote is of no moment except as example. There may be straightforward political conclusions to draw from unmasking. In so far as serial killing is an especially American conception (the British rippers notwithstanding) is its 'extra-theoretical force' intended to deflect attention from gun control, inner-city mayhem, and so forth?

What is to be unmasked? Above all, the unpleasant. Even when we pass from specific kinds of people, such as serial killers, to quite general attributes of people, we are not astonished to find the construction of anger (Miller, 1983) or dangerousness (Webster, 1985). The construction of joy or tenderness would astonish us. Doubtless the all-too-good are in for it: We would be disheartened, but not astonished, by a construction analysis of Médecins Sans Frontières or Mother Teresa. But unmasking must be strongly distinguished from exposure. When the American evangelist

Bakker was shown to be sexually involved with acolytes and to be salting away a fortune, he was exposed, not unmasked. The difference between exposing and unmasking at the personal level is the equivalent of Mannheim's distinction between challenging the extra-theoretical effectiveness of a doctrine, and simply refuting it, showing it to be false.

*

5   Analyses that chiefly aim at unmasking are to be distinguished from those that primarily aim at refuting or discrediting, but which also show how what is to be refuted or discredited was constructed in the first place.

In 1925 Mannheim distinguished unmasking from refuting. The distinction has become less sharp, because we now sometimes try to refute a thesis, or show a practice to be mistaken, by showing (a) that it is wrong, and simultaneously showing (b) how the thesis or practice was put in place. Why does not (a) suffice? If something is mistaken, refute it! The answer is that often the establishing of a thesis, or a practice, involves a series of rhetorical or polemical moves which must be unmasked in order for one to look the thesis or practice squarely in the face.

Mannheim made plain that pure unmasking addresses extra-theoretical effects that have to be undone. Formally speaking there is a close analogy between unmasking and Russell's theory of logical constructions. Both types of analysis work outside the level of what is put in question. They seek not to refute at that level but to criticize at a quite different level.

The construction metaphor is severely weakened by not distinguishing pure cases of unmasking, and mixed cases of unmasking and refuting. Two remarkable books by Donald MacKenzie illustrate the difference. In 1990 he published *Inventing Accuracy*, subtitled *An Historical Sociology of Nuclear Missile Guidance*. This book unmasks, but it also refutes the claim of any cold warrior (or of today's sons of cold warriors) to have 'correctly' defined missile accuracy. The measured comparisons of 'our' with 'their' missiles are proposed in order to satisfy various political or technical agendas. The point is not that missiles are not sufficiently accurate to be lethal. The point is that exceedingly delicate, competing and incompatible measures of accuracy are defined to cater to two distinct interests. The paymasters and the public must be convinced that our missiles deliver excellent accuracy per dollar, but also that enemy missiles are so accurate that we need to build yet more missiles, or else introduce multiple entry missiles that leave a large enough footprint (the jargon of the trade) to cancel out inaccuracies. MacKenzie's historical sociology shows how experts and the lay public are taken in by the assertions of the weaponeers, engineers and policy-makers alike. We walk away from MacKenzie's book knowing that in terms of the accuracy debates themselves, the standard measures of accuracy correspond not to some ideal measure of accuracy but to the interests of the parties involved. The measures are better or worse to the extent that they serve the goals of maintaining or expanding arsenals.

Contrast this with MacKenzie's 1981 *Statistics in Britain: The Social Construction of Scientific Knowledge*. This is a fascinating account of how statistical knowledge was produced in order to satisfy certain class interests of Victorian and Edwardian England. Eugenics became a dominant research interest of the later part of that period, and featured, in a major way, in the contributions of such influential pioneers as Francis Galton and Karl Pearson. But we do not leave this book with the sense that correlation, regression or the chi-squared test have been refuted. They may still be abused. We know from Herrnstein and Murray's *Bell Curve* (1994) that the use of these tests, to pass from correlation to spurious causal claims about race, is alive and well. Correlation and chi-squared nevertheless remain cornerstones of statistical inference, and MacKenzie did not even think of dislodging them. His missile book described the social construction of missile accuracy *and* refuted measures of accuracy. His statistics book described the social construction of statistical methods, and left those methods intact.

If these two books are run together as two undifferentiated works of all-purpose constructionism, their distinct merits and contributions are altogether lost. I write with some feeling here, having published a book about multiple personality (Hacking, 1995b). In one chapter I explain how a certain continuum hypothesis about dissociative behaviour was set in place. It has become almost a dogma that a tendency to dissociate – whose extreme form is multiple personality – forms a continuum. I describe how this dogma became established by reprehensible psychological testing and abuse of statistical tools. Yes, I show how the continuum of dissociation was constructed before our very eyes, a micro-social construction of a supposed psychological fact if ever there was one. But I also demolish the evidence and the techniques; I refute the claim to fact. Because of the current enthusiasm for social construction, I have to say, pedantically, that this chapter is not a piece of social constructionism, even though I describe the wilful construction of an unwarranted 'pseudo-fact' by a small but very influential social group of psychiatrists and psychologists. The ghost of Karl Popper is at work in this chapter, denouncing bad science. That ghost is untainted by all-purpose constructionism.

The assault on the dissociative continuum is not a piece of constructionism but straightforward refutation. Yet the refutation also shows how the dogma was constructed by a ginger group. My book has been and will be read by some as the claim that multiple personality disorder is a social construction – with the chapter on measurement being part of the argument. That misreading is possible because of the all-purpose casual use of the idea of construction that I oppose in the present chapter. I never claim that multiple personality (or dissociative identity disorder, as it has been renamed) is a construction. It became rampant in North America only because of a complex interaction of social ingredients. But it was not, in any literal way, constructed.

*

6   Construction analyses have been applied primarily (a) to ideas about people, knowledge of people, or practices that involve the interactions of people. They have also been applied to (b) knowledge of inanimate nature. The unmasking aimed at in analyses of type (b) has been essentially different from that in type (a). Type (b) unmasking has metaphysical aims; while type (a) has socio-political ones.

Mannheim had an attitude to physical science very different from that of our modern constructionists. 'Scientific-technical thought,' he wrote, 'completes just one and the same system during successive periods. . .'.

> Because it is the same system that is being built up in science in the course of the centuries, the phenomenon of change of meaning does not occur in this sphere, and we can picture the process of thought as direct progress toward ultimately 'correct' knowledge which can be formulated only in one fashion. In physics, there are not several different concepts of 'force', and if different concepts do appear in the history of physics, one can classify them as mere preparatory steps before the discovery of the correct concept prescribed by the axiomatic pattern of the system. (Mannheim, 1952 [1925]: 170)

This attitude is characteristic of sociology of knowledge from Durkheim through Mannheim. It took men trained in the sciences to apply sociology to the sciences themselves. The first such, known to me, was Ludwik Fleck. Referring to Durkheim, Lévy-Bruhl and less well-known figures such as Gumplowicz and Jerusalem, Fleck wrote caustically:

> All these thinkers trained in sociology and classics, however, no matter how productive their ideas, commit a characteristic error. They exhibit an excessive respect, bordering on pious reverence, for scientific facts. (Fleck, 1979 [1935]: 47)

The examples of Latour and Woolgar on endocrinology, and Pickering on quarks, show that the era of excessive respect has passed. But that does not mean that quarks and serial killers are exactly parallel. Latour and Woolgar made plain: 'We do not wish to say that facts do not exist or that there is no such thing as reality. In this simple sense our position is not relativist' (Latour and Woolgar, 1986: 182).

These authors reject a picture of discovering facts. Their world is full of scientific facts, but those facts are the historical product of 'microsociological processes'. There is a substance, TRF, secreted in minute amounts by the hypothalamus, and whose structure is that of a tripeptide, a string of three amino acids. That is a fact. But it became a fact. Latour and Woolgar do not say that something in the hypothalamus changed in 1969. But they think that what logicians would call the modality and tense structure of assertions of fact is misunderstood. Let F be a relatively timeless fact, say the fact that TRF has such and such a chemical structure. The official view would be: before 1969 one was not entitled to assert, categorically, that F is a fact, nor that F has always been a fact. But since then we know enough to be justified in asserting that F is a fact, and has always been so. Latour and Woolgar say no: only after 1969 and a particular series of laboratory events, exchanges and negotiations did F become a fact, and only after 1969 did it become true that F was always a fact. The grammar of our language prevents us from saying this. Our very grammar has conditioned us towards the timeless view of facts. But it is not only our grammar. In their own italics they write: *'our argument is not just that facts are socially constructed. We also wish to show that the process of construction involves the use of certain devices whereby all traces of production are made extremely difficult to detect'* (1986: 176). Their picture of what is happening is this. In the beginning of research people do not have much sense of which statements are even in the cards, certainly not which are true or probable. But when a discovery is made, a statement begins, as they put it, to stabilize. We get a 'split entity', namely a statement about an object, and on the other hand the object that the statement is about: 'It is as if the original statement had projected a virtual image of itself which exists outside the statement' (ibid.). 'The past becomes inverted. TRF has been there all along, just waiting to be revealed for all to see' (ibid.: 177).

Mannheim's phrases are especially apt for *Laboratory Life*. The authors do not refute assertions about TRF, but they wish to get rid of the extra-theoretical force of such assertions. True statements about TRF invite a picture of reality as populated by facts. Moreover the statements must be true because they match up with the facts that inhabit that reality. The true statements about TRF in no way imply that metaphysical picture. Latour and Woolgar wanted to unmask certain practices so as to get rid of a certain metaphysics.

Pickering's *Constructing Quarks* is in much the same vein. He wrote of constructing not facts but a type of entity. The difference is not all that great, here; he might have written about constructing the facts about quarks. Pickering does not mean to deny that quarks exist. He has many reservations about high-energy physics (the discipline in which he was trained). They do not, however, amount to claiming that it is simply mistaken. Instead Pickering aims at the extra-theoretical force of the physics: the metaphysical picture of one necessarily true account of the microcosmos. Pickering emphasizes contingency. Physics need not have developed in this way.

Pickering is faithful to Kuhn, who taught that although there is progress away from a previous state of knowledge, there is not progress towards any ideal state. Although he seems never to have actually said as much, we can see that a state of Kuhnian crisis does not necessarily lead to the actual scientific revolution that ensues. There might have been a different achievement, a different exemplar, a different paradigm. It is a contingent matter, that a particular revolution set a special science in the direction it did. Modern constructionists in the natural sciences emphasize contingency even more than Kuhn. It is a cardinal watchword for Pickering in *Constructing Quarks* and his subsequent studies.

Thus constructionism about the natural sciences is metaphysical. It is directed at certain pictures of reality, truth, discovery and necessity. It joins hands very naturally with Nelson Goodman and what he calls irrealism. Such metaphysics can have ideological consequences. The natural sciences may seem less appealing. The sciences, for some researchers, seem to involve getting to know the essence of creation, the mind of God. Constructionism must be felt as a threat to such a worldview. Likewise feminist critiques of the natural sciences may form alliances with constructionism in order to undermine the idea that the sciences proceed along an inevitable, pre-ordained track. But there is nothing essentially political or ideological about constructionism in the natural sciences. A constructionist could be totally committed to the current enterprises of the natural sciences, and just as full of admiration for past genius and present achievements as the most gung-ho science journalist, who weekly announces the latest discovery.

There is a body of constructionist work on the natural sciences, but it is as nothing compared to work on human affairs. Politics, ideology and power matter more than metaphysics to most advocates of construction. Talk of construction tends to undermine the authority of knowledge and categorization. It challenges complacent assumptions about the inevitability of what we have found out or our present ways of doing things – not by refuting or proposing a better, but by 'unmasking'. Let us, one last time, consider the types of items, connected with people, that tend to be analysed in terms of construction. We can sort them like this:

Conditions, states of affairs, involving people: childhood, gender, youth homelessness, dangerousness, deafness, illness, madness, lesbianism, literacy, authorship. (All the examples come from published monographs.)
Relations between people: inequality.
Kinds of individual: women refugees, the child viewer of television, the (psychologist's) subject.
Kinds of human behaviour or feeling: serial homicide, anger.
Freestanding objects arising from people: homosexual culture, vital statistics, postmodernism, Franco-Ontarian interests.
Super-general: persons, science, reality, facts, knowledge.

Some of this classification is arbitrary. Youth homelessness is a condition; the homeless youth, or the runaway, is a kind of person. Why distinguish this great variety of items from kinds of inanimate entities, such as the quark, or knowledge, for example about TRF? Why are people and social relationships different? We get an intimation of the answer from the motivation of much constructionism. Constructionists are greatly concerned with questions of power and control. This point of unmasking is to liberate the oppressed, to show how categories of knowledge are used in power relationships. It is widely taken for granted in these studies that power is not simply exercised from above. Women refugees or deaf people participate in and assist in the power structure. One hope of unmasking is to enable the deaf or the women refugees to take some control over their own destiny, by coming to own the very categories that are applied to them. I call kinds of people, of human action, human behaviour, *human kinds*. It is an important feature of human kinds that they have effects on the people classified, but the classified people can also take matters into their own hands. I call this phenomenon the looping effect of human kinds (Hacking, 1995a).

The conclusions are obvious. People are self conscious. They are capable of self-knowledge. They are moral agents for whom autonomy has, since the days of Rousseau and Kant, been a central Western value. Quarks and TRF are not moral agents and there is no looping effect for quarks. Hence the interest of constructionism applied to the natural sciences must be primarily metaphysical. When applied to the moral sciences, the interest must first of all be moral. Assuredly there are uncertain boundaries. We do not need Latour's 'actants' to remind us that the non-human may increasingly be invested with moral qualities – species, forests, ecosystems, Gaia. Yet the modelling of the moral remains firmly rooted in human values. One of the defects of all-purpose talk of social construction has been to deflect attention from moral issues. This is doubtless partly because of a nervousness, noticed in some constructionists, in admitting the possibility of the very idea of morality. But if the point of the exercise is moral, one should not be squeamish about saying so. Likewise when the point of the exercise is primarily metaphysical, one should not hesitate to say that too.

References

Anastasi, A. (1988) *Psychological Testing*. New York: Macmillan.

Beck, L.W. (1950) 'Constructions and inferred entities', *Philosophy of Science*, 17: 74–86.

Bijker, W.E., Hughes, T.P. and Pinch, T. (eds) (1987) *The Social Construction of Technological Systems*. Cambridge, MA: MIT Press.

Bishop, E. (1972) *Constructive Mathematics*. New York: Wiley.

Carnap, R. (1967 [1928]) *The Logical Structure of the World*. Berkeley, CA: University of California Press.

Cook-Gomperz, J. (ed.) (1986) *The Social Construction of Literacy*. Cambridge: Cambridge University Press.

Danziger, K. (1990) *Constructing the Subject: Historical Origins of Psychological Research*. Cambridge: Cambridge University Press.

Fleck, L. (1979 [1935]) *Genesis and Development of Scientific Fact*. Chicago: University of Chicago Press.

Fowler, H.W. (1926) *A Dictionary of Modern English Usage*. Oxford: Oxford University Press.

Galison, P. (1990) 'Aufbau/Bauhaus: logical positivism and architectural modernism', *Critical Inquiry*, 16: 709–52.

Goodman, N. (1990 [1940]) *A Study of Qualities*. New York: Garland.

Goodman, N. (1951) *The Structure of Appearance*. Cambridge, MA: Harvard University Press.

Goodman, N. (1978) *Ways of Worldmaking*. Indianapolis, IN: Hackett.

Hacking, I. (1988) 'The participant irrealist at large in the laboratory', *British Journal for the Philosophy of Science*, 39: 277–94.

Hacking, I. (1991) 'The making and molding of child abuse', *Critical Inquiry*, 17: 253–88.

Hacking, I. (1992) 'World-making by kind-making: child abuse for example', in Mary Douglas and David Hull (eds), *How Classification Works: Nelson Goodman among the Social Sciences*. Edinburgh: Edinburgh University Press. pp. 180–238.

Hacking, I. (1995a) 'The looping effects of human kinds', in D. Sperber, D. Premack and A.J. Premack (eds), *Causal Cognition: A Multidisciplinary Approach*. Oxford: Clarendon Press. pp. 351–94.

Hacking, I. (1995b) *Rewriting the Soul: Multiple Personality and the Sciences of Memory*. Princeton, NJ: Princeton University Press.

Harraway, D.J. (1991) *Simians, Cyborgs and Women: The Reinvention of Nature*. London: Free Association Books.

Herrnstein, R.J. and Murray, C. (1994). *The Bell Curve: Intelligence and Class Structure in American Life*. New York: Free Press.

Jenkins, P. (1994) *Using Murder: The Social Construction of Serial Homicide*. New York: A. de Gruyter.

Kitzinger, C. (1987) *The Social Construction of Lesbianism*. Newbury Park, CA: Sage.

Knorr-Cetina, K. and Mulkay, S. (eds) (1983) *Science Observed: Perspectives on the Social Study of Science*. London: Sage.

Laqueur, T.W. (1990) *Making Sex: Body and Sex from the Greeks to Freud*. Cambridge, MA: Harvard University Press.

Latour, B. (1987) *Science in Action: How to Follow Scientists and Engineers through Society*. Milton Keynes: Open University Press.

Latour, B. (1993) *We Have Never Been Modern*. Cambridge, MA: Harvard University Press.

Latour, B. and Woolgar, S. (1979) *Laboratory Life: The Social Construction of Scientific Facts*. Beverly Hills, CA: Sage.

Latour, B. and Woolgar, S. (1986) *Laboratory Life: The Construction of Scientific Facts*. Princeton, NJ: Princeton University Press.

Lorber, J. and Farrell, S.A. (1991) *The Social Construction of Gender*. Newbury Park, CA: Sage.

MacCorquodale, K. and Meehl, P.D. (1948) 'On a distinction between hypothetical constructs and intervening variables', *Psychological Review*, 55: 95–107.

MacKenzie, D.A. (1981) *Statistics in Britain: The Social Construction of Scientific Knowledge*. Edinburgh: Edinburgh University Press.

MacKenzie, D.A. (1990) *Inventing Accuracy: An Historical Sociology of Nuclear Missile Guidance*. Cambridge, MA: MIT Press.

Mannheim, K. (1952 [1925]) *Essays on the Sociology on Knowledge*. London: Routledge & Kegan Paul.

Miller, J.B. (1983) *The Construction of Anger in Women and Men*. Wellesley, MA: Wellesley College.

Mitchell, J.V. (ed.) (1992) *The Eleventh Mental Measurements Yearbook*. Lincoln, NB: Buros Institute of Mental Measurements.

O'Neill, O. (1989) *Constructions of Reason: Explorations of Kant's Practical Philosophy*, Cambridge: Cambridge University Press.

Pickering, A. (1986) *Constructing Quarks*. Edinburgh: Edinburgh University Press.

Russell, B. (1918) *Mysticism and Logic, and Other Essays*. London: Longman Green.

Searle, J.R. (1995) *The Construction of Social Reality*. New York: Free Press.

Webster, C.D. (1985) *Constructing Dangerousness: Scientific, Legal and Policy Implications*. Tornoto: Centre of Criminology, University of Toronto.

PART II
THE LIMITS OF CONSTRUCTIONISM

4

What Does the Sociology of Scientific Knowledge Explain?

Paul A. Roth

Beginning in the 1950s, philosophical critiques (primarily by positivists themselves or apostates) made plain major conceptual difficulties with the positivist account of natural science and its attendant analysis of rationality. However, absent was a means of translating these problems into creative insights regarding the study of scientific practice. This creative translation arrived in 1962, with the publication of Kuhn's *The Structure of Scientific Revolutions*. Indeed, effecting this change remains one of that work's enduring accomplishments. What Kuhn's work suggested to some social scientists was how the story of belief acquisition, maintenance, and change in the natural sciences could be told in a way that ignored the encomiums to scientific method by the philosophical orthodoxy.[1]

By the mid-1970s, new schools of the sociology of scientific knowledge laid claim to the conceptual space created by Kuhn with regard to filling out the explanation of belief evaluation in the natural sciences. The claim, of course, was that the sociology of scientific knowledge could discern the relevant mechanisms, ones which had eluded philosophers. However, sociologists looked for causal explanations of beliefs (both true and false) well beyond the narrow range of methodological ideals sought by philosophers.[2] Today, after barely two decades, proponents of the sociology of scientific knowledge (SSK) confidently cite numerous case studies as evidence for the success of SSK as a research programme.[3]

What has been explained about the evolution of beliefs in scientific communities since Kuhn? I approach this question by examining two key methodological assumptions animating SSK case studies. First, there is the symmetry principle, which proclaims that all beliefs – true or false – stand in need of causal explanation by the same sorts of factors.[4] Secondly, SSK is itself understood as a scientific undertaking. In particular, its method is naturalistic. This means that all phenomena, be they rocks or beliefs, are legitimate subjects of scientific scrutiny and causal explanation. Naturalists, that is, eschew appeals to a priori knowledge and view the traditional philosophical hope of underwriting the standards of science as a lost cause.

These tenets crucially distinguished the new, sociological explainers of science from the old, philosophical ones. The first tenet explicitly replaces the view that the rationality of scientific practices explains the beliefs that scientists accept or reject. The first and second tenets together authorize the characteristic result of SSK case studies, namely that the standards and practices of any group of scientists are historically contingent and culturally specific. This 'localism' constitutes the substance of the relativism to which sociologists in SSK subscribe.[5]

However, recent in-house debates in the SSK community raise basic questions regarding how to reconcile these principles in practice, basic though they may be. For, *qua* sociologists, some in SSK are sensitive to a pull to restrict the causal explanations to social and cultural factors. Yet, *qua* naturalists, their commitment to disciplinary hegemony proves unjustifiable. For naturalism does not establish any prior restrictions on just which factors may prove causally relevant or appropriately scientific. Unlike positivism, that is, naturalism does not have a built-in view regarding the hierarchy of sciences. Naturalists may look for causes, but naturalism does not license the presumption that all or even any sociological factors must be explanatorily relevant.

More importantly, debates in SSK over who is a naturalist (or not) and whose interpretation of the symmetry principle is acceptable (or not) point to a deeper problem. The issue which these controversies help bring into focus concerns whether the putative advance in the explanation of scientific practice offered by SSK has proven more apparent than real, and for precisely the reasons that made its project plausible to begin with. Positivists wanted to explain belief maintenance and change within science by reference to the inherent rationality of scientific practices; SSK insisted that they had a more empirically adequate account, albeit one which found the causes of belief within a cultural nexus other than that canvassed by philosophers. But, I argue, no genuine causal explanations are to be found in that literature.

Upon examination, the sociological stories invariably offer no more than narratives of the *post hoc, ergo propter hoc* variety, or allege that they have represented scientific practice *wie es eigentlich gewesen*.[6] Indeed, for all the undeniable interest of the numerous case studies generated by this movement, their methodological principles render hollow their claims to have provided causal explanation. The case studies are no more than just-so stories about science. In what follows, I explore how the professed naturalism of the SSK is at odds with its commitment to the symmetry principle – the claim to provide causal explanations.[7]

A naturalist takes human knowledge as a product of our interactions with the world, to be studied by the best methods available for that purpose. In contrast with the foundational epistemological tradition stemming from Descartes, naturalism, in the form championed by W.V. Quine, denies that there is some special method, prior to science, which yields knowledge more certain than that of the sciences with which we are familiar.[8] The naturalist studies, for example, claims about what knowledge is, using whatever intellectual resources have been developed for the scientific study of any other phenomenon.

Philip Kitcher, in a recent work on naturalism in a Quinean spirit, empha-sizes what a naturalist does not do, that is, appeal to a priori principles or atemporal conceptions of reasoning.[9] The substance and method of natural-ism, on this view, are supplied by the various special sciences which one brings to bear on the phenomena of interest. Naturalism, in this respect, is less a set of explicit methodological prescriptions and more a denial of any attempt to exempt some elements basic to science (logic, clear and distinct ideas, God, etc.) from the purview of science.[10]

This way of characterizing naturalism, brief as it is, suffices to bring forward a central point of contention regarding proposals to naturalize epistemology. In brief, there is the recurrent claim that in so far as epistem-ology concerns the search for optimal criteria of human epistemic function-ing, then a naturalized epistemology is an oxymoron. The reason is that a naturalized account appears inherently *descriptive*, i.e. it concerns the mechanisms (causes) generating and sustaining certain states of belief. Epis-temology, however, is nothing if not *prescriptive*, i.e. an effort to specify how reasoning/justification (or any other epistemic notion) ought to be pursued.

This tension between the descriptive concerns of naturalism and the prescriptive goals of epistemologists is evident in the writings of both sociologists of science and philosophers. Social constructivists, by and large, characterize themselves as naturalists in the *descriptive* sense just noted. Their naturalism contrasts with what they identify as a philosophical – prescriptive – account of scientific practice.[11] For example, Andy Picker-ing glosses the notion of naturalistic explanation in the following way: 'one should try to explain how science is actually done in laboratories, offices, seminar rooms, and so on, without reducing one's account to any pre-given basis like logic. The explanatory framework should be developed hand-in-hand with empirical research' (Pickering, 1991a: 575). Pickering goes on to explicitly contrast this 'naturalizing impulse' (ibid.) with what he under-stands as the project of traditional philosophy of science.

The received SSK view on naturalism owes its essentials to Barry Barnes's notion of natural rationality. Barnes suggested that studies 'which relate to how people actually reason rather than how ideally they should reason, are concerned with *natural rationality*; they relate to our natural reasoning proclivities or capacities' (Barnes, 1976: 115). Natural rationality should interest all those 'with a naturalistic interest in cultural change and the growth of knowledge' (ibid.: 116). Barnes contrasts this concern with normative or prescriptive characterizations of human reason (ibid.: 117).[12]

Natural rationality competes with evaluative notions of rationality as an account of positions held in the sciences.

Most significantly, Barnes distinguishes between 'tolerant' and 'intolerant' theories of (natural) rationality. Intolerant theories sort beliefs into those which are rationally held and those which are not. A tolerant theory, however, treats differences in modes of reasoning as one would regard differences in, for example, manners. On the tolerant sort of view which Barnes endorses, characterizing certain cultural practices, such as magic, as irrational reflects no more than a cultural prejudice (Barnes, 1976: 123). Applied *intra-culturally*, this implies that 'no distinctiveness can be attributed to our existing natural science. All institutionalized systems of belief and action appear to embody natural rationality alike – science no more than any other institution. It follows that science should be treated as a part of culture like any other, to be studied by the same methods, explored by the same techniques' (ibid.: 124).[13] A naturalistic study of rationality, Barnes is insisting, must be tolerant, not prescriptive.

There is no small irony, given this background, in the fact that questions raised by those advocating the 'reflexive turn' in SSK should now be accused of abandoning their scientific/naturalistic credentials because they question the legitimacy of the scientific/naturalistic method favoured by some. In their essay 'Epistemological chicken', Harry Collins and Steven Yearley offer a highly critical review of recent developments, stemming primarily from work by Bruno Latour and Steve Woolgar, challenging the faithfulness of this work to the principles of symmetry and naturalism (Collins and Yearley, 1992a, 1992b). Latour (and those following his lead) are accused of abandoning the faith because their studies sin against symmetry. Woolgar's scepticism about social objects is seen as making it impossible to construct causal accounts. By exploring these charges, one gains insight into just how those advocating SSK misunderstand their own principles.[14]

Woolgar's preferred characterization of the reflexive turn emphasizes the dualism involved in any notion of representation. Objects are presumed to exist prior to the methods and criteria used to study and identify them, but (the reflexive thesis goes) these very methods and criteria are implicated in constituting the objects. Reflexive analysis shows how disparate experiences must first somehow be stitched together in order to constitute the putative unity being studied. Woolgar exploits philosophical critiques of the notion of natural kinds in order to detail how we fabricate through social artifice what is called 'natural'.[15]

Against this, Collins and Yearley complain that Woolgar's procedure provides no methodologically firm ground for the important business of demystifying the epistemological pretensions of the natural sciences. An attitude of social realism, they assert, is needed for that purpose (Collins and Yearley, 1992a: 309). Moreover, Collins and Yearley maintain, by depriving himself of a causal vocabulary Woolgar forfeits his claim to naturalism (ibid.: 323, fn. 21).

Social realism permits the sociologist, in that mood, to provide close descriptions of the world in which the scientist operates. 'Detailed description dissolves epistemological mystery and wonder' (Collins and Yearley, 1992a: 309). The method of close description, under the assumption of social realism, yields the signature SSK conclusion: 'The methodological prescription that emerges . . . is that explanations should be developed within the assumption that the real world does not affect what the scientist believes about it' (Collins and Yearley, 1992b: 372). Descriptions done in the SSK mode license the position, as a result, that 'all cultural enterprises . . . [have] roughly the same epistemological warrant' (ibid.: 384). The legitimacy of their descriptions is taken to underwrite, then, both their particular explanations and their general epistemological evaluation of the natural sciences.

How does reflexive critique enter in here? In order to appreciate the power of a reflexive critique of methodology, recall the role of such critique in the overthrow of positivism. The methodological linchpin of positivism was the verifiability criterion of meaning. This held that for any sentence to be cognitively significant/meaningful, it must either be so by virtue of its logical form (either analytic or self-contradictory), or, if contingent, have empirically specifiable truth conditions. However, when the question was raised whether this principle itself is believed to be true either by virtue of its logical form or because of evidence, no good answer could be given.[16] The positivists did not want to contend that they had simply stipulated a definition of meaningfulness; that would have taken any critical edge off their critiques of other views on meaning. Yet they could not maintain that the account was an empirical hypothesis, because the criterion delimited the realm of empirically meaningful sentences; hence, any 'test' would be question-begging.

The reflexive equivalent in the context of SSK, in turn, would demand a naturalistic justification of claims made for close description by the SSK. But then a paradox analogous to the one that plagued the verifiability criterion arises for sociologists committed to social realism. On the one hand, the method of close description *per se* does not require excluding the sort of descriptions Collins et al. find offensive. On the other hand, social realism is not an empirical hypothesis sustained by sociological practice using the method of close description, since such descriptions can be used to precisely the opposite effect. In short, the Collins and Yearley position is neither true by definition nor a hypothesis that can be sustained without begging the question of which accounts 'make sense'. What, then, legitimizes the limits on which they insist?

Faced with a demand to substantiate the legitimacy of their approach, Collins and Yearley turn from bold challengers into reactionaries, much in the manner of positivists who could neither justify the verifiability principle nor bring themselves to give it up. In particular, they can neither legitimize the elevated status given descriptions in the mode of social realism nor give them up. For example, the criticism of Woolgar and other reflexivists turns out to be *not* that they fail to provide close description, but that they provide the 'wrong kind' of close description, namely descriptions that

make problematic the sort of causal account Collins and Yearley favour
(Collins and Yearley, 1992a: 308–9).

But the problem goes deeper than a stubborn preference for one mode of
description over another. Avoided entirely is the crucial question of what
makes one description, from any perspective, either worthy of attention in
its own right or preferable to that of a competitor in the same style. It just
will not do to insist, however repeatedly, that such descriptions 'demystify'
science, that their approach 'makes science look like any other kind of
practical work' (Collins and Yearley, 1992a: 309). Thin wires made Mary
Martin, when playing Peter Pan, look like a creature that could fly. The
issue is *not* how SSK can make scientists 'look'; the challenge concerns what
makes these descriptions (however 'close') worth taking seriously. Otherwise, there is no reason whatsoever to credit the rhetoric that now, thanks to
SSK, we have learned that all disciplines have the same epistemological
warrant, etc.[17]

Having, like their positivist forebears, glimpsed the fact that their method
of explanation has no immediate or automatic standing given their own
principles, they dig in their heels and declare their faith: 'We have our
methods; they include participation in forms of life. To deny this on
grounds of unobservability would be to resurrect the scientific sociology of
the early sixties' (Collins and Yearley, 1992b: 381). 'We have our methods'
indeed![18] 'Participation in forms of life' is not a method, but a claim.
Questions of how to substantiate this sort of claim have never been
resolved. The suggestion that one empirically unjustified account of scientific belief formation – the positivists' – be replaced by an empirically
unjustifiable one is, for all its delightful irony, still quite unsatisfactory.[19]

Consistent with the thought that their favourite close descriptions are
somehow self-substantiating, one also finds appeals to historicism as the
method of choice for underpinning the explanations of science which the
SSK prefer. By 'historicism' is meant 'the programme dedicated to analysing historical action in historical actors' terms' (Shapin, 1992: 354). Shapin,
whose characterization this is, acknowledges that 'historicism is accompanied by its own methodological baggage', most infamously 'atomiz-
ing particularism' (ibid.). Traditionally, of course, this generates charges
that historicism is *anti-scientific*, inasmuch as particularism precludes any
generalizations, and is unverifiable, in so far as there is no good test of
whether or not one has reconstructed the categories particular to participants correctly. Shapin's historicist programme is Barnes-inspired (Shapin,
1992: 352–3). As with Collins, Shapin appeals to the most localist of all
localist methods in order to sustain the general sociological thesis that
certain factors – the ones sociologists favour – are causally determinative
(ibid.: 353).[20]

Further muddying the explanatory waters is a recent effort by Pickering
to combine historicism and an account of science which brings the world
back in as an explicit player in the sociological story, what Pickering calls

the 'mangle of practice' (Pickering, 1991b). For Pickering, being a historicist means eschewing appeal (for purposes of explanation) to a

> realm of regulatory or guiding principles – standards or interests – that endure
> through particular acts of knowledge production and evaluation. . . . Traditional
> thought in philosophy and the social sciences on human action and cognition in
> general begins from just this assumption. Nevertheless, the historicist view that I
> advocate . . . suggests that science can, and indeed does, function in the absence
> of these. (Pickering, 1991b: 411)

Rather, he sees inquiry as a matter of resistance – 'emergence of obstacles
on the path to some goal' – and accommodation – 'the revision of open-
ended modeling sequences' (Pickering, 1991b: 412). The interplay of resistance and accommodation comprises what he terms 'the mangle of practice'.[21]

The puzzle here is how this account of the mangle extends, or rather fails
to extend, to those accounts on which Pickering does not smile. For while,
on Pickering's account, resistances can lead scientists he discusses to modify
their practice, Pickering vigorously chastises philosopher of science Ron
Giere for suggesting that experimental resistance can make one theory
appear strongly preferable to another.

The problem, I suggest, lies not in any deep methodological divide
between Pickering and Giere but consists, rather, in the sort of description
of the case that Giere favours. For when Giere describes matters in a way
that suggests that experiments provide evidence for rationally preferring
one view to another, Pickering argues *ad hominem* by attempting to tar
Giere's position with some tinge of positivism: 'here we are, back in a good
old-fashioned context of justification in which the data tell scientists what to
believe' (Pickering, 1991a: 578). The reason that Giere, but not Pickering,
commits the sin of letting nature guide the scientist is that, on Pickering's
view, Giere does not see the process as sufficiently open-ended. Nature can
guide a scientist's hand, but not when described, Pickering believes, in
Giere's way.

To this, Giere could and does reply that it is strange indeed for a
sociologist to insist that all logical possibilities must count, since, in actual
situations, scientists will have before them a rather limited repertoire of
theories by which to accommodate various resistances (Giere, 1992: 100–1).
Furthermore, Pickering, in his own work, employs a distinction between
'free' and 'forced' moves which seems not at all unlike the kind of description he finds so offensive in Giere.[22] Indeed, by emphasizing the historically
situated options confronting the scientists he discusses, Giere appears the
better historicist and naturalist than does Pickering.

What divides naturalizing sociologists from naturalizing philosophers,
once the red-herring charge of positivism is seen for what it is? The issue,
it now appears, turns not on competing methodologies, but on *competing
descriptions* of ethnographic or historical material. As previously argued,
attending to the details of a case does not preclude the formulation of

incompatible accounts or prevent investigators from drawing different conclusions from the data based on different\descriptions of what they observe.

In addition, I have emphasized, celebration of close description as a method and appeals to historicism can only impugn SSK claims to have followed the symmetry principle – to have provided a causal explanation of both true and false beliefs in terms of the same sorts of factors.[23] For their view of themselves as naturalists relies on their form of historicism, i.e. the particularism of their descriptive work. But, as a result, their accounts can provide neither insight into why their explanations are comparatively superior to competing interpretations or descriptions, nor any test of their explanations, for no predictions issue from close description or historicism.

I began this discussion by claiming that two tenets basic to SSK – symmetry and naturalism – are in tension with one another. My diagnosis of the reasons for this tension focused on the view, stemming from Barnes's work on natural rationality, that the sociology of scientific knowledge can only be descriptive. However, I noted, there is a growing dissensus within SSK regarding what the proper parameters of description are. On the one hand, reflexivists like Woolgar are charged with using descriptive techniques to undercut the type of facts on which sociological explanations depend. On the other hand, philosophers of a naturalizing sort are berated for reinserting prescriptive notions of rationality. Thus, experimental results can work into the story if described as a 'mangle', but not if described as probative. But, I have indicated, there is no apparent basis for the sort of limitations – ban reflexivity! ban accounts that see experimental results as probative! – on which some insist.

I questioned, as well, whether the sociologists have actually explained, even on their own terms, the scientific practices in question. In particular, I maintained, the appeal to interests, to close description, and to recovering how things actually were, raise questions about the scientific status of the studies that have yet to be answered.[24]

The status of SSK as a science is tied by key practitioners to a form of naturalism. This naturalism, in turn, is grounded in descriptions or historicism (or some combination of these). But none of these approaches can be reconciled with the symmetry principle – at least when interpreted, as the sociologists themselves do, as the claim to provide causal explanations. For all lack relevant attributes of causal explanation – testability and generalizability. Thus two basic tenets of SSK conflict.

Can a naturalist approach teach us, in the end, anything about science? Collins and Yearley express the hope that SSK will level the cultural playing field, letting us perceive scientists as people with expertise, but without a window on reality (Collins and Yearley, 1992b: 384–5). I applaud this goal, but fail to see how their version of the programme advances it. They leave no account of why scientists (or sociologists) should be credited with any expertise. More interesting, I suggest, are various proposals to naturalize science studies which do put forward methods for ascertaining and evaluating mechanisms, particularly ones which might help ensure that the scientific enterprise continues to produce helpful results. At the present time, several such programmes have been proposed.[25]

In order to explain anything, one needs to ascertain, *inter alia*, what difference various differences might make. By linking explanation to prediction, by insisting on clear standards of verifiability and falsifiability, positivists developed important and suggestive ideas regarding explanation. Recovering what is sound in these ideas suggests that a normative programme ought to be linked with the descriptive one, for one can serve as a check on the other. Quine remarks somewhere that whistling in the dark is not the method of true philosophy. I have suggested that the sound and fury within SSK regarding their naturalism, their advances over positivism, and their identification of causal mechanisms, is just so much whistling in the dark. Three decades ago, Kuhn made vivid how little we understand of how scientists do the work they do. For reasons rehearsed above, I remain unconvinced that SSK fully appreciates the questions about science that Kuhn bequeathed us. SSK remains, rather, a part of the puzzle they claim to solve.

Notes

I would like to thank Jim Bohman, Ron Munson and Stephen Turner for helpful comments on an earlier draft of this chapter.

1 For the story from the sociologists' perspective on this matter see Barnes (1985). However, Barnes's reading of Kuhn is idiosyncratic in many respects. For a rather different reaction by social scientists to Kuhn's work, see the essays in Gutting (1980).

2 I have detailed the philosophical foundations of the Strong Programme in the sociology of scientific knowledge (and related sociological projects) in Roth (1987: Ch. 7). For a good overview of how the sociology of scientific knowledge rode to respectability on the coat-tails of philosophy see Shapin (1982). This article also contains a very nice bibliography of the field to that data.

3 For bibliographies, see Shapin (1982, 1992).

4 Traditional philosophy of science maintained that the processes of belief acceptance, rejection and change could be accounted for, in the natural sciences anyway, by discerning how the canons of some logical method guided scientists. Appeal to procedures sanctioned by some ideal method was to explain the acceptance of true beliefs. The acceptance of false beliefs, e.g. Lysenkian biology, was the only sort of case where external factors needed to be cited, and then for purposes of showing how the ideal process of belief evaluation was distorted or otherwise corrupted. The plausibility of this philosophical picture of matters died in the second half of this century. The symmetry principle is its proposed replacement. The symmetry principle, in contrast to the philosophical story regarding belief evaluation in science, emphasizes that one does *not* cite one type of process or set of factors for purposes of explaining the embrace of true beliefs by the scientific community and another, and different, kind of consideration by way of explaining false ones.

5 For a good statement of the position emphasizing the gloss just given see Barnes and Bloor (1982).

6 The German phrase is Ranke's famous injunction to historians to report the past 'as it actually was'. In what follows, I focus on this twist, i.e. the view now being promoted by a

number of representatives of SSK to represent scientific practice 'as it actually is (or was)'. The invocation of historicism as a methodological principle by way of bolstering claims to scientific practice is just one of the many ironies which works its way into current efforts, including those of a growing group of philosophers, to be more naturalistic than the next researcher.

The *post hoc* nature of interest explanations is, moreover, a topic which has been well discussed and amply documented. Early articles by Steve Woolgar remain the classics here, especially Woolgar (1981) and (1983). Detailed critiques of the efforts to use case studies to support causal accounts include Roth (1987: Ch. 8), Roth and Barrett (1990a) and Yearley (1982). The last-mentioned piece is, if nothing else, a testimony to the steadfast refusal of those in SSK to think seriously about their own practice. The article represents an internal critique of explanatory practices typically found in SSK case studies. For a classic instance of an inability to fathom the point that their own practices might not deliver as promised, see Pickering (1990). Barrett and I replay the missed points in Roth and Barrett (1990b).

7 Strictly speaking, the symmetry principle says only that the same sort of factors should be used to explain both true and false beliefs; the canonical formulations do not state that the explanations must be causal. However, despite their vocal criticisms of positivist accounts of scientific practice, the sociologists associated with the Strong Programme and their fellow travellers accept *in toto* the basic Hempelian line on scientific explanation. This means that any proper scientific explanation is not just causal, but also of the covering law type. (For an excellent discussion of this aspect of the new sociology of science, see Bohman 1991, especially pp. 40–50.) Given the wholesale acceptance of the positivist notion of what constitutes an explanation by the sociologists in question here, the symmetry principle may be fairly interpreted as requiring that the same sorts of factors causally explain both true and false beliefs. This is how symmetry is, in fact, understood for purposes of argument in this chapter.

I thank Malcolm Ashmore who, when I presented a version of this chapter at the Constructing the Social conference at Durham in 1994, quite properly pointed out to me that my emphasis on the causal interpretation symmetry principle was not required by the principle alone.

8 Quine is, I would argue, the philosopher most responsible for bringing naturalism back to the philosophical fore. His classic essay here is Quine (1969). For an account of how Quine's philosophy relates to SSK, see Hacking (1990) and Roth (1987). Roger Gibson provides a general overview of Quine's naturalism. See, for example, Gibson (1993).

9 Philip Kitcher notes this convergence as well, in his survey of the resurgence of philosophical naturalism. See Kitcher (1992: 74–83), where he explicitly notes the complaint that a naturalized inquiry into knowledge cannot also be prescriptive, made by various sociologists of scientific knowledge.

10 Arthur Danto puts the point nicely when he writes, 'naturalism is polemically defined as repudiating the view that there exists or could exist any entities or events which lie, in principle, beyond the scope of scientific explanation' (Danto, 1967: 448).

11 Richard Rorty's distinction between *philosophy* and *Philosophy* develops some of what is alluded to here. See Rorty (1982).

12 The contrast is sometimes put as a distinction between natural and normative notions of rationality. See, for example, Bloor (1981: 207).

13 This commitment to a 'tolerant' conception of natural rationality remains undiminished, so far as I can tell, for Barnes. Indeed, he still tends to divide the good guys from the bad (mostly, sociologists from philosophers) based on a willingness to go naturalistic. See Barnes (1991: 322). Barnes also goes on to remark that 'with "naturalistic epistemology" like that of Quine, Campbell, or Goodman, and with philosophy firmly grounded in empirical historical study, such as for example Giere, there is no fundamental clash' (ibid.: 334). Steven Shapin also acknowledges in passing both the importance of Barnes's early article and the fact that some philosophers have naturalistic inclinations. See Shapin (1992: 367, fn. 66).

14 In what follows, I discuss only the charges against Woolgar. But the other issues are not unrelated. If Woolgar sins against symmetry and naturalism by eschewing a causal idiom, Latour stumbles, Collins and Yearley insist, by stretching the concept of symmetry beyond the bounds of intelligibility. In particular, they charge, 'French-style radical symmetry draws no

boundary between objects that have been created and those that occur naturally' (1992a: 312). They illustrate this by examining two landmark papers, Callon's on scallop fishermen and Latour's on automatic door openers (Callon, 1986; Latour and Johnson, 1988).

Much of the debate here is over who is using (or misusing) the symmetry principle. Interested readers should also consult Latour (1990) and Schaffer (1991). There is a disquieting aura of 'political correctness' surrounding this debate, with each side suggesting that the other has broken the faith which the symmetry principle represents. In addition, much of the criticism of Latour's position centres on the question of what sort of entities can be ascribed agency. In this regard, the debate echoes controversies in ethics over the moral status of non-human animals. The odd result is that Collins, Yearley and Schaffer want to rule out a priori the position that Latour and Callon take. But what is the argument for showing that it is wrong to treat scallops or microbes as Callon and Latour do? Only, it seems, that it does not result in an account to the political pleasure of Collins et al.

15 For a good overview linking philosophical critiques of natural kinds to work in SSK, see Hacking (1990). Woolgar's own development of these ideas can be found in Woolgar (1988) and Lynch and Woolgar (1988), especially their introductory essay. Case studies in this area include classics such as Hacking (1991) and Latour and Woolgar (1979).

16 For a brief consideration of the problems here, see the 'Introduction' (Ayer, 1952). This edition was originally published in 1946.

17 There is a further deep puzzle here. Collins and Yearley speak of three methods for making progress with regard to our relation to 'machines and other artifacts'. These are the methods of modelling, natural science and that of the SSK. 'What sociology of scientific knowledge provides is a third method, no longer subservient to accounts of the work of the scientists and technologists and the stories of philosophers but rooted in special understanding of social life' (Collins and Yearley, 1922a: 321). What is puzzling is that this method is explicitly contrasted with 'the false ally of the counterfactual method' (ibid.). Yet causal explanations are taken to support counterfactuals – if being exposed to a virus caused Jones's disease, then, presumably, if not exposed, Jones would not have had the disease. More generally, in non-laboratory sciences, explanations that could not support counterfactuals would not usually be thought to be providing causal explanations at all. If, as Collins and Yearley complain, in 'their emphasis on form, the reflexivity and actor-network theory approaches both exclude explanation' (ibid.: 323), it is difficult to see where Collins and Yearley imagine their account provides for it.

18 These comments also exhibit the favourite fallacious argument form of the SSK – *argumentum ad hominem*. No one should be cowed by this SSK version of guilt by association. Find an aspect of an opponent's position that is also some view that any positivist ever held and, *voilà*, the argument is refuted. In this case, the fact that positivists made light of claims to understanding does not show, now that we are all properly post-positivist, that suddenly all is well with the so-called method of empathetic identification. Collins and Yearley are correct to maintain that there is nothing particularly methodologically *outré* about an appeal to unobservables. However, when the appeal is for the purpose of justifying one's entire way of proceeding, without additional empirical check, then some more compelling reasons for accepting the posit is needed. Use of this argument form is also rampant in Pickering's work. See, for example, Pickering (1991a). Setting up straw men and knocking them down occupies most of Pickering (1990) as well.

19 For balanced historical overviews of this particular controversy, which concerns primarily the status and the nature of the distinction between the *Geisteswissenschaften* and the *Naturwissenschaften*, see Habermas (1988) or Apel (1984).

20 This despite Shapin's characteristically candid acknowledgement of the shortcomings of his preferred approach on the critical issue of causality. See especially Shapin (1992: 345–51). While Shapin cites as exemplary his own work here (Shapin and Schaffer, 1985), it is instructive to note how their account can be challenged by another self-professed naturalist and read to the advantage of a more philosophical account, i.e. one that emphasizes just the factors as determinative that Shapin would discount. See the discussion in Kitcher (1993: 294–302). The point here is that the historical data too is underdetermined and so can be read to many

different effects. If the issue is who has the best explanation of the shape which scientific practice takes, appeals to historicist matters hardly strengthens the SSK position.

The problems with a historicist methodology are well canvassed by historians. See, for example, the magisterial Iggers (1968). One might say that the time has come for the SSK to stop worrying about Karl Popper et al. and start thinking seriously about their relation to Hayden White. Although it is not directly tied to the issues of this chapter, I remain fascinated by how the two most influential schools pursuing social constructivism – those who, like the SSK, claim to follow Kuhn and those who take their lead from Hayden White and various schools of semiotics (see, e.g., work by James Clifford in anthropology) – ply their trades in apparent ignorance of one another. Moreover, the types of relativism to which each school subscribes have important differences as well. For an account of how the notion of historical objectivity has played out on the American scene, told in a way in which the SSK ought to be sympathetic, see Novick (1988). Novick's book should convince them that attempts to found their account of scientific objectivity on historicist notions is building on quicksand.

21 The notion of mangle is to emphasize the contingent nature of scientific productions, how they are jury-rigged rather than constructed by some cook-book of scientific method. 'The particular resistances and accommodations that give content to *this* new instrument, fact or theory arise unpredictably in the real-time of scientific practice and cannot be explained by reference to any catalog of enduring regulatory principles. What emerges from the mangle has therefore a truly historical character, and this is what I mean by describing the appreciation of knowledge outlined here as a historicist one' (Pickering, 1991b: 412). 'Historicist', for Pickering, connects then to the gloss by Shapin cited above; the point is to emphasize the localism and particularity of the object or theory under discussion.

22 See Pickering and Stephanides (1992). Note particularly p. 163, fns. 23 and 24.

23 For a very incisive analysis of Harry Collins's work emphasizing how the issue turns, not on issues of who is a naturalist or not but on whose description of the historical data is better or not, see Hesse (1986).

24 The *éminence grise* here is, of course, Foucault. Foucault was criticized for refusing to specify mechanism. A Foucauldian history is not an explanation, at least in the traditional sense of explanation to which the practitioners of SSK subscribe. It is a sensitivity to Foucault's work which separates, I suggest, Hacking's work on social construction from that of most others in this area.

25 Steve Fuller, for example, argues for an epistemological evaluation of science by examining the institutional structures which promote science. He has urged this position in a number of books and articles. See, for example, Fuller (1992a, 1992b, 1993). Alternative proposals within a naturalist framework are also promulgated by Kitcher (1993), Laudan (1987), and others.

Barnes's view that a theory of natural rationality has to be tolerant, in short, has become an unexamined dogma of SSK.

References

Apel, K.-O. (1984) *Understanding and Explanation*. Cambridge, MA: MIT Press.

Ayer, A.J. (1952) *Language, Truth, and Logic*, 2nd edn. New York: Dover Publications.

Barnes, B. (1976) 'Natural rationality: a neglected concept in the social sciences', *Philosophy of the Social Sciences*, 6: 115–26.

Barnes, B. (1985) *T.S. Kuhn and Social Science*. New York: Columbia University Press.

Barnes, B. (1991) 'How not to do the sociology of knowledge', *Annals of Scholarship*, 8: 321–35.

Barnes, B. and Bloor, D. (1982) 'Relativism, rationalism, and the sociology of knowledge', in M. Hollis and S. Lukes (eds), *Rationality and Relativism*. Cambridge, MA: MIT Press. pp. 21–47.

Bloor, C. (1981) 'The strengths of the strong programme', *Philosophy of the Social Sciences*, 11: 199–213.

Bohman, J. (1991) *New Philosophy of Social Science: Problems of Indeterminacy*. Cambridge, MA: MIT Press.

Callon, M. (1986) 'Some elements of a sociology of translation: domestication of the scallops and the fishermen of St Brieuc Bay', in J. Law (ed.), *Power, Action, and Belief: A New Sociology of Knowledge*. London: Routledge & Kegan Paul. pp. 196–233.

Collins, H.M. and Yearley, S. (1992a) 'Epistemological chicken', in A. Pickering (ed.), *Science as Practice and Culture*. Chicago: University of Chicago Press. pp. 301–26.

Collins, H.M. and Yearley, S. (1992b) 'Journey into space', in A. Pickering (ed.), *Science as Practice and Culture*. Chicago: University of Chicago Press. pp. 369–89.

Danto, A. (1967) 'Naturalism', in P. Edwards (ed.), *The Encyclopedia of Philosophy*, Vol. 5. New York: Macmillan. pp. 448–50.

Fuller, S. (1992a) 'Epistemology radically naturalized: recovering the normative, the experimental, and the social', in R. Giere (ed.), *Minnesota Studies in the Philosophy of Science*, Vol. 15: *Cognitive Models of Science*. Minneapolis, MN: University of Minnesota Press. pp. 427–59.

Fuller, S. (1992b) 'Social epistemology and the research agenda of science studies', in A. Pickering (ed.), *Science as Practice and Culture*. Chicago: University of Chicago Press. pp. 390–428.

Fuller, S. (1993) *Philosophy, Rhetoric, and the End of Knowledge*. Madison, WI: University of Wisconsin Press.

Gibson, R. (1993) 'Two conceptions of philosophy', *Grazer Philosophische Studien*, 44: 25–39.

Giere, R. (1992) 'The cognitive construction of scientific knowledge: response to Pickering', *Social Studies of Science*, 22: 95–107.

Gutting, G. (ed.) (1980) *Paradigms and Revolutions*. Notre Dame, IN: University of Notre Dame Press.

Habermas, J. (1988) *On the Logic of the Social Sciences*. Cambridge, MA: MIT Press.

Hacking, I. (1990) 'Natural kinds', in R. Barrett and R. Gibson (eds), *Perspectives on Quine*. Oxford: Basil Blackwell. pp. 129–41.

Hacking, I. (1991) 'The making and molding of child abuse', *Critical Inquiry*, 17: 253–88.

Hesse, M. (1986) 'Changing concepts and stable order', *Social Studies of Science*, 16: 714–26.

Iggers, G. (1968) *The German Conception of History*. Middletown, CT: Wesleyan University Press.

Kitcher, P. (1992) 'The naturalists return', *Philosophical Review*, 101: 53–117.

Kitcher, P. (1993) *The Advancement of Science*. New York: Oxford University Press.

Latour, B. (1990) 'Postmodern? No, simply amodern! Step towards an anthropology of science', *Studies in the History and Philosophy of Science*, 21: 145–71.

Latour, B. and Johnson, J. (1988) 'Mixing humans with non-humans: sociology of a door-opener', *Social Problems*, 35: 298–310.

Latour, B. and Woolgar, S. (1979) *Laboratory Life*. Beverley Hills, CA: Sage.

Laudan, L. (1987) 'Progress or rationality: the prospects for a normative naturalism', *American Philosophical Quarterly*, 24: 19–31.

Lynch, M. and Woolgar, S. (eds) (1988) *Representation in Scientific Practice*. Cambridge, MA: MIT Press.

Novick, P. (1988) *That Noble Dream: The 'Objectivity Question' and the American Historical Profession*. Cambridge: Cambridge University Press.

Pickering, A. (1990) 'Knowledge, practice and mere construction', *Social Studies of Science*, 20: 682–729.

Pickering, A. (1991a) 'Philosophy naturalized a bit', *Social Studies of Science*, 21: 575–85.

Pickering, A. (1991b) 'Objectivity and the mangle of practice', *Annals of Scholarship*, 8: 409–25.

Pickering, A. and Stephanides, A. (1992) 'Constructing quaternions: on the analysis of conceptual practice', in A. Pickering (ed.), *Science as Practice and Culture*. Chicago: University of Chicago Press.

Quine, W.V. (1969) 'Epistemology naturalized', in *Ontological Relativity and Other Essays*. New York: Columbia University Press.

Rorty, R. (1982) 'Introduction: pragmatism and philosophy', in *The Consequences of Pragmatism*. Minneapolis, MN: University of Minnesota Press. pp. xiii–xlvii.

Roth, P. (1987) *Meaning and Method in the Social Sciences*. Ithaca, NY: Cornell University Press.

Roth, P. and Barrett, R. (1990a) 'Deconstructing quarks', *Social Studies of Science*, 20: 579–632.

Roth, P. and Barrett, R. (1990b) 'Reply: aspects of sociological explanation', *Social Studies of Science*, 20: 729–46.

Schaffer, S. (1991) 'The eighteenth Brumaire of Bruno Latour', *Studies in the History and Philosophy of Science*, 22: 174–92.

Shapin, S. (1982) 'History of science and its sociological reconstructions', *History of Science*, 20: 157–211.

Shapin, S. (1992) 'Discipline and bounding: the history and sociology of science as seen through the externalism–internalism debate', *History of Science*, 30: 333–69.

Shapin, S. and Schaffer, S. (1985) *Leviathan and the Air Pump*. Princeton, NJ: Princeton University Press.

Woolgar, S. (1981) 'Interests and explanation in the social study of science', *Social Studies of Science*, 11: 365–94.

Woolgar, S. (1983) 'Irony in the social study of science', in K. Knorr-Cetina and M. Mulkay (eds), *Science Observed*. Beverly Hills, CA: Sage. pp. 239–66.

Woolgar, S. (1988) *Science: The Very Idea*. London: Tavistock Publications.

Yearley, S. (1982) 'The relationship between epistemological and sociological cognitive interests: some ambiguities underlying the use of interest theory in the study of scientific knowledge', *Studies in the History and Philosophy of Science*, 13: 353–88.

5

The Reflexive Politics of Constructivism Revisited

Steve Fuller

The history of realism is the best argument for constructivism, but that is only the start of constructivism's troubles! Although constructivism is typically seen as existing within the human sciences, the perils that await constructivism have already been foreshadowed in the history of the natural sciences. After surveying the various instabilities inherent in the realist position, I consider the natural science whose self-understanding has been most consistently constructivist: chemistry. After drawing some lessons from chemistry's ill-fated attempt at socio-epistemic prominence earlier this century, I then examine recent constructivist efforts to avoid the 'context-captivity' that befell chemistry. However, these depend too much on the 'normal science' image of inquiry that constructivism is supposedly designed to subvert. Nevertheless, a precedent for this position may be found in rhetoric's historical retreat from political involvement to the pursuit of 'interpretation'. Next, I argue that one way of repoliticizing constructivism is to consider alternative social formations within which constructivist projects can be pursued. Surprisingly, this sense of 'reflexivity' has been under-represented in the constructivist literature. Social movements appear to be an especially good alternative to, say, disciplinary paradigms, for reasons that I go on to explain. Finally, the entire discussion is epitomized by contrasting 'Right' and 'Left' constructivisms according to the features of realism that constructivists have felt worthy of simulation.

Realism and its Constructivist Devolutions

Philosophers sometimes argue that the success of constructivism depends on the truth of realism. After all, things must be constructed out of something ('real' stuff), and not all constructions succeed (only 'real' ones do). However, the rhetorical strength of these appeals to realism is inversely proportional to the specificity with which one defines 'realism'. For, as the history of realism itself shows, definitions of 'realism' are hopelessly unstable. In terms Kierkegaard could appreciate, realism is a 'both/and' philosophy for 'either/or' beings. Let me briefly illustrate this point by

indicating the instability implicit in three cases where realist positions have
been advanced in philosophy. In each case, after a realist thesis is presented,
two aspects of that thesis are shown to pull in opposite directions, leading to
alternative 'constructivist devolutions' of realism.

Science is both value-oriented and univocal.
(a)   *Science is value-oriented but multivocal.* Example: Relativism, which uses
       the plurality of value orientations to ground a multiplicity of incommensur-
       able sciences.
(b)   *Science is univocal but value-neutral.* Example: Instrumentalism, which
       explains the 'universality' and 'objectivity' of science in terms of its ability
       to be used as a means for any number of ends.

*History respects the integrity of each moment in time while admitting of an overall
temporal direction.*
(a)   *By manifesting an overall temporal direction, history undermines the
       integrity of each moment in time.* Example: Rational reconstructionism,
       whereby the significance of the past can be determined by its contribution
       to the present.
(b)   *By unfolding one moment at a time, history undermines any overall
       temporal direction.* Example: Decisionism, whereby history consists of
       many turning points which may issue in any of a number of alternative
       futures, depending on what one decides to do.

Society is the concrete instantiation of social relations.
(a)   *Society is nothing but the reproduction of social relations.* Example:
       Sociologism, which treats individuals as symbols or placeholders who
       exert little control over the shape of social relations.
(b)   *Society is nothing but the sum of concrete individuals.* Example: Liber-
       tarianism, which treats social relations as exerting no constraint of their
       own aside from what aggregates of individuals do.

Realism in its pure 'both/and' form corresponds most closely to the
Aristotelian conception of *formed matter*. Aristotle's paradigm case of
formed matter was a statue, the specific product of design applied to stone.
Each of the above devolutions may be seen as regressing to the prior state
of (a) *matterless form* (the specific statute as only one of many ideas for
statues in the sculptor's mind) and (b) *formless matter* (the stone as something that can be sculpted into a number of different statues). Notice that
even these constructivist devolutions imply resistances: limits on the sculptor's imagination and the stone's malleability, respectively. At first glance,
these resistances may seem to suggest that realism has been smuggled in the
back door. However, the history of chemistry – the science most closely
associated with the properties of building materials – reveals a continual
interpenetration of 'form' and 'matter' that the constructivist should readily
recognize. But because chemistry remains a philosophically underappre-
ciated science, its history is not widely known (cf. Bernal, 1969). Let me,
then, sketch the four major phases of that history, which shows successive
reconstructions of material resistance.

The first phase, corresponding to the period of alchemy, consisted of
(largely unsuccessful) efforts to transform one substance into another with
rather different physical properties, typically by appealing to forces able to

transcend the differences. The second phase, the Chemical Revolution in the late eighteenth and early nineteenth centuries, introduced techniques for obtaining 'pure' samples of the substances defined by modern chemical theory as 'elements'. Both the purifying agents and the purified substances were soon seen to have commercial value. The third phase, marked by the industrial domination of chemistry from the mid-nineteenth to the early twentieth century, focused on synthesizing new materials by rearranging the molecules of naturally occurring substances. These 'synthetics' were designed to heighten certain humanly relevant properties, such as resilience to weather changes (in the case of synthetic fabrics). The fourth phase, which covers the rest of this century, has involved the gradual replacement of naturally occurring substances by synthetic ones, but more with an eye to satisfying consumer demand (and corporate profits) than to reproducing the physical properties of natural substances. Indeed, chemistry's role in the depletion of natural resources in our time has arguably put it in a position of eliminating nature as it replaces it.

The Rise and Fall of a Constructivist Natural Science

Chemistry is rarely accorded much philosophical respect because it is seen as 'applied physics', with physics itself being the ultimate science of matter. However, only over the course of this century has physics become the indisputable foundation of the sciences, out of whose domain all the other sciences are constructed. A major turning point was Max Planck's victory over Ernst Mach in a series of debates about 'the ends of science' in 1908–13. These debates arose, in large part, because of the widespread perception that physicists – in their search for the fundamental units of matter ('the atomic hypothesis') – were pursuing a line of research that exhibited diminishing marginal returns on investment. Thus, the question was framed in terms of whether science has its own ends independent of the benefits people derive from science. Planck said yes, Mach no. In this way scientific realism was posed for the first time as a clear *alternative* to instrumentalism or any other philosophy of science that makes the ends of science dependent on human interests (Fuller, 1994a).

Planck's arguments for the foundational status of physics rested – as such arguments do today (cf. Weinberg, 1992) – on the field's supposedly unique ability to define the limits of human comprehension and control. On the one hand, physics could encompass the intellect with its unified worldview; on the other, it could determine the final point at which matter resists the will. However, scientists less ensconced in the physics establishment than Planck ridiculed these grandiose claims when they were first presented. Philosophers of science are familiar with Pierre Duhem's (1954: 320–35) critique that physicists are concerned only with the 'hows' but not the 'whys' that characterize the great theological and metaphysical worldviews. Less known, but more pertinent here, is Wilhelm Ostwald's (1910: 13–15) argument that the advent of synthetic materials has rendered the search for immutable atoms obsolete because any resistance in nature can be either overcome or circumvented by some kind of chemical process. Ostwald regarded the idea of a final 'end' to inquiry as a vestige of earlier eras when people expected to run up against some insurmountable barrier in nature.

The Promethean image of science projected by chemists like Ostwald figured prominently in German rhetoric during the First World War (Johnson, 1990). But after Germany's humiliating defeat, leaders of the scientific community came around to Planck's opinion that scientists needed to define their interests as distinct from those of their state and corporate sponsors (Heilbron, 1986). Only in this way would scientists have a chance to escape the taint of betrayal that was driving citizens of the Weimar Republic to turn toward explicitly anti-scientific movements (Forman, 1971). From this environment, then, arose the image of natural science as a self-determining pure inquiry, so-called scientific realism, thanks initially to the efforts of Planck's student, Moritz Schlick (1974), the founder of the Vienna Circle. This was followed up with a rhetoric that stressed sharp contrasts between 'science and technology' and 'theory and application' – all of which served to protect the integrity of science precisely during the period when technological and economic development was increasingly driven by 'basic research', and scientific techniques were introduced to integrate educational systems and labour markets (Fuller, 1994c).

The lesson to be learned from the brief rise and precipitous fall of chemistry's socio-epistemic prominence is that a science that does not postulate its own intrinsic, or 'internalized', ends runs the risk of becoming captive to its context, much as an organism can become 'overadapted' to its environment. Planck consistently maintained that the ends of science must be served before science can serve the ends of society, or neither end will be achievable. Thus, scientific realism acquired sociological status. This argument recurs throughout the twentieth century to justify the funding of basic research. The US atomic bomb project during the Second World War appeared to be an especially successful case of this strategy, in that the bomb was portrayed as the application of already existing knowledge to a new situation, not merely knowledge made to order, as the misbegotten fruits of Nazi and Soviet science policy were thought to be (Fuller, 1994b).

However, it would be misleading to conclude simply that science maintains its integrity by successfully imposing its demands on society. After all, the other major sectors of society have not automatically complied with science's wishes. Thus, science has also had to prevent their demands from being superimposed on its own. Herein lies the Faustian bargain that Planck and his successors have struck that has enabled the insinuation of science in the regulation – and not merely the facilitation – of societal functions. Perhaps the most vivid legacy of this bargain is the control that academics have over the credentials that people need for holding jobs that have little or no specifically academic content. The overall lesson, then, would seem to be: *Use or be used!*

Chemistry's Lessons for Constructivist Human Sciences

Now, how does all of this bear on the problems of constructivism in the human sciences? In answering this question, it is worth recalling the extent to which recent developments in the human sciences were anticipated by those in the natural sciences earlier this century. Three anticipations are especially noteworthy.

First, in the course of his lifelong battle with the physics establishment, Mach (1960) pioneered the 'critico-historical' approach to understanding science by presenting the progressive consolidation of Newtonian mechanics as the result of the systematic suppression of voices that challenged the Newtonian commitment to absolute space, time, matter and motion. In recovering these voices, Mach cleared the way for Einstein's relativity theory. Since then this approach has become a general strategy for undermining the realist status of normal science, as in these latter-day exemplars of constructivist research: Shapin and Schaffer (1985), on the emergence of experimentation as the paradigm of all natural knowledge in the seventeenth century; Mirowski (1989), on the rise of constrained utility-maximization as the paradigm of economic activity in the nineteenth century; and Danziger (1990), on psychology's multifarious appropriations of natural scientific methods in the twentieth century.

In normal science, each successive puzzle solved, each case study added, is supposed to deepen and broaden our knowledge of a reality that is independent of inquiry but whose form had been originally grasped by the inquiry's paradigm. However, this image is deconstructed by showing that the paradigm is less indubitable fact than irreversible decision. By returning to the key decision points in the past that established the paradigm, the constructivist then recovers a variety of contesting parties with stakes in inquiry following alternative paths. Some of these paths are counterfactually projected and shown to have been improvements on the path historically taken. In addition, the constructivist reveals the subsequent efforts taken – the rewriting of history as well as the silencing and co-opting of potential opponents – to prevent the original disagreements from ever again being aired in public. These efforts incur a cost that can be seen in the paradigm's current practices, notably its studied blindness to certain questions, facts, theories and/or people. But like the adept psychoanalyst, the constructivist often raises these blind spots to self-consciousness.

A second naturalistic anticipation of constructivist human science was the idea of matter, not as an ultimate barrier to human construction with, so to speak, 'a mind of its own', but rather as raw material, a potential (or *dynamos*, in Aristotle's Greek) that can be formed in many, perhaps even

mutually incompatible ways. Whatever limits there are to matter's con-
structibility would become apparent only as construction proceeds, as the
pursuit of one project precluded the subsequent use of that matter for other
projects. For Duhem, Ostwald and other opponents of the dominant
physics worldview, the constructivist conception of matter often went by
the name of 'energy'.

Already in Duhem (1954) we can witness the extension of 'energeticism'
from the natural to the human realm, through what has since come to be
called the 'Duhem–Quine Thesis' or the 'underdetermination of theory by
data'. Although a trained physicist himself, Duhem was sufficiently marginal to the physics establishment to embrace a chemist's understanding of
the history of physics. This understanding turns on attributing progress in
physics to its increasing artificiality. Specifically, physicists have become
able to reproduce theoretically pure conditions in laboratory experiments
to such an extent that the artificial settings have effectively replaced natural
ones as the arbiters of physical reality – much as synthetic materials have
increasingly replaced natural ones in chemical research and industry. Thus,
only the ends of the physicist – especially his or her commitment to the
theory under investigation – can determine the appropriate response to any
data generated in such artificial settings. Nature as such offered no direct
assistance, but merely reminded the physicist of the need for overall consistency in his or her resolution of theory and data. But clearly, some
resolutions required more effort than others, and so the need to 'conserve
energy' provided an intuitive sense of direction to the physicists' inquiries.

As constructivism moves more completely into the human sciences, the
artificiality of physical discourse and its experimental applications is generalized to all of social life. Thus, an ordinary language-in-use becomes the
paradigm case of a socially constructed world, a raw material that enables
and constrains its inhabitants in various ways. While it may be a strict
grammatical fact that all languages can convey all thoughts, it is also true
that for any given thought, some languages have traditions of speaking and
writing that make the thought's conveyance relatively easy. Imagine, say,
the difference between talking about automobiles in English and in Latin.
No doubt, automobile-talk can be translated between the two languages,
but given the complexity and clumsiness of the Latin expressions, it is
unlikely that the automobile would have ever been invented by anyone
who thought exclusively in Latin. It could be done, of course, but it would
be an uphill battle from the start.

A third and final way in which the earlier natural science debates antici-
pate contemporary constructivism concerns the problem of 'context-captivity'. In refusing to postulate an intrinsic end to its inquiries, constructivism
opens itself to becoming captive to the ends of whoever constructs the
context in which constructivist research occurs. Here the 'reflexive politics
of constructivism' is clearest. And so, because German chemists had tied
their fate to that of the Kaiser, the Kaiser's defeat had become their defeat
as well. In terms of our first pair of constructivist devolutions of realism,

chemistry's instrumentalist philosophy of science had relativized its epistemic authority to specific imperial interests.

Turning to the human sciences, consider a constructivist social epistemology that portrays disciplines as corresponding more to producer-dominated markets than to natural ontological domains (cf. Fuller, 1993a). In an academic environment faced with a variety of political and economic pressures, as well as faculty failure to respond adequately to those pressures, university administrators may find such a social epistemology convenient for undermining the intellectual entitlements of disciplines. This, in turn, would facilitate the consolidation and elimination of academic posts, if not entire departments (Lynch, 1994). And once the crisis has passed and/or the university administrators are deposed, the constructivist social epistemology similarly suffers the fate of the other parties to that episode.

In partial awareness of this prospect, constructivists who study 'science in action' have recently tried to escape context-captivity by adopting a weak version of Planck's strategy (Collins, 1985; Lynch, 1985; 1993). Perhaps practitioners of the human sciences cannot muster the ethos needed to regulate societal functions, but at least they can resist being used to facilitate them. Specifically, constructivist ethnographers and discourse analysts of science have increasingly encased themselves in a studiously empiricist rhetoric fraught with 'close readings' and 'close observings' which have all the circumspection one would expect from someone 'trying to get it right'. But are card-carrying constructivists entitled to adopt this rhetoric for their own purposes?

The Ambiguous Lessons of the History of Rhetoric for Constructivism

Nowadays, constructivist conference presentations invariably begin with the ceremonial castigation of some generalization about 'the nature of science', typically one uttered by a philosopher, which is then subject to detailed refutation in terms of a particular case. At the end, the constructivist portentously observes that more of such research is needed if we are truly to understand the full complexity of scientific practices. Pressed in the question-and-answer period, the constructivist will refuse to draw any normative implications from his or her study, again remarking that we really do not know enough to offer any meaningful advice about the conduct of science policy.

But what does 'now knowing enough' mean for the constructivist? In constructivist narratives scientists are not adherents to what John Dewey called 'the spectator theory of knowledge', trying to get a clear picture of a pre-existent reality. Rather, they are portrayed as actively transforming their work environments so as to bring into existence new entities and new forms of life. Scientists seem to have little to do with 'knowledge' in the way a realist would recognize it, namely, 'justified true belief'. Indeed, the point of the scientific enterprise would seem to be to make the world conform to one's will rather than to grasp the world with one's intellect. All the more puzzling, then, why constructivists should scrupulously adopt the very rhetoric they are trying to demystify.

Of course, some constructivists are being ironic here, not really meaning to have their 'case studies' add more bricks to the edifice of empirical knowledge (cf. Woolgar, 1988). Rather, they strategically adopt the rhetoric of their opponents, typically neo-positivists and historicist philosophers and sociologists of science, who happen to abide by this empiricist image of inquiry. The idea, then, is to beat them at their own game. The ultimate goal, however, is to play some other game entirely.

Despite the prominence of some of its members, these constructivists remain in the minority. More common is a 'business as usual' normal science attitude, which argues that a genuine transformation of the socio-epistemic order is not possible without an adequate understanding of it. In short: interpretation must precede action, and failures of action result from failures of interpretation. This seems a sensible view, until one considers the kind of action that 'interpretation' itself is. Historians of hermeneutics have remarked that the need to 'interpret' a text before acting upon it implies that the reader is somehow estranged from the text, typically by not having been the text's intended or primary audience (Tompkins, 1980). When texts are intended for us – as when someone addresses us directly – we do not ponder their meaning but simply respond in an appropriate fashion. A look at the history of rhetoric bears out the significance of this point.

It is fashionable nowadays in the human sciences to work with an elastic conception of 'rhetoric' that refers indifferently to both the instrumental-motivational skill of the author/speaker and the critical-interpretive skill of the reader/hearer. However, in classical Athens the latter skill came into prominence as a result of a decline in the former skill. The earliest rhetoric manuals – to which the Sophists attached their names – clearly regarded words as tools to move people to act or feel in certain ways. There is little talk of what words mean or whether ideas have been grasped. The manuals appeared in the midst of a democratic culture where speakers knew their audiences well, especially the constraints within which they had to operate in order to achieve a desired effect. More to the point, every citizen regarded himself as a potential speaker, even when listening to someone else talk.

All of this changed, however, with the end of democracy in Athens, an event first formally registered in Aristotle's *Rhetoric*, a book that shifted the criteria for good speech from qualities associated with the speech context to qualities associated with the speech text. As the sphere of public action had become restricted, the need to act upon a speaker's words became less pressing. This transition is semantically marked by a change in the meaning of *kairos* (literally 'timeliness') from a multiply constructible opportunity to an already constructed occasion (Kinneavy, 1986). Instead of causing action, speeches would now decorate action. This detachment of speech from action encouraged the formulation of general interpretive principles that were indifferent to the speech event itself. Thus, with Aristotle began the tradition of depoliticizing rhetoric by distinguishing the 'critical value' of a speech from its reception at the time it was spoken.

Of course, the turn to interpretation sometimes has had subversive consequences, as when humanist scholars in the Renaissance called for a re-examination of classical and biblical texts in their original languages. But it was not this call alone that challenged the grounds on which the Scholastics legitimized much of their teaching. In addition, the call was targeted at specific, politically empowered audiences who would be flattered by the thought that they were wise enough not to fall prey to the tired nostrums of their Scholastic teachers. However, for the most part, it remains true that the turn in interpretation has been a temporizing gesture, one made to delay action when it is not clear how, when or where one should act. Indeed, in the recent period, whenever interpretation is promoted as a field of study, it is done typically in order to foster a sense of ambiguity or scepticism amongst those who would otherwise act in a decisive, but presumably coarse, manner. The pedagogical project of 'practical criticism' associated with the New Critics is a case in point, but much the same could probably be said of critics with a more muted pedagogical agenda, such as the structuralists and post-structuralists (Siebers, 1993).

In bringing the history up to date, I court the objection that the post-structuralists – and even the structuralists and New Critics – have revived a Sophistic attitude toward rhetoric. After all, the reason that the original rhetoric manuals said little about the meanings of words or the grasping of ideas was that the Sophists held these things to be either impossible or, if possible, irrelevant to good speech – a response that Plato (via Socrates) always tried to turn into a symptom of the Sophists' intellectual bankruptcy. And while it is certainly true that the best constructivist analyses of scientific discourse often seem quite self-consciously based on Sophistic strategies (e.g. Ashmore, 1989), a big difference between the original Sophists and today's neo-Sophists is that the originals had not yet colonized all of social life as 'texts' in constant need of interpretive mediation. They did not even care much to preserve their own texts or launch great traditions of commentary. Indeed, the Sophists often compared effective speech with the use of the voice to choreograph listeners in a dance performance.

This comparison, far-fetched though it may seem, raises three interesting points of difference between the Greek Sophists and today's neo-Sophists. (1) In the Greek context, probably no one had access to a written copy of the text used in the speech – certainly not the listeners. Even though they may share many life experiences, listeners would not be presumed to belong to a common 'interpretive tradition' that would allow the speaker the luxury of making fine-grained references to the texts of earlier speeches. (2) In his role as choreographer, the speaker receives constant feedback from his audience, which enables him to adapt his speech as their response changes. In no sense is the speech a 'message in a bottle', which one launches and then prays for the right response. The relevant sense of 'knowledge' desired by the speaker does not remain hidden in some indefinite future – 'the end of inquiry' – but is regularly revealed so as to inform further action. (3) The audience itself is at first simply a group of disparate individuals who find themselves exposed to the speech, but who over the course of the speech begin to see that they are implicated in a common fate, one symbolized by the dance they perform together. Thus, the audience does not appear as a ready-made group whose identity is ceremonially reaffirmed by the speech; rather, the group identity of the audience itself comes into being during the speech.

Against what is implied here, it may be argued that interpretation is a perfectly proper self-sustaining practice that need not be seen as an arrested or deferred form of 'real action'. In this spirit, constructivist sociology of science has increasingly moved toward 'new literary forms' that experiment with ways of writing that straddle fact and fiction, thereby highlighting the constructed character of the distinction (Mulkay, 1985). However, what remains 'arrested' or 'deferred' in these forms is the possibility of constructing new audiences motivated to engage in collective projects that would otherwise not have seemed feasible to its members. Instead, what we have here is a subset of the original constructivist sociologists (and their students) moving on to what they regard as the next phase of their project, one that only makes sense to those capable of retracing their textual steps.

Consequently, while the genres may now be blurred, the relationship between constructivists and their audience remains unchanged. And it will stay that way, unless constructivists start to take seriously their own insight that texts are merely tools for constructing audiences, hopefully ones that will do interesting things once constructed. In this respect, Mirowski (1989) and Danziger (1990) come closer to the ideal I am projecting, given their success in dividing economists and psychologists, respectively, over whether their fields are progressing or stagnating, which has, in turn, served as an open invitation for science studies practitioners to participate in their debates.

An Alternative Proposal: Movements as Vehicles of Epistemic Devolution and Dynamic Credibility

My proposal here may be read as a plea for constructivists to allow the realist conception of knowledge to devolve openly in their own work. 'Justified true belief' – a staple in both philosophical epistemology and scientific methodology – enshrines a sociological syncretism, one that reflects the modern origins of the problem of knowledge in the clash of sacred and secular authorities in sixteenth- and seventeenth-century Europe:

Knowledge is justified true belief.
(a)   *Because knowledge is ultimately a justified truth claim, it does not require a personal commitment of belief, simply conformity to the procedural rules of evidence and inference.* Example: Legalism, or the public acceptance of secular authority.
(b)   *Because knowledge is ultimately a matter of belief, it can never be fully justified, except by the strength of the commitment and its consequences for action.* Example: Voluntarism, or the private acceptance of sacred authority.

It may seem that the (b) side of the devolution has virtually disappeared from scientific discussions of knowledge, with William James's version of pragmatism being the exception that proves the rule. However, such a verdict would be much too hasty. Current debates between 'realists' and 'instrumentalists' typically turn on whether one truly needs to 'believe' in the entities referenced in one's theories or simply act 'as if' one believed in them. Moreover, one plausible way of encapsulating recent philosophical debates over scientific rationality is in terms of when one should make and forsake commitments to particular research programmes, especially in the face of less than adequately justified knowledge claims. Finally and most importantly, both Polanyi (1957) and Kuhn (1970) have located the 'genius' of science in the personal commitment that each scientist presumes of his or her colleagues. This mutual presumption creates a climate of tolerance for somewhat divergent paths of research and even temporary disagreements over matters of fact and interpretation. In that sense, (a) and (b) remain bound together because (a) is taken to govern the micro-level of day-to-day research and (b) the macro-level of overall epistemic orientation.

However, an interesting point raised by Kuhn's account of paradigmatic crisis is that enough divergent and unresolved judgement calls at the (a) level – standing anomalies – can cause scientists to doubt each other at the (b) level, which then leads to sectarian formations, ideological struggles, and ultimately to a 'scientific revolution'. Once a new paradigm is ensconsed, the history of the revolutionary episode is retold to make it seem as though the winners were bound to win because the strength of their commitment was commensurate with the epistemic warrant of their theory. Kuhn himself believes that the long-term survival of science depends on these rationally reconstructed histories being taught to the next generation of scientists, so that they perceive a natural fit between the (a) and (b) levels (Kuhn, 1970: 167).

But what if Kuhnian crises are regarded not as threats to order within science but as catalysts to societal transformations outside of science? Paradigmatic disorder may thus be reinterpreted as the emergence of *inquiry as a social movement*. Let us briefly pursue this possibility as an alternative to constructivists' retreating to the rhetoric of normal science (cf. Fuller, 1993b).

There is a vulgar way of thinking about social movements that makes them seem purely reactive entities composed of disgruntled – if not down-right irrational – individuals, entities which lack the sustained purposeful-ness of proper institutions. Indeed, sociologists have traditionally treated movements as transient or degenerate social formations. However, Eyerman and Jamison (1991) have recently resurrected the integrity of movements by portraying them as 'flexibly organized cognitive praxes'. What differentiates the American civil rights, environmental, and peace movements from, say, academic disciplines is their sense of organization, not necessarily their goals, their longevity or their sense of inquiry. Success-ful movements manage to retain their dynamism as they gain credibility. They do not simply 'evolve' into paradigms. The dynamic credibility of movements is maintained precisely by continually displaying the tension between (a) and (b), which correspond, respectively, to the 'resource-mobilizing' and 'consciousness-raising' sides of the movement.

By 'consciousness-raising', I mean the role of movements in forming a collective identity among people who may be disparately located (in both space and status), but who nevertheless share experiences that hitherto had been ignored or trivialized – even by those individuals themselves. Familiar examples of such heightened experiences can be found in the reinterpreta-tions that people of colour and women have given to routinized forms of discrimination. A favourite Marxist example is Luther's campaign to get the peasants to stop discounting the cognitive significance of their own sensory and spiritual experience. This campaign was at once directed against helio-centric astronomy and Catholic theology, which, in their quite different ways, were bastions of cognitive authoritarianism. However, as Marx himself had already realized in *The German Ideology*, a movement that thrives entirely on consciousness-raising is likely to be confined, ever more dogmatically, to just those people who have had the relevant sensitizing experiences. In short, it becomes cultish to the point of losing all hope of establishing society-wide credibility.

In contrast, the 'resource-mobilizing' side of movements aims to achieve goals on an agenda. Here we find the efforts to reduce utopian aspirations to planks on a party platform, which enable the movement to make a series of short-term alliances with more mainstream interest groups. Not surprisingly, the sheer increase in the movement's dimensions is taken by its members as a sign of progress, even if it involves diluting the movement's identity and exaggerating the significance of getting a compromise bill passed as part of an omnibus legislative package. The advantage of seeing movements as agenda-pushing vehicles is that it provides concrete reference points for the movement's activities, continu-ally reminding the movement's members – especially those who have *not* had the relevant sensitizing experiences – that it is heading the entire society in the right direction. However, a movement that is exclusively focused in this way easily falls victim to its own success, as the move-ment's ability to adapt to the mainstream gets mistaken for its ability to bend the mainstream to its will. Thus, we see another version of context-captivity at work.

So far, we have only defined the tension that makes movements vehicles of 'dynamic credibility' or 'epistemic devolution', depending on whether one sees instability as a good or a bad thing. But under what circumstances is this tension amplified or dampened? Sociologist Robert Wuthnow (1989) has taken a major step toward answering this question by trying to explain the transformations in European society wrought by the Protestant Reformation, the Enlightenment, and nineteenth-century socialism. He is interested in how discourse fields manage to acquire the political and economic resources that enable them to become vehicles for large-scale cultural change. By necessity, I will have to distil the complexity of Wuthnow's account into an overall plot structure.

The movement gestates during a period of economic expansion, which allows many people to enter discourse-intensive occupations, such as the clergy, the academy and the bureaucracy (cf. Gouldner, 1979). This is followed by a period of economic contraction that causes considerable social dislocation as different sectors of society adapt differently to their new situation. Professions that had been prestigious or rich lose status, and vice versa. People in the discourse-intensive fields, who have themselves become dislocated, compete with one another in offering new criteria of legitimation. They convert their collectively threatened position into an opportunity for expansion. Their doctrinal disputes are played out in the public forum, thereby enabling specific interest groups to see their own fates reflected in the outcomes of the disputes. Since these disputes already have a momentum of their own, and the interest groups are struggling to redefine themselves, the disputes turn out to shape the intergroup dynamics more than vice versa – even when the intellectuals are explicitly hired to do a group's bidding. Typically, this leads to a realignment of interests in society at large.

Thus, the intellectuals exercise transformative power on the society at large as their disagreements become the terms in which the major interest groups define their own differences. For example, a nobleman may see his political fate as tied to how he decides between contesting Protestant faiths; a factory owner, despite his aversion to or incomprehension of socialism, may nevertheless refer to his workers as belonging to a certain 'class' and treat them as the term would suggest. In this respect, a striking feature of the history of Wuthnow's three movements is that their source of strength does not seem to have been any tendency toward doctrinal consensus. These were not cases in which the resolution of intellectual questions provided the model for the rest of society to follow. On the contrary, these movements became more transformative, the wider the circle of people who felt that their interests were somehow implicated in the swirl of discourse.

Here it is worth recalling Wuthnow's own roots in the sociology of religion, which, following Max Weber, has traditionally regarded institutionalization – the formation of doctrinal consensus and its ritualized reinforcement – as sapping the spirit that marked a religion's charismatic origins. Established churches are thus commonly portrayed as domesticating more ecstatic forms of religious experience. Indeed, would it be so far-fetched to think of each consensus-based normal science as a withdrawal, a splintering, from the spirit of inquiry? Similarly, the sort of divisiveness that eventually diminished the impact of the movements Wuthnow studied took the form of sectarian withdrawals, often under the guise of 'purity': either a refusal to argue with doctrinal opponents or a refusal to acknowledge the legitimacy of *any* existing authority (cf. Frey et al., 1992, for contemporary corroboration of this point). Wuthnow (1989: 577) astutely observes that the Reformation, the Enlightenment and socialism each left the state stronger, not because the intellectuals supported the status quo (they did not) but because their disputes reinforced the idea that there was a single source of authority, control over which could be determined by public means. A stronger state was thus a by-product of the movement's refusal to be identified primarily by its own institutional forms.

Are Wuthnow's tales of movements ultimately offering anything more than alternative accounts of how constructivists fall captive to context? Although I cannot do full justice to this question without introducing more detail from Wuthnow's accounts, the fact that specifically the *state* – and not industry or other private interests – proved to be the direct beneficiary offers at least a ray of hope that movements will contribute to the preservation of the public sphere.

Reinscribing the Politics of Constructivism in the Metaphysics of Realism

The preference for 'movement' versus 'paradigm' as the mode of constructivist inquiry reflects a profound difference in metaphysical taste over the features of realism that constructivism needs to simulate. Corresponding to 'movement' and 'paradigm' are, respectively, Left and Right constructivisms. Whereas Right constructivists simulate the *stability* of metaphysical reality, their Left counterparts are drawn to the *depth*, or non-apparent quality, attributed to such reality. Stability and depth are correlated in metaphysical realism by supposing that reality's changing appearances are grounded in permanent deep structures that manifest themselves differently under different conditions. The Right constructivist tries to reduce depth to stability by arguing that 'depth' is nothing more than a reification of the more regular appearances in ordinary social interaction. The Left constructivist pulls in the opposite direction, reducing stability to depth by arguing that 'stability' is nothing more than organized resistance to possible but currently non-apparent forms of social interaction. In terms of our devolutionary schema, we have the following:

Reality extends beyond the appearances and is invariant.
(a)   *Reality extends beyond the appearances but is variable.* Example: Left constructivism or possibilism, whereby all that can be is not limited to what already has been. *Motto*: 'Philosophers have so far only interpreted the world; the point is to change it' (early Marx).
(b)   *Reality is invariant but limited to the regularity of appearances.* Example: Right constructivism or actualism, whereby all that can be already has been. *Motto*: 'Philosophy leaves the world alone' (early Wittgenstein).

As essentialist views of human nature broke down in the eighteenth century, Right and Left constructivisms came into their own. Right constructivism emerged from the Scottish Enlightenment's preoccupation with social orders maintained by tradition and convention without appeal to either Providence or Leviathan. Collins (1987) exudes this sensibility in contemporary science studies, drawing upon Berger and Luckmann (1968), who, in turn, draw upon that sociological sympathizer of Austrian economics, Alfred Schutz (Prendergast, 1986). All of these thinkers share a prima facie interest in levelling the distinction between elite and ordinary forms of knowledge. However, this levelling occurs only at an analytic level – in the use of a common method to study all epistemic communities – but not at a substantive level that would make the communities more permeable to each other. In fact, the analytic levelling is integrally tied to the reinforcement of community boundaries, in that each epistemic community is a 'form of life' whose legitimacy rests on its having been constituted by its members. Under those circumstances, any attempt to reconstitute the community from the outside by, say, a speech that criticizes the external conditions needed to maintain the community would involve a violation of the community's right to self-determination.

On the contrary, Left constructivism emerged from an interest in shaking off tradition and convention, Rousseau's revolutionary impulse to make oneself and one's society anew. The most thoughtful recent articulation of this position is Roberto Unger (1987). A Brazilian native who is both a Third World radical democrat and a Harvard law professor, Unger founded the Critical Legal Studies movement, which is designed to 'denaturalize' the legal system so that people will see it at least as much as enabling as constraining action. According to Unger, the feeling of 'necessity' attached to certain social arrangements is simply the fear of what might follow from breaking them. Effective political action consists of dividing and recombining agents, so that the promised threats can no longer be enforced. Unger observes that two of the main signs that such 'plasticity' is at work occur when people see their assigned social roles as no longer adequate to the work they are actually doing and when they fail to find useful a strong distinction between the tasks involved in defining and executing a plan of action. A fully self-realized constructivism would bring these points back home to the academy and, once and for all, do away with the institution of normal science.

te

This chapter is a substantially expanded and revised version of Steve Fuller (1994) 'The reflexive politics of constructivism', *History of the Human Sciences*, 7: 87-94.

References

Ashmore, M. (1989) *The Reflexive Thesis*. Chicago: University of Chicago Press.

Berger, P. and Luckmann, T. (1968) *The Social Construction of Reality*. Garden City, NY: Doubleday.

Bernal, J.D. (1969) *Science in History*, 4 vols. Harmondsworth: Penguin.

Collins, H. (1985) *Changing Order*. London: Sage.

Collins, H. (1987) 'Certainty and the public understanding of science', *Social Studies of Science*, 17: 687–702.

Danziger, K. (1990) *Constructing the Subject*. Cambridge: Cambridge University Press.

Duhem, P. (1954) *The Aim and Structure of Physical Theory*. Princeton, NJ: Princeton University Press.

Eyerman, R. and Jamison, A. (1991) *Social Movements: A Cognitive Approach*. Cambridge: Polity Press.

Forman, P. (1971) 'Weimar culture, causality, and quantum theory: 1918–1927', *Historical Studies of the Physical Sciences*, 3: 1–115.

Frey, S., Dietz, T. and Kalof, L. (1992) 'Characteristics of successful American protest groups', *American Journal of Sociology*, 98: 368–87.

Fuller, S. (1993a) *Philosophy, Rhetoric, and the End of Knowledge*. Madison, WI: University of Wisconsin Press.

Fuller, S. (1993b) 'Social constructivism teaching itself a lesson: science studies as social movement', *Danish Yearbook of Philosophy*, 28: 47–60.

Fuller, S. (1994a) 'Retrieving the point of the realism–instrumentalism debate: Mach vs. Planck on science education policy', in D. Hull, M. Forbes and R. Bruian (eds), *PSA 1994*, Vol. 1. East Lansing, MI: Philosophy of Science Association. pp. 200–7.

Fuller, S. (1994b) 'Teaching Thomas Kuhn to teach the Cold War vision of science', *Contention*, 10: 81–106.

Fuller, S. (1994c) 'Towards a philosophy of science accounting: a critical rendering of instrumental rationality', *Science in Context*, 7: 591–621.

Gouldner, A. (1979) *The Future of Intellectuals and the Rise of the New Class*. London: Macmillan.

Heilbron, J. (1986) *The Dilemmas of an Upright Man: Max Planck as Spokesman for German Science*, Berkeley, CA: University of California Press.

Johnson, J. (1990) *The Kaiser's Chemists*. Chapel Hill, NC: University of North Carolina Press.

Kinneavy, J. (1986) '*Kairos*: A neglected concept in classical rhetoric', in J. Moss (ed.), *Rhetoric and Practice*. Washington: Catholic University Press. pp. 79–105.

Kuhn, T. (1970) *The Structure of Scientific Revolutions*, 2nd edn. Chicago: University of Chicago Press.

Lynch, M. (1985) *Art and Artifact in Laboratory Science*. London: Routledge.

Lynch, M. (1993) *Scientific Practice and Ordinary Acton*. Cambridge: Cambridge University Press.

Lynch, M. (1994) 'Review of Fuller's *Philosophy, Rhetoric, and the End of Knowledge*, *Contemporary Sociology*, 23: 312–14.

Mach, E. (1960) *The Science of Mechanics*, 6th edn. La Salle, IL: Open Court.

Mirowski, P. (1989) *More Heat than Light*. Cambridge: Cambridge University Press.

Mulkay, M. (1985) *The Word and the World*. London: Allen & Unwin.

Ostwald, W. (1910) *Natural Philosophy*. New York: Henry Holt.

Polanyi, M. (1957) *Personal Knowledge*. Chicago: University of Chicago Press.

Prendergast, C. (1986) 'Alfred Schutz and the Austrian School of Economics', *American Journal of Sociology*, 92: 1–26.

Schlick, M. (1974) *The General Theory of Knowledge*. Berlin: Springer-Verlag.

Shapin, S. and Schaffer, S. (1985) *Leviathan and the Air-Pump*. Princeton, NJ: Princeton University Press.

Siebers, T. (1993) *Cold War Criticism and the Politics of Skepticism*. Oxford: Oxford University Press.

Tompkins, J. (1980) 'The reader in history: the changing shape of literary response', in J. Tompkins (ed.), *Reader-Response Criticism*. Baltimore, MD: Johns Hopkins University Press. pp. 201–32.

Unger, R. (1987) *Politics: A Work of Constructive Social Theory*, 3 vols. Cambridge: Cambridge University Press.

Weinberg, S. (1992) *Dreams of a Final Theory*. New York: Pantheon.

Woolgar, S. (ed.) (1988) *Knowledge and Reflexivity*. London: Sage.

Wuthnow, R. (1989) *Communities of Discourse*. Cambridge, MA: Harvard University Press.

6

Unconstructive

Wil Coleman and Wes Sharrock

The notion of 'social construction' currently in use seems to us seriously confused. Here we can only highlight some aspects of that confusion. Our argument must, of necessity, have a perfunctory character, with room only for the assertion and comparatively superficial argument on behalf of a handful of mainly critical points.

The fundamental reservations we express pertain to (a) what we see to be the conflation of epistemological and sociological issues and (b) the extent to which the pursuit of epistemological concerns subverts the realization of the sociological objectives which might have been sought through the implementation of the notion of 'social construction'.

Slippage between Sociology and Epistemology

One of the critical moments in the formation of the idea of 'social construction' was the publication of Peter Berger and Thomas Luckmann's *The Social Construction of Reality: A Treatise on the Sociology of Knowledge* in 1966 (1967). In Berger and Luckmann's case, the specifically sociological purpose of their inquiries is made plain and a sharp separation of these from epistemological issues is insisted upon. The basis for this insistence is the recognition on Berger and Luckmann's part that the two kinds of problem are quite different, and that the attempt to treat the epistemological problems in sociological terms would be, in their memorable phrase, equivalent to attempting to push the bus upon which they are riding. However satisfactory or otherwise Berger and Luckmann's understanding of the nature of epistemology might be, they were at least clear that the determination of the validity or otherwise of persons' claims to knowledge were beyond the competence of the sociologist – whether witchcraft beliefs or nuclear physics is valid is not a sociological question (Berger and Luckmann, 1967: 13–30). The problem which Berger and Luckmann thereby surface is one inherent in the very idea of a sociology of knowledge – namely, it is beyond the competence of the sociologist to identify the purported phenomenon of that putative field of inquiry.[1]

The term 'knowledge' is, of course, an evaluative one, and someone who characterizes something as knowledge thereby provides endorsement for it.

There is nothing in the competence of sociologists, however, which provides them with any capacity to endorse (or to refuse to endorse, for that matter) the claim that bewitchment has caused an illness or that the physical structure of matter is particulate. Hence the sociologist *qua* sociologist cannot identify any bona fide instances of knowledge.[2] Recognizing this situation, Berger and Luckmann resort to the only solution available to them, which is to undertake a change of subject matter for their putative domain of inquiry, the substitution of knowledge-in-inverted-commas for knowledge. Their proposal is for a sociological study of 'what passes for knowledge in society' instead of the study of knowledge as such. Berger and Luckmann recognize that neither the modes of investigation nor their objects are equivalent.

Whether or not Berger and Luckmann's diagnosis and attempted remedy for their difficulties was the most effective response to the situation in which they found themselves can provide the occasion for another discussion. Here our sole concern is to explore the nature of their initiative and the way in which this has subsequently been developed – or misapplied.

The study of knowledge as such, involving as it does the question 'What is knowledge?', Berger and Luckmann cede to epistemology. They do so on the assumption that it must fall to epistemology to provide criteria for identification of bona fide instances of knowledge. Members of society can and do speak of certain matters as, or as instantiating, knowledge. Yet, according to Berger and Luckmann, they must defer to the epistemologist if the validity of their bona fides is to be assessed. In similar fashion must the member *qua* sociologist defer to the epistemologist in these matters: sociology's remit is strictly delimited – it consists solely in the registration of 'what passes for knowledge', what we have called knowledge-in-quotation-marks. Thus, following Berger and Luckmann, the projection of a sociology-of-knowledge-in-quotation-marks is to effect two operations:

1   The disaffiliation of the sociologist from any putative endorsement of the characterization 'knowledge', for the sociologist is incompetent to determine – *qua* sociologist – whether something is or is not a matter of knowledge.

2   The use of the term knowledge is therefore a matter of citation. This means, effectively, that one is speaking of what someone else identifies as, what someone says is, what someone *calls* knowledge.

The sociology of 'knowledge' thus becomes the sociology of, so to speak, knowledge claims. 'The sociology of "knowledge"' is not, on Berger and Luckmann's scrupulous terms, identical with 'the sociology of knowledge', for they have surrendered the possibility of the latter. 'What passes for knowledge in society' is not by any means the same as 'what knowledge is', but is the closest that the sociologist can come to the study of knowledge.[3] That the study of 'what passes for knowledge' must displace the study of knowledge need not, thereby, be a disadvantage for sociology but might, to the contrary, be to its advantage and the proposal to turn attention to 'claims to knowledge' might be the basis for a radicalization of sociological conceptions.

It seems to us, however, that rather than being employed for its specifically sociological implications, Berger and Luckmann's work has been read against its own grain, taken as an epistemologically oriented and radicalizing doctrine.

Naturally, we cannot endow Berger and Luckmann with anything like our set of sociological preoccupations, and the direction in which these authors developed their initial premises – which were a combination of the above considerations with the pre-sociological ideas of Alfred Schutz – seem to us to proceed in a disappointingly Parsonian fashion.[4] Thus, we certainly do not suppose that the advantages we might perceive in Berger and Luckmann's premises with respect to the development of sociological analysis were those that Berger and Luckmann perceived in them. Our regret, then, that subsequent elaboration of the idea of 'social construction' has taken it ever further away from the potential that we might have seen in it does not provide an occasion for criticism, as such. The advantage we could perceive in the idea of 'the social construction of reality' would be that it could permit the further elaboration of Schutz's central concern with the adequate identification and description of 'the actor's point of view' and, most particularly, with the *socially organized ways* in which (what Schutz termed) 'the accent of reality' was bestowed from within social settings.[5]

The notion of 'social construction' might then have been developed in a direction which would have enabled it to strengthen that strand of sociological thought which questions the stock assumption that it is sociology's role to 'debunk' members' understandings. It seems to us, however, that far from being drawn upon to support such opposition, helping to challenge the easy assumption that the sociologist knows best, it has been absorbed into the prevailing conception and has come to play just such a 'debunking' role. In doing so it has, in addition, preserved the inclination to which it seemed to us a corrective was necessary, which was to provide relatively impoverished characterizations of 'the actor's point of view'.[6] But to reiterate, these disappointments of ours are not themselves objections to the turn that the notion of 'social construction' has taken since Berger and Luckmann. What is more cogent in the way of objections is the possibility of questioning whether *illicit* transitions have taken place in the development of the idea after Berger and Luckmann's initiation of it that have been essential to its reformulation in the service of its 'debunking' role.

The post-'Strong Programme' development of the 'The Sociology of Scientific Knowledge' must be something that we have in mind in making our allegations, for SSK now stands as one of the paradigms of the 'social construction' conception. The brief but energetic history of that enterprise has meant that there is a very dense, complicated and, above all, entangled story to be told about the way in which the notion of 'social construction' has developed, but there can be no doubt that the dissociation of sociological and epistemological issues which Berger and Luckmann laid down has by no means held,[7] and that the import which is seen in SSK (both by those who practise it and by those who draw upon it for intellectual legitimation of their own concerns) is an epistemological one.[8]

Given the dissociation which Berger and Luckmann seek to effect between the sociological and the epistemological, how can epistemological concerns not merely be reinstated but come to acquire such predominance? One of the ways in which this may be done is, we argue, precisely by the misreading of Berger and Luckmann's position as an epistemological one, by disregarding, by overlooking, the extent to which Berger and Luckmann's proposals had effectively changed the subject of 'the sociology of knowledge'.

The work of the founders of the so-called Strong Programme, David Bloor and Barry Barnes, by no means took matters in the direction in which they have subsequently been carried but they did incorporate many of the confusions that have resulted in the subsequent instability of standpoints within SSK and that stimulated the purportedly progressive 'radicalizations' which have seemed necessary to give sense to the programme of SSK.[9] That work did, however, make the transition that we contest.

The crucial step in the transition is a simple one, and no doubt one which, without great wariness, is easily made. It involves no more than the supposition that to speak of 'what passes for knowledge in society' is to give an account of the nature of knowledge. The fact is that 'what passes for knowledge in society' is not, in Berger and Luckmann's formulation of it, an account of what knowledge is. That their formulation is not and cannot be, any form of response to the questions of epistemology is a constituent feature of it. The formulation that their subject matter is 'what passes for knowledge in society' is a *methodological* step for demarcating their domain of inquiry, and a way of bypassing epistemological issues, of confining their enquiries to empirically accessible topics. The study of 'what passes for knowledge in society' is *substituted* for the study of knowledge.

If one disregards these (necessary) caveats one will no doubt develop the conviction that one is in possession of an account of knowledge, that the account is one which says that knowledge *is* 'what passes for knowledge in society'.[10] The account then permits, indeed requires, a degree of elaboration in order to see how this provides an understanding of what makes something knowledge. If knowledge is 'that which passes for knowledge in society' then the way in which to understand how it comes to 'pass for knowledge in society' is, of course, to identify the mechanisms which give rise to such 'passing', to ask how some item's status as knowledge comes to be disseminated within society. How do people come to agree (in so far as they do) that something is knowledge? This sounds just like the doctrine which causes so much anxiety amongst the would-be 'realists' in the philosophy of science, for it sounds as though it carries the suggestion that the way in which something comes to be knowledge (or counted-as-knowledge, which is misleadingly – we say – presented as the same thing) is by virtue of agreement. It is because, so to speak, everyone says that something is knowledge that it is knowledge, and thus it is just everyone's agreeing that it is correct which makes it correct.[11]

Note that we do not dispute the possibility of giving a sociological account of what makes something 'knowledge', in terms, say, of an empirical investigation into scientific controversy. We make no objection to *causal* (or genealogical) accounts of how something acquires the status of 'knowledge', i.e. of how it comes to be installed and disseminated within the scientific community or within society more generally. But we deny that such studies have any epistemological import, our point being that in the very formulation of the Strong Programme (and we have Bloor in mind as a key figure here) there is conflation of causal and, for want of a better word, 'conceptual' investigations.

Perhaps the tendency to ask the question as to what makes something knowledge misleads Bloor, for the word 'makes' is one which is often employed in a causal fashion. However, it is not invariably employed in such a causal way, and the fact is that the question 'What makes something knowledge?' is characteristically not a causal question but a conceptual one. Berger and Luckmann at least go some way to recognizing this when they allocate epistemology the task of identifying criteria for the identification of knowledge. Such a conception does differ, and profoundly, from Wittgenstein's view that grammar drives out epistemology, but does acknowledge that the question 'What makes something knowledge?' does not call for the provision of any kind of causal account. There is a difference between a causal and a 'conceptual' story, and the conflation of these is the source of much philosophical trouble, as it is (again) in the recent history of SSK. To provide a conceptual story is to provide not an account of the causal circumstances that lead us to assert that we know something but is to give an account of *what we are saying about something* when, for example, we say that we know it.

In Wittgenstein's *On Certainty* (1969), for example, an account is given of the expression 'know' which holds, in sum, that when someone says 'I know', they are saying 'I am not mistaken'. This might seem a trivial and irrelevant business, except and in so far as, if Wittgenstein's arguments are sound, the fundamental supposition of philosophical scepticism has been that someone who says 'I know' is saying 'There is no conceivable possibility that I might be mistaken.' Wittgenstein shows that 'I am not mistaken' is not the same as 'There is no conceivable possibility that I am mistaken', arguing that 'I know' is normally used in the face of ways in which I might be conceived to be mistaken. *On Certainty* is intended to dissipate philosophical scepticism,[12] but is brought in here only to indicate the extent to which the provision of an account of 'what we are saying of something when we say that it is knowledge' does not involve any kind of causal story and does not, therefore, depend upon the outcome of scientific inquiries of any sort (including sociological ones).

The context in which we located the previous paragraph was that of the prior contention that it is the word 'makes' which perhaps misleads Bloor, who mistakes it for one that invariably makes a causal story relevant. To ask 'What makes something knowledge-in-inverted-commas?' is indeed to ask a question to which a causal answer may be given, perhaps even one that involves the citation of the conventionally sociological factors of the sort that those in the Strong Programme like to invoke. However, in the question 'What makes something knowledge?' (wherein the latter term is of course to be read without inverted commas) the word 'makes' does not necessarily, if at all, figure as a causal expression. What makes the proposition 'The earth is round' an item of knowledge, what makes it true, is the earth's being round. To say this is not, however, to offer a theory of any sort in which the shape of the earth plays a causal role. The bogey of the constructionists is, of course, realism, and what we say might sound as if we were committing ourselves to some form of realism, even, despite our denials, to a correspondence theory which says that truth involves a correspondence between a linguistic expression and an external, non-linguistic state of affairs. To suppose this, however, would be to overlook the fact that we have put forward no theory of any kind, and have advanced nothing of a controversial character whatever. Indeed, we have stated what are virtually tautologies.

What we are seeking to do is to issue reminders of the difference between causal and 'internal' connections – in the present case they impinge upon the different uses of the word 'makes'. In doing so, we wish to disabuse those who argue that (for example) the world's being round plays a causal role either (a) in the statement 'The world is round' being an item of knowledge, being true; or (b) in someone's coming to know that the world is round. At the same time, however, we draw attention to the internal relation of the (fact of) the world's being round *vis-à-vis* (c) the truthfulness of the statement (its status as knowledge) 'The world is round', and (d) being able to say of someone that they *know* that the world is round. In emphasizing the logical role played in our example (which must stand for a multitude of other cases) by the state of affairs, the world's being round, we seek to disabuse social constructionists who would claim that it is *just* human agreement that decides matters pertaining to truth and knowledge. It is the case that people generally assent to the proposition that the earth is round. But the social constructionist fails to give that 'agreement' its full weight. The 'agreement' does not inhere in persons happening to give voice to the identical utterance. For what people agree (or disagree) on is the facts (Wittgenstein's point: their agreement on the facts is different from their agreeing – or not – on whether an occasion is an appropriate one for voicing the assertion 'The earth is round'). It is the independent order of fact that makes the statement 'The world is round' true. And to say this is to point to the grammatical (internal) role played by an independent realm of states of affairs in knowledge claims and statements of fact.

Conclusion

We have presented several arguments in a compacted and assertive form to indicate the extent to which it is possible, beginning from sources which are much the same as those from which 'constructionism' is allegedly drawn, to form some profoundly dissenting views. We are well aware that we cannot hope convincingly, in such small compass, to show that our objections to 'constructionism' are justly applied to a significant proportion of the many (perhaps different) things which travel under its name; or substantiate that there are indeed the misreadings we allege; or demonstrate convincingly that our objections have genuine substance. Further, we have primarily made reference to works which are now quite dated, and these cannot be taken as good guides to the character of current work: things have moved on. However, if the formulation of our own views must be intensely compacted, then even more so must the treatment of that now expansive topic of 'constructionism', and we certainly do not imagine that we have given a full and fair account of constructionism, nor sought to confront it in its most up-to-date form. All we have tried to show is that if 'constructionism' does indeed confront the problems we identify, then these may have been built in at an early stage.

Notes

1 A comparable realization with respect to the phenomenon of 'deviance' resulted, particularly via ideas of 'labelling' made a parallel and equally crucial contribution to the formation of the idea of 'social construction'.

2 Which is not to say that sociologists as members of the culture are bereft of convictions with respect to the respective bona fides of 'primitive magic' and 'Western science'.

3 The sociologist might be studying a bona fide instance of knowledge but could not – *qua* sociologist – be aware that this was in fact the case. All that the sociologist could know is that this was what passes for knowledge within the society.

4 Given the widespread antipathy to Parsons, we should make it plain that we ourselves are far from finding Parsons's work inherently objectionable or as being in fact subject to the criticisms which are commonly levelled against it. Our complaint is that Berger and Luckmann's account of 'the social construction of reality' reads as remarkably similar to Parsons's account of the institutionalization of culture in terms of double contingency (see, for example, Parsons and Shils, 'Values, motives and systems of action', in Parsons and Shils (1966: 47–233) and that it is not, therefore, a very distinctive development from premises which might permit the formulation of a very different conception of sociology to that found in Parsons. The formulation of the latter, from very similar premises, particularly Schutz's presociological work, was provided in Harold Garfinkel's *Studies in Ethnomethodology* (1967).

5 An advantage which, again, was primarily – virtually exclusively – developed by ethnomethodology.

6 And thus to perpetuate the characterization of actors as, in ethnomethodology's jargon, 'dopes'. The form this has taken under the influence of 'social constructionism' involves treating the actors as 'reality dopes', i.e. as though they were persons who conducted their everyday affairs on the basis of a philosophical theory, namely that of 'naive realism'. For a comparable objection, cf. Lynch (1993).

7 We will note that relatively recent 'deconstructionist' inclinations in SSK would maintain that such dissociations cannot prevail, that they must unravel, but will disregard such possible lines of objection since these 'deconstructionist' inclinations arise from and are persuasive only in the light of the transitions which we will, shortly, oppose.

8 Such that those who are involved in it come to read their venture's short history as a form of 'epistemological chicken', with successive positions seeking to take ever more radical epistemological steps.

9 For arguments of the type we are about to oppose, cf. Barry Barnes and David Bloor, 'Relativism, rationality and the sociology of knowledge', in Hollis and Lukes (1982). We can also note that it is one of those paradoxes which pervade the sociological thought of the last thirty years or so that yet again a theorist's ideas have been brought into service of the very strategies those ideas were formed to oppose. The irony we have in mind here is that Alfred Schutz's work, which was specifically directed against what he disparaged as 'the so-called sociology of knowledge', was – via Berger and Luckmann – used to underpin conceptions which were then, courtesy of Barnes and Bloor, deployed to justify the resuscitation of that selfsame 'so-called sociology of knowledge' (for, of course, Barnes and Bloor sought to revitalize the Mannheimian tradition in 'sociology of knowledge', which was the very paradigm of Schutz's 'so-called sociology of knowledge').

10 There is a sense in which this assertion is true, but only if it is understood in its fully and properly qualified sense but, however, the fully, properly qualified sense is not one which is likely to be noted by the unwary. The assertion is true in so far as it is assigned an 'operational status'. If it is stated in the following fashion, for example, it is correct but, at the same time, the reservations of Berger and Luckmann are also preserved: from a sociological point of view, knowledge is 'what passes for knowledge in society'. It is an operational contention which says that what, in practice, sociological inquirers study – for this is all they *can* study – are people's claims to knowledge. Disregarding the necessarily qualified, operational character of this assertion can, of course, result in the conversion of what is actually a statement of (epistemological) impotence into one which sounds as if it expresses the most potent and overriding (epistemological) conception.

11 The role of Thomas Kuhn's account of science and the co-optation of Wittgenstein's later philosophy cannot be neglected in considering how this transition came about. Both were pivotal figures in forming the Strong Programme in SSK, though it cannot be overlooked that both Kuhn and Wittgenstein were devoted to arguing against the conclusions that were drawn from their work by such as Barnes and Bloor – cf. Barnes (1983) and Bloor (1983). Kuhn's emphasis upon the role of the 'scientific community' perhaps provides his would-be adapters with some justification for supposing that he is offering an epistemological view, not least since Kuhn does intertwine his reflections with epistemological considerations. In that respect, his work can be read as holding that it is agreement within the scientific community which comprises knowledge, though his own denials must be borne in mind. However, the capacity to extract from Wittgenstein any suggestion that truth is a matter of agreement is one which neglects, to begin with, the fact that the purpose of his later philosophy was to displace epistemology with 'grammar', not to formulate epistemological positions at all. For a detailed rebuttal of the idea that Wittgenstein conceived truth as a matter of agreement see Hacker (1990), especially Part 1.

12 Providing yet another indicator of the extent to which contemporary work in SSK is simply at odds with work which it typically presents as licensing its project.

References

Barnes, B. (1983) *T.S. Kuhn and Social Science*. London: Macmillan.
Barnes, B. and Bloor, D. (1982) 'Relativism, rationality and the sociology of knowledge', in M. Hollis and S. Lukes (eds), *Rationality and Relativism*. Oxford: Blackwell.

Berger, P. and Luckmann, T. (1967 [1966]) *The Social Construction of Reality: A Treatise on the Sociology of Knowledge*. Allen Lane: Penguin Press.

Bloor, D. (1983) *Wittgenstein: A Social Theory of Knowledge*. London: Macmillan.

Garfinkel, H. (1967) *Studies in Ethnomethodology*. Englewood Cliffs, NJ: Prentice-Hall.

Hacker, P. (1990) *Wittgenstein: Meaning and Mind*, Vol. 3 of *The Analytical Commentary on Wittgenstein's Philosophical Investigations*. Oxford: Blackwell.

Hollis, M. and Lukes, S. (eds) (1982) *Rationality and Relativism*. Oxford: Blackwell.

Lynch, M. (1993) *Scientific Practice and Ordinary Action*. Cambridge: Cambridge University Press.

Parsons, T. and Shils, E. (1966) 'Values, motives and systems of action', in T. Parsons and E. Shils (eds), *Toward a General Theory of Action*. New York: Harper Torchbooks.

Wittgenstein, L. (1969) *On Certainty*. Oxford: Blackwell.

7

The Limits of Social Constructionism

Stephen Turner

What is social constructionism? Is it a form of relativism that is essentially similar to cultural relativism and historical relativism? Is it a thesis about the contingency of knowledge? What is the point of saying constructionism is 'social'? Partly as a result of the fact that the term 'social construction' had its origins in sociology, in Berger and Luckmann's influential book *The Social Construction of Reality*, these simple 'philosophical' questions have not been systematically addressed. In this chapter I will give a kind of genealogy of relativism in terms of which these questions may be posed. I will distinguish two historically important forms of relativism, which I will call cold and hot relativisms. Cold relativisms are those that appeal to notions like 'culture' and 'epoch'. Cultures and epochs are totalizing notions. But precisely because they are totalizing notions, change is difficult to account for. Hot relativisms are those, like Thomas Kuhn's (1964) model of scientific revolutions, in which change plays a more central and dramatic role. But change is a puzzle for Kuhn as well. Does it really always involve a moment of irrationality and the psychology of the mob?

Constructionism solves the problem of explaining changes between divergent 'frameworks'. The narratives detailing the 'social construction' of a fact are accounts of change of the sort missing in both hot and cold relativisms. But the accounts work by appealing, often covertly, to a particular model of social life. So constructionism depends on a distinctive social theory. On the surface, constructionist change narratives appear to be radically different from familiar change narratives appealing to such notions as rational superiority. The 'relativistic' character of constructionist accounts, it seems, arises entirely from the importation into these accounts of notions that derive from either cold or hot relativism. Whether these imported notions add anything to a detailed account of the construction of a fact or concept is an open question. In the end, it seems, there are few differences between an account of conceptual change in terms of reasons that makes some innocuous concessions to the notion of the historical contingency of knowledge and a 'social constructionist' account.

Cold Relativism

Claude Lévi-Strauss made a famous distinction between hot cultures, by which he meant cultures in a constant state of change, those of modern societies, and cold cultures, those of the static world of the 'primitive'. The latter, he presumed, were structured by fundamental principles of mental ordering that modern thought has transcended. The distinction between our thought and that of cold cultures is dubious. Derrida, indeed, turned the tables on Lévi-Strauss by suggesting that his whole project was itself an exercise in mythic thinking (1972: 258). But the distinction is useful as a way of categorizing modes of thought about culture, and about the objects in terms of which we account for the facts of culture.

The relativism of Diderot in his *Supplement to Bougainville's Voyage* (1964) and the relativism of Burckhardt in his reconstruction of the mind of Renaissance Italy are relativisms of cultures and epochs respectively. For Diderot's audience, the perspective on sexuality of his (ethnographically quite mythical) Tahitians was exotic, but it was nevertheless open to recapture in the language of European civilization of the eighteenth century. Indeed, Diderot valorized it as sensible and humane. Burckhardt's task was defined by the fact that in the nineteenth century an aesthetic sensibility so different from that of the Renaissance had taken hold that the reasons why particular works of art and architecture in the past were regarded as great had to be reconstructed or supplied by the historian of culture.

Burckhardt was happy enough talking of 'the Italian mind' (1975: 279). From Burckhardt's time forward, however, a different locution has become entrenched. The term of choice is 'presuppositions'. The neo-Kantians were the first to use the term 'presuppositions' as a term to describe the contents of the mentality of an epoch or *Fach* (speciality, field or discipline). The idea of presupposition, used in this way, is based on a complex analogy. The model is the missing premiss in a formal logical argument. What the neo-Kantian analyst does for a specialized discipline, for example, is to supply the missing premisses that would make the discipline's arguments valid – these are its 'presuppositions'. It was understood that the presuppositions were ordinarily tacit. But it was also understood that the things taken for granted were shared among members of a discipline, such as the law, and that these common things could be identified and recovered.

Presuppositions are cold things. To think that they are shared is to think that something unchanging is shared. So this model of the cognitive character of culture lent itself to a particular range of cases, such as epochs or disciplines in which there is presumably little change and much commonality. Epochs, however, end; disciplines undergo radical changes. The historiographic convention of constructing periodizations fits nicely with a certain view of these changes, namely that there must be a breakdown of order – a rupture between epochs or a moment of revolution in which the presuppositions of the next epoch are formed.

The model of rupture and revolution fit best with *external* explanations of change. Presuppositions could be identified with historical classes, and their rise and fall could be accounted for externally by the political or economic fact of the rise and fall of classes. This was the basis of Marx's theory of the *Überbau* (superstructure). The same strategy, of identifying systems of thought with their class-bearers, and accounting for the historical fate of ideas in terms of the historical fate of their bearers, is equally central to Weber. For Durkheim, moral facts (which he conceived of as collectively charged presuppositions) were established in crucible-like moments of flux and collective 'fusion' that marked the transition between epochs.

In these models, change is exceptional – a hot moment between periods of presuppositional glaciation. Ruptures and revolutions are exceptional moments, such as the birth of a new class, a period of moral collapse and ferment or the emergence of a charismatic leader with a moral or religious ideology. These moments are themselves mysterious. So change itself remains a mystery. What is the source of the bourgeois ideology for Marx? What determines the new moral facts for Durkheim? What is the cause of the charismatic leaders' message for Weber? In the case of Marx, there is no answer, other than the general teleological claim that the bourgeois ideology serves to justify bourgeois claims to power and legitimize its scheme of domination. In Weber and Durkheim, the claim is that in general nothing constrains the messages of the charismatic leader or the results of a period of collective fusion.

There has been a good deal of discernible change in Western society that cannot be traced to the rise and fall of class positions, to periods of moral flux, to moments of collective fusion, or to charismatic moral ideologists. Indeed, the dominant 'liberal' narrative and explanation of moral development in Europe at the time that these three thinkers wrote was the story of the extirpation of superstition, the slow triumph of rationality, and the advance of secularism. Weber himself was a proponent of this model. For him, the process of rationalization was more or less normal. The explanations of non-Western cultures that he advanced were essentially accounts of the impediments to this process.

Hot Relativism

The inner sanctum of the narrative of secularization, and indeed the putative motor of rationalization, was science itself. Yet the history of science by the middle of the present century was itself subjected to an analysis of a cold relativist kind, particularly by historians of science influenced by neo-Kantianism. The most important of these was James Bryant Conant (1951), who stressed the idea that the science of a particular period served as a kind of reception device that received and accepted only those ideas for which it was ready, so that a scientific idea born out of its time would need to wait until the discipline had changed enough for new ideas to be received. Conant's teaching assistant, Thomas Kuhn, was to restate these ideas in a way that undermined the rationality and rationalization narratives decisively.

By marrying the notion of periods of flux to the notion that the presuppositions of science change, Kuhn produced the idea of periods of scientific revolution in which the first principles of science themselves were replaced. This was hot relativism, a relativism that recognized not just the alien character of the presuppositions of the dead and distant but the alienness of the presuppositions of the last generation of scientists. Change in fundamental premises was still an exceptional event – 'normal' science was the norm. But revolutions were now seen as, if not normal, historically ubiquitous, necessary, and central to intellectual life.

The problem of the mechanism of change, which could be safely neglected by writers like Burckhardt or Diderot, or treated in terms of corruption by outside influences, now became more problematic. There were no 'outside influences' on physics, no classes that declined or rose, no *Bau* (or underlying 'structure') that changed, no charismatic prophets. What was needed to explain change in presuppositions was some sort of internal mechanism. Kuhn's own attempts to provide such a mechanism, famous though they became in the 1960s, were poor answers. The difficulty Kuhn faced was this. On the one hand, Kuhn argued that the world of the scientist was constituted by the presuppositions of a given discipline and period. On the other, he needed reasons why these fundamental presuppositions should be abandoned. But if the reasons were constituted *in terms of* the presuppositions, they could not be reasons *for abandoning* the presuppositions. So something had to give.

Constructionism

Hot relativism was not a machine that could go of itself. It was, rather, a dramatic description of the phenomenon of change in search of a mechanism of change. Social constructionism supplied an internal mechanism of change of precisely the kind that hot relativism required. Constructionism enabled one to explain how facts could be constructed as 'anomalies' that gave grounds for abandoning fundamental presuppositions, and thus enabled one to explain how fundamental presuppositions came to be established, how novelties came to be established, and how presuppositions came to be replaced. The secret of constructionism, and the source of its power, is that it provides an account of the creation of conceptual practices.

A characteristic constructivist argument goes something like this. Something is constructed as a fact through means that are available to the constructor. The 'means' are such things as practices of representation that are shared between the constructor and the audience of the constructor. By applying these practices or by construing the world or representing it in accordance with these practices one establishes something as a fact. 'Facts', of course, are not the only things that can be constructed. What holds for 'facts' can also be understood to hold for moral arguments or claims, practical facts, inventions, 'isms' like racism and sexism, and a whole variety of other things.

A (constructed) fact is also an object of conduct – something to use in relation to others. By treating a novel 'fact' as a fact one allows for the accretion around it of standard actions and forms of reasoning. Facts acted upon as facts become practices – shared between those who act upon them in a similar way and thus open to use among those who share in the actions and forms of reasoning. We may call the step in the reproductive cycle of constructions in which practices result from treating things as facts 'embedding': facts become embedded as practices through shared action, successful imitation of the usages of others, and so forth. The power of facts to produce practices through their use by a given group of persons – the ability of facts to become tacitized or embedded as practices – creates audiences with shared practices. The possession of shared practices in turn enables audiences to be persuaded, joint conduct of various kinds to be undertaken, and so forth. The possession of shared practices also makes it possible to establish new facts – in just the way that the original practices were used to establish the fact with which we began.

Fact-making and representation is not the whole of a body of practice, typically, but only a part of the joint uses of the practices. So the bed of practices within which facts are established has a kind of stability that is a result of the role of practices in joint actions, and at the same time ensures that practices are community-relative, which is to say that a given body of practices attains this stability (or facts become practices through their appropriation in action) only within 'local' settings.

The relativism of constructivism derives from the local character of practices. Only those who share in the activities, such as the laboratory activities within which facts are created and used, are in possession of the practices in terms of which facts are made. It takes another step, what Bruno Latour calls translation, to turn facts that are the products of joint action within a community into products of joint action in other communities, and typically the actions that come to surround a fact will differ and produce different practices in different communities.

An Example: Hacking on 'Child Abuse'

This structure may not be obvious in all constructionist texts, and indeed may seem like a very inaccurate description of the main work of constructionism, for example in the sociology of scientific knowledge. Especially where these narratives have become routinized, they have become partial, so the larger story in terms of which they have a point is suppressed or ignored. However, if we take a standard case of a constructivist narrative, Hacking's 'The making and molding of child abuse' (1991), we can identify most of these main narrative elements quite readily. Hacking's account, like those of the sociology of scientific knowledge, begins with a showing of the point before the newly constructed idea is established as a fact. In the case of child abuse, Hacking stresses 'the malleability of the idea' and the fact that it did not exist in its present, though widely agreed, form even a few years ago (1991: 259). The story he tells is one about how, through the use of some very specific and widely accepted (in the medical community) techniques of medical representation, a new syndrome of 'child abuse' was first established. He then explains how it was, to use Latourian language, translated into the public domain, notably through the efforts of journalists, academics, politicians and pressure groups, how the definitions were gradually extended, and how various numbers games came to be played with the new 'fact' of the prevalence of child abuse. X-ray evidence was only the first in a long series of constructions of child abuse, as Hacking shows. Each step in the extension or reconstruction of the concept of child abuse depended on the establishment of a previous construction. These reconstructions are mostly, in Hacking's account, successful attempts to define things that had not previously been labelled in this way, such as incest, as 'child abuse' (1991: 276). The creation of a new object of joint action, as I call it, is the point of the constructionist narrative. It is Hacking's point as well. He tells us that his concern is not simply with 'the construction of the idea of child abuse' but rather with how 'we uncritically and spontaneously "make up people"' (1991: 254). People, he says,

> are affected by what we call them and, more importantly, by the available classifications within which they can describe their own actions and make their own constrained choices. People act and decide under descriptions, and as new possibilities for description emerge, so do new kinds of action. (1991: 254–5)

This is a description of the way in which a fact becomes a practice. In this case it is a practice of classification that has a power of constraint. Only some version of the social theory of practices I have sketched above can account for the phenomenon of collective constraint to which Hacking's discussion refers.[1]

Construction and Contingency

This dependence on the notion of practices comes in many forms. In some constructivist arguments, the term 'practices' is used, in others it is not. The range of concepts that can be used to refer to collectively shared tacit presuppositions, methods of classification, and so forth are, as I have suggested in the history given above, quite large. But the appearance of these concepts in constructionist arguments raises a basic question. To what extent do constructionist narratives depend on the notion of practice for their relativistic conclusions? Is the scepticism that constructivist accounts generate a product of convincing narrative, or is it simply a by-product of the role of a relativistic object in the accounts? Does constructionism assume relativism, or are relativistic conclusions the outcome of constructionist analyses? Hacking's explicit aim is to induce a certain kind of scepticism about the constructed fact of child abuse – not to deny it exists, but to make it more difficult for us to take the concept for granted. If we are, so to speak, constrained by our practices or socially contingent presuppositions to take this notion of child abuse seriously, Hacking offers, if not freedom from constraint, a loosening of the fetters. This is a familiar enough aim – it was Diderot's as well. In each case we show that the usage that we took for granted is historically contingent, in the specific sense of being relative to a specific historical community, and not given by God or nature. One might think that constructionism is an extension of this insight. But there are two quite distinct claims mixed up in this formulation, and only one of them supports any sort of radical scepticism or relativism.

Consider three claims. The first is this: all knowledge is historically contingent, and what we believe to be true about the world is conditioned by circumstances some of which are beyond our control. The second is this: 'the world' (and therefore what can be true for us about the world) is constituted for us by culture, language, scientific paradigms and so forth, and these rise and fall for contingent reasons that cannot be reduced to a uniquely valid story of 'rational advance', in part because all stories of rational advance are internal to cultures, paradigms and the like, and their validity is relative to a particular culture or paradigm. The third claim is this: particular constitutive conceptual frameworks or bodies of practice have a genealogy which involves motives that in some way compromise the claim of the practitioners within this framework to truth. One might claim, for example, that the modern idea that numbers are especially objective is a framework that arises and serves the interest of patriarchy.

Contingency alone perhaps justifies a certain form of scepticism, but a somewhat innocuous one. Even if one believes that fundamental categories come from God or nature, one is hard put to deny that the discovery of the categories or the establishment of their validity was a process in history, governed by various contingencies. At any given moment the state of our beliefs could have been different. It could have been that Watson and Crick gave up on DNA, and that others also decided their efforts were better spent elsewhere. It could have been the Warren Wilson had never made the investment in molecularizing biology that created the resource base that favoured Watson and Crick's efforts. People in history had to make the discoveries and do the validating, and they might not have done so. Similarly, someone may overturn previously 'established' truths or categories in the future. We do not know whether our beliefs were formed under the most favourable auspices. The activity of discovering and validating truths and categories, in short, is no more free of contingency than other activities, even if the ultimate truths and categories are themselves fixed. If one is not committed to the notion of ultimate truths or categories, one is free from the worry that present concepts, produced under present circumstances, do not correspond to those 'ultimates'. One can simply concede that our ideas are what they are partly as a result of contingencies (whose effects are usually unknown to us), and ask instead whether they are the best ideas available, and whether they can be made better.

If 'frameworks' or 'practices' are what is held to be the product of contingencies, however, it seems that this last activity is itself rendered problematic. Standards of goodness of theories are relative to frameworks; judgements of factuality and validity are internal to bodies of practice. The thought that our evaluations are themselves the product of historical contingencies, however, is only unsettling if we think that standards of evaluation ought to be different from facts, not subject to revision as our beliefs about the world are. If we believe that our cognitive standards are given by God or nature, we are in the same difficulty as those who believe that their categories come from God or nature. The contingencies that, we now think, shaped past evaluations are not different in kind from those that operate today and might in unknown ways shape present evaluations.

Kuhnianism was indeed an unpleasant revelation for those philosophers who thought that standards of theory-choice could be spared historicity. But acknowledging that standards are just as contingent as discoveries is only a problem for philosophers who hold that standards are and always have been not only fixed and universal but universally known. If constructionism is only a club to beat this largely lifeless corpse, it adds nothing to hot relativism. But there is more to it than this. Contingency at the level of basic frameworks seems to imply something more than contingency of factual belief. It seems to bear on the possibility of improving basic frameworks. Hot relativism says that basic frameworks are 'basic'. We can leap from one to another as we can leap from one rock in a stream to another rock in a stream, but we have to stand on one rock at a time. We can judge other rocks only from the vantage point of the particular rock we are standing on. Hot relativism thus rules out the possibility that one can improve one's basic framework and be on the same evaluative footing as someone who has not yet improved it. Improvement is a leap; recognizing improvement only comes with the same leap.

The existence of such things as 'paradigms', that is to say self-grounding cognitive objects shared by some group and conceived as stable, is the source of the difficulty. By definition, such objects are not revisable. Change only comes in the form of leaps, or as Kuhn called them, revolutions, and piecemeal changes 'within' the paradigm do not challenge its self-grounding bases. The problem of explaining change and the problem of 'improvement' arise from the same source: the leaps can neither be explained nor justified in a way that is permitted by the theory of paradigms.

'Practices' for 'Paradigms'

The zone in which constructionism's claim to account for change operates is more or less the zone in which rationalizing narratives, progress and improvement narratives, and 'bowing to necessity' narratives have operated in the past. In the case of cold relativistic objects, like the Italian mind, and hot relativistic objects, like paradigms, there was no such competition. The objects themselves were novel. Because they were such novel objects, there were no existing answers to questions like 'How do they progress?' Existing notions of progress and change did not apply to these objects, but rather to such things as errors and superstitions. Constructionism, however, faces a more crowded field. The changes explained by social constructionists are usually already explained, if not precisely in the same terms, by the people who argued for the changes and by historians of science and ideas.

The smaller the object, the more extensive its applications and the more direct the competition. 'Italian minds' and paradigms are relatively rare objects; practices are ubiquitous and plentiful. So to turn to the concept of practices to solve the explanatory problems of hot relativism is to invite new problems. We can ask how constructionist narratives differ from ordinary historical narratives and the narratives of participants, and how they lead to apparently different conclusions.

Hacking's account of the making and moulding of the concept of child abuse provides a clear illustration of the kind of competition that occurs in this zone. Hacking identifies a series of successful attempts by individuals to define or redefine different phenomena as instances of child abuse. The initial act is the definition of a particular identifiable pattern of bone injuries as a 'syndrome' (1991: 267–8), later relabelled 'battered-child syndrome'. This basic concept is then remade and moulded by various people to suit various purposes. Hacking's main effort is spent on the general question of the 'contingency' of the concept of child abuse that has ultimately emerged from the battered child syndrome, but two specific kinds of contingency concern him most. At each step along the way of the path between the X-ray observations and the present concept Hacking identifies individuals who promoted the expansion of the concept to cover more ills, and stresses the contingent character of the circumstances under which this expansion occurred, that is, under which these individuals 'constructed' the concept and under which it was received and accepted by various audiences. One set of contingencies of expansion and acceptance involves power. Indeed, at one point Hacking summarizes his general argument by saying that 'in the power struggle over who owns child abuse the doctors triumphed' (1991: 287), by which he means that the definition of child abuse promoted by physicians, which employed a medical model and implied that the appropriate expert authorities in this domain were physicians, became the dominant or most widely accepted definition. He goes on to suggest that 'this was a foregone conclusion because child abuse is seen in a framework of normalcy and pathology' (1991: 287). 'Normal', he argues, is a notion that in the nineteenth century replaced 'human nature'. In another work, *The Taming of Chance* (1990), Hacking gave a constructionist account of the rise to dominance of this concept. So the origin of the concept of child abuse

and its triumph depended on the previous establishment of the rhetorical
rails on which the argument expanding the notion of child abuse travelled.
These rails were simply a set of pre-existing practices that had arisen
through construction and a subsequent forgetting of their origins, in the
same manner as the concept of child abuse itself did.

Despite calling the triumph of the physicians a foregone conclusion,
Hacking makes a great deal of the ways in which the details of the moulding
of the concept of child abuse reflected the existence of particular institutions with particular power interests. He notes, for example, that 'the
name "social work" was unknown before 1900' and goes on to say that
when social work was established 'a new kind of expert had emerged and
insofar as anyone was to be responsible for cruelty to children it was . . . to
be the social worker' (1991: 266). This was an anterior condition for one
step in the moulding of the category of child abuse. It gave rise to a group of
people with professional interests. The immediate occasion for one organized effort to promote the notion of child abuse was the organizational need
of the Children's Bureau of Health Education and Welfare for something to
do: it was 'a bureaucracy in search of a job' (1991: 267). This bureaucracy,
presumably motivated by the need to survive, found the 'job' of dealing
with child abuse (ibid.).

Hacking also tells the story of the effort to interest the mass media in the
new framework of child abuse and its successful promotion as the object of
public policy and public concern. The effort, Hacking stresses, also rode
along pre-established rhetorical tracks. The terminology of abuse itself was
morally loaded and connected to notions of pollution and purification that
were already established elements of the practice of moral representation in
American society. Hacking suggests that the connection between the notion
of self-abuse and the notion of pollution provided the terminology with a
specific moral charge (1991: 279).

These are representative steps in Hacking's argument. The possession of
a practice is a contingency. The physicians 'won' because they could appeal
to the pre-existing practice of their audience of thinking in terms of normality. If there were no such practice, there could have been no such
successful appeal. There is no reason to think of the audience as duped. In
and of itself, this contingency is like contingencies of discovery in science in
which one fact or method needs to be discovered or established before
another can be. But Hacking wishes to say something more than this.
Using terms like 'own' and 'power struggle' to characterize the wide acceptance of a particular notion of child abuse and appending such institutional
facts as the creation of a profession of social work suggests that these other
contingencies are neither neutral nor innocuous, and that their role in the
history of the concept of child abuse taints it. It is here that Hacking's
account collides with its competitors.

At one point Hacking gives an example of what he regards as a particularly visible extension of the notion of child abuse by a physician. The
example is a discussion by the author of a medical textbook on child abuse

by a paediatrics professor and physician. The author points to the problem of abuse by siblings. From Hacking's point of view, this is another instance of the tendency of physicians and other professionals to assert authority over domains previously left to the family. As it happens, I spoke to the author when he was writing the book, and I can supply some of the context for the point he makes. The author is a clinician who works with children who are patients at a large clinic serving the urban poor of Baltimore. He is often asked to testify in court on child abuse cases. Typically he is asked to make a judgement about whether a particular injury could have been produced by accident, for example by a child falling down stairs. Medical diagnoses do not ordinarily take the form required by the courts: 'very unlikely' is not a good enough answer. The problem of identifying physical bases for distinguishing child abuse in a legally adjudicable sense from all the other kinds of injuries to which children are prone is a problem produced by the courts and their procedures. But dealing with child abuse, protecting the child, requires something more of the physician than guarded answers. The physician as caregiver has responsibilities that the cautious researcher does not. So the physician's concern with 'non-medical' aspects of child abuse is imposed by circumstance. Sibling abuse, meaning the same injuries but produced by siblings rather than parents or caregivers, is medically indistinguishable from child abuse, and it presents the physician as caregiver with the same problem. What is medical prudence here? Send the child back to be injured again? Report the case as abuse (something that is typically required by law)?

Hacking's presentation of course ignores this specific context. The effect of ignoring it is to exoticize the notion of sibling abuse, to lump it together with a long series of similarly exoticized, taken out of context, extensions of the concept of child abuse. These extensions are made to seem like a series of accidents which can be fitted into a pattern of professional power-seeking. It is at this point that the accounts collide. The collision, however, is quite unequal. The constructionist account has no attraction once one knows the things Hacking leaves out.

Hacking's larger story, of course, leaves many things out as well. It can also be told in a less sensitive way. Some physicians identified a series of Roentgenological artefacts, constructed an explanation of them, and thus created a medical notion of child abuse. Other professions with a responsibility for children accepted and then revised this notion, and publicized the idea. Ultimately, the revisions of the idea came into conflict with common ideas about child-rearing and parental authority. Such conflicts are not surprising. People under different circumstances will revise concepts in different directions. When, for whatever reason, they come into conflict, the conflicts may need to be resolved, by new revisions of our ideas, by institutional changes, and so forth. Child abuse is a typical case of this. Practical considerations – even professional interests – may bear on the process and motivate revisions. One would be surprised if they did not.

Sorting out these conflicts is a genuine problem. Reconstructing the paths by which a widely accepted classification emerged, with attention to the special circumstances under which they developed, may serve a constructive purpose. But at some point the machinery of constructionism ceases to contribute much to this task. We can tell these stories without exoticizing, without reference to 'practices' and 'interests'. When we tell them better in a more prosaic way, by filling in facts and context, we have reached the limits of constructivism.

Note

1 I have argued elsewhere, at length, that this theory is defective as social theory and ought to be discarded (Turner, 1994).

References

Berger, Peter L. and Luckmann, Thomas (1967) *The Social Construction of Reality: A Treatise in the Sociology of Knowledge.* Garden City, NY: Anchor Books.

Burckhardt, J. (1975) *The Civilization of the Renaissance in Italy*, Vol. 2. New York: Harper & Row.

Conant, James B. (1951) *On Understanding Science.* New York: New American Library.

Derrida, J. (1972) 'Structure, sign, and play in the discourse of the human sciences', in R. Macksey and E. Donato (eds), *The Structuralist Controversy: The Languages of Criticism and the Sciences of Man.* Baltimore, MD: Johns Hopkins University Press. pp. 247–65.

Diderot, D. (1964) 'Supplement to Bougainville's Voyage', in *Rameau's Nephew and Other Works.* Indianapolis, IN: Bobbs Merrill. pp. 179–228.

Hacking, Ian (1990) *The Taming of Chance.* Cambridge: Cambridge University Press.

Hacking, Ian (1991) 'The making and molding of child abuse', *Critical Inquiry*, 17: 253–88.

Kuhn, Thomas (1964) *The Structure of Scientific Revolutions.* Chicago: University of Chicago Press.

Turner, Stephen (1994) *The Social Theory of Practices.* Cambridge: Polity Press.

PART III
APPLYING CONSTRUCTIONISM

8
Relations, Communication and Power

Ian Burkitt

In this chapter I will concentrate on problems surrounding social constructionism and realism as alternative ways of approaching central problems in
the social sciences. The debate between these two positions centres on
such problems as the nature of reality and the relative certainty or uncertainty of knowledge about it; what exactly it is to know something; and
who it is who does the knowing – in other words, the constitution of the
identity of the knower. Common sense would seem to tell us that we are
surrounded by a world that forms our basic reality, which has its own
separate existence and internal processes that sustain it, things that we are
gradually understanding more adequately through increasingly complex
and realistic knowledge. In turn, this advanced knowledge and understanding shapes our own thought processes which are, accordingly, coming into
tune with reality as it exists. This way of seeing things posits an unchanging
world viewed dispassionately by a single independent observer, who
adjusts his or her mental perspectives and verbal descriptions so as to
better represent reality.

Although the above is something of a caricature, a more complex and
subtle form of this view is reflected in certain branches of philosophy, and
some aspects of it can be found in realism. Here, there is the notion that
transcendental structures exist in the world which are partly independent of
human knowledge, and that knowledge changes in order to account for
these structures or to reveal them. Therefore, aspects of the world are
always partially hidden and are laid bare by the penetration of the rational
cogito. This rational subject (or potentially rational subject) stands at the
centre of realist philosophy and is one of the pivots on which it rests.

On the other hand, Kenneth Gergen (1994) has argued that constructionism is ontologically mute, because certainty in the actual existence of
objects as constituted in knowledge can never be secure. We can never,
with certainty, know a world beyond knowledge, and so constructionism

cannot bolster us with ontological security. This position is also reflected in the work of John Shotter who argues that the 'realities' we deal with – the certainties we have in the permanent ontological foundations that seem to support our lives – are actually a product of everyday language. The way we talk about the world and construct an understanding of it in joint activities becomes our reality and forms the basis for daily ontological certainties and uncertainties.

In this chapter, then, I want to concentrate on the debate between constructionism and realism, because while I have great sympathy with the constructionist approach I recognize that it has limitations and that realism raises points of vital concern. My aim is to try to think beyond some of the oppositions between these two approaches, questioning the division made between ontology and epistemology in realism and also the extreme onto-logical scepticism found in varieties of constructionism. While construction-ists like Gergen and Shotter do not subscribe to such extremism, nevertheless constructionism is not always successful in addressing issues of the real and of the construction of knowledge in reality. In suggesting possible ways forward in resolving some of these problems I want to build upon Gergen's view of humans engaged in ongoing relationships; however, I will offer some variations on this theme by looking at selves, not only in relation to other selves, but also in relation to the non-human world. As Bruno Latour (1993) has pointed out, this relationship produces another dimension of life that subverts the traditional opposition between nature and society, an aspect of life in which artifacts, quasi-objects and hybrids emerge – objects which are at one and the same time natural, discursive and social. This helps us to overcome the resistance that can sometimes be found in constructionism to address questions of the natural world and the way in which it influences knowledge (Murphy, 1994). The focus here is not, then, on oppositions and dichotomies, but on relationships and the trans-formations that occur in what Norbert Elias calls 'the three basic coordi-nates of human life: the shaping and the position of the individual within the social structure, the social structure itself and the relation of social human beings to events in the non-human world' (1991: 97).

As social action gradually changes these coordinates, these relationships, the non-human world becomes partially humanized as cultures infuse it with meaning and give objects (both those produced in societies and those which are naturally occurring) a specific purpose. But equally, the human world is always intermingled and interdependent with the non-human world which emerges in various ways in our relationships and practices. Similarly, the mind is not an entity separate from the relationships which define humanity and human selves – a realm of pure intelligence or ration-ality which gazes on its surroundings from some degree of separation. Instead of this view I will consider ideas that suggest there is no such 'thing' as the mind, and that thought cannot be separated from its place in the relationships and practices that define social selves within particular cultures and historical periods. The position I will be taking here rests on a rejection of the dichotomy between mind and matter. I agree very much with Tom Kitwood, who says of his own approach:

> The position which I shall outline here rejects the Cartesian idea of two funda- mentally different 'substances': matter and mind. Instead, [my position] is monistic, in that it assumes the existence of one (exceedingly complex) reality. We can call it material reality, but we must at once bracket commonsensical ideas of materialism. As human beings we act upon and within this reality, and in reflection upon our experience we create sets of categories. Our capacity for receiving, processing and storing information is extremely elaborate; it is excel- lent for securing our survival as a social species, but it could never provide a complete understanding of what is 'really' there. Thus every discourse which human beings create in order to give coherence to their experience is limited in its scope. (Kitwood, 1996: 270–1)

There is, then, one reality with many different epistemic and discursive positions upon it and these are created by people in relationships, and also in relationships with non-humans. Indeed, I want to extend a way of think- ing about these things begun in my earlier work (Burkitt, 1993) which utilized the stance taken by Foucault (1980), who claimed that humans are engaged in relations that transform the real, relations of communication, and relations of power. For me, this encapsulates the scope of relationships both between humans and between humans and non-humans. It also conveys that humans are related in every instance to the non-human world, so that explanations of activity cannot be couched solely in terms of discourse, but must extend to relations that transform the real. Following from this, the discussion here will be organized around these different aspects of social relations, beginning with relations of communication.

Relations of Communication

For constructionists, language is not a means of picturing or representing a reality that exists separately and independently of it, but a means of com- munication that only has meaning in the context of relationships, inter- dependencies and joint action. The conversation between people does not represent some ontological realm that is unchanging, and which acts as the foundation for linguistic meaning and knowledge: rather, conversations create and sustain everything that the social group takes to be the ontologi- cal foundation of life, the taken-for-granted 'reality'. Words do not stand for things but are an element of the constantly contested meanings in the arena of social life, involving claim, counter-claim and disputation. Within the social sciences, then, there can be no appeal to independent 'facts' or 'realities', nor to underlying cognitive structures, as a guarantee of the validity of knowledge. All knowledge is generated in a community of speak- ing subjects and is an aspect of communication within relations and inter- dependencies. As Gergen puts it:

because disquisitions on the nature of things are framed in language, there is no grounding of science or any other knowledge generating enterprise in other than communities of interlocutors. There is no appeal to mind or matter – to reason or facts – that will lend transcendental validity to propositions. (1994: ix)

Meaning is generated in relationships, in the hurly-burly of daily interchange, and not by language corresponding to some extra-linguistic or non-social reality. Constructionism is therefore very much against the idea of representation, that words used in daily life or in scientific explanations can mirror or reflect reality. It also opposes realist philosophies which suggest that language can create an analogue or model of structures that generate events in the world, but which are not observable on the surface of appearances. In this view, there is an ontological realm of transcendentally ordered structures waiting to be discovered if only we could devise a scheme of representation for them. However, this raises the problem of how we could be certain of the existence of something – be it an object or underlying structure – that exists beyond the range of our knowledge and outside the linguistic boundaries of understanding. Instead, constructionists insist on the realization that objects of knowledge cannot be independent of the accounts given of them, and that our understanding cannot be separated from the sociolinguistic practices in which it is achieved. Rejecting a grounding for social science in an ontology of objects or things, Shotter follows Wittgenstein in taking as his task 'to "see" what confronts us as "what" actually it is within the form of life within which it has its being' (1993: 114). In other words, like Wittgenstein's notion of the language game, there is nothing outside of this game to understand because intelligible reality is created within it. This is the form of life in which humans create their understanding of everything that exists, and therefore making sense of social life involves an understanding of how it is produced on a daily basis from within the bustle of social practices.

Furthermore, this style of constructionism rejects the notion that knowledge is produced by a single, rational individual, engaged in solitary reflection upon the world. Understanding is not achieved through the penetration of reality by outstandingly rational individual minds, but through the communicative construction of knowledge within relationships. Knowledge and understanding is therefore constructed by interdependent people who are practically engaged in joint practices with one another, not by detached and disengaged observers. It is feasible, then, to have an account of the joint production of knowledge which does not refer to individual mental events or cognitive frameworks, but is instead focused on the network of communicating persons. For Shotter, such a position helps us to understand social action without any reference to a priori and reified notions such as the 'mind'. Just as constructionism has subverted the realist notion that events are produced by hidden causal and generative structures, so it also undermines the cognitivist position in which unseen mental processes or structures are construed as the causal mechanisms that produce the actions of the individual. Instead, the 'mind' is simply a word used in everyday and scientific language (Shotter, 1993) which calls up images of a container, usually located 'inside' the head, which stores the knowledge and experience of the subject, or a series of 'internal' mental grids or networks which give a capacity for reflection upon internal sensations or external objects. Once we have done away with the notion of the mind and all the above connotations that go with it, we can begin to think of selves as existing in and taking their identity from a community of interrelated and communicating people, rather than as isolated and self-sufficient monads. Following Shotter (1993) and his notion of 'knowing of the third kind', we can also account for the actions of individuals as practical, sensuous joint actions involving tacitly understood commonalities of feeling and meaning, rather than as ordered interchanges generated by prior social or cognitive structures. Social selves are thus understood as embodied beings, responding to one another in their joint actions by drawing on tacit and corporeal levels of understanding through which the social world is constantly made anew.

Knowledge, then, is created in relations and joint activities – in what Latour (1987) would call the actor-networks – and not by a Cartesian rational cogito inanimately poised to grasp a transcendental world just beyond its view. We do not create knowledge and understanding through logic but through a sociologic. As Gergen says, 'there is good reason for privileging the reality of the social' (1994: 47), by which he means that language, knowledge and text are best understood as part of a broader social process. However, constructionism does tend, on the whole, to have a problem in dealing with the reality of things – that complex materiality that Kitwood mentioned in the quotation earlier in this chapter. It has become caught up in the 'turn to language' which has enveloped much of the social sciences through the influence of post-structuralism and postmodernism, reducing all social analysis to that of the text. As Gergen says of this reduction of all social life to signification: 'The play of signifiers is essentially a play within language, and this play is embedded within patterns of human action in what we call material contexts' (1994: 262). Furthermore, 'it is human interchange that gives language its capacity to mean, and it must then stand as the critical locus of concern. I wish then to replace *textuality* with *communality*' (1994: 263–4).

Yet, this insistence on language as embedded in social relations which are themselves located in material contexts has yet to be fully developed in constructionism. Shotter has, of course, stressed the material and sensuous relatedness of joint action, but has done so only in respect of the human world. What is missing from constructionism is an attempt to explicate the meaningful relationship of humans to the non-human world, and thus to show how our constructed, communal reality can also be in many complex ways a changing (as opposed to transcendental) material reality. This brings us to the other coordinate of human life – relations that involve the non-human.

Relations that Transform the Real

One of the ways in which the realist position, as expounded by Roy
Bhaskar, has certain advantages over constructionism is in taking the relationship of human groups to their complex material contexts more seriously. Like constructionism, Bhaskar's critical or transcendental realism
takes the relational formation of the social world to be its primary characteristic, yet 'the natural and social worlds [are] conceived as in dynamic
interrelationship' (Bhaskar, 1991: 148–9). However, 'the faster dynamics
. . . and the associated spatial features of social life impart to it a more
geo-historically specific character than the arcs of biological, geological
and cosmological being within which it is successively inscribed' (Bhaskar,
1989: 185). This inscription marks the interrelation of the social and natural
worlds because it is not just social relations, but also the geophysical
context, that provides a structured location for praxis. In Bhaskar's *transformational model of social action* society is the ensemble of positioned
practices and interrelationships reproduced or transformed by activity. So
whilst no one ever makes their relationships, because we all come into a
world which is historically already made for us, people have the power
either to reproduce or transform their society with the materials at hand.
Similarly, following Marx, humans are able to transform nature through
their labour, and so Bhaskar has some notion of relations that transform the
real. This also includes changing the basis of human nature, for individuals
are embodied minds who are partially the products of nature, but also of
historically developing ensembles of social relations through which we appropriate stocks of skills and competencies (Bhaskar, 1991: 163; Geras,
1983; Sève, 1978).

   However, despite this notion of relations that transform the real, Bhaskar
maintains a distinction in his work between ontology (the nature of being
and the existence of things) and epistemology (the nature and source of
knowledge). The reason for this is that he believes it to be important that we
understand there is a realm of the objective existence of things which is
independent of human knowledge and action. Bhaskar accuses philosophers such as Richard Rorty and constructionists like Shotter of falling
into what he calls the *epistemic fallacy* which is the definition of all being
in terms of our knowledge about it, thus reducing all of existence to human
knowledge. Instead of this, Bhaskar wants to retain in his work a distinction
between the transitive, social-epistemic dimension and the intransitive,
ontological dimension. This means that while socially constructed knowledge is transitive, often going through rapid and dynamic changes in terms
of the way things are conceptualized, the ontological domain remains relatively unchanged by this. The causal laws of the structured ontological
sphere are transcendental, while knowledge is a social process the aim of
which is to produce a model of the laws that generate phenomena in the
social and natural worlds. This is why the approach has been labelled
'transcendental realism'.

However, in my view Bhaskar is wrong to take this position because in the distinction between the transitive and intransitive he has separated out what appear to be two distinct realms and, despite his own best intentions, divided the ontological from the social. That is, reality appears to be governed by its own laws in some independent realm that is distinct from humans, and transformational activity seems confined only to the social-epistemic. Yet Bhaskar has himself shown that this is not so; unfortunately, the philosophical dualism he adheres to does not allow him to build upon the notion of relations that transform the real, and he is left in static theoretical dichotomies. If instead we follow a sociological line more akin to constructionism, then we can see that relationships between humans, and those between humans and non-humans, mean that there is no break between the ontological and epistemological. Social relations are lodged in material contexts and knowledge is another dimension of those contexts. Knowledge can be constructed in many different ways but it is always knowledge-in-the-world, to paraphrase Heidegger, and therefore the non-human is always absorbed in knowledge. The best examples of this are artifacts, quasi-objects and mediating tools, which I will come to shortly.

One final point about Bhaskar's critical realism is that while he clearly sees the self as socially and historically constituted, he does nevertheless have a residual cognitivism in his approach. It is claimed that the production of knowledge depends on the utilization of antecedently existing cognitive materials (1989: 68), which comes perilously close to the idea of a developing rational cognitive system which could penetrate the layers of appearance to create models that approximate the transcendental causal mechanisms of the ontological realm. We seem to be edging back to a form of rationalism here which posits the (albeit collective) mind laying bare reality as it is in itself. This is seen most clearly in Bhaskar's critical use of his philosophy, where he claims that to transform society into a more equal and just socialist system depends on the knowledge of underlying social structures, so that 'the world cannot be rationally changed unless it is adequately interpreted' (1989: 5). But as Shotter (1992) points out, this means that Bhaskar tends to put theory before practice, in that he sees action flowing from a rational, cognitive analysis rather than from communities of shared practice or moral values. And as Gergen (1994: 75) points out, realism cannot say how underlying structures could ever be identified so that the validity of the rational, structural account could be established as an adequate model of the generative mechanisms supposedly in operation.

For an alternative account of transformative practice and the relation between the human and non-human, I want to turn to the work of Evald Ilyenkov and Bruno Latour, particularly for their ideas on the production of artifacts by human groups. Taking from Marx and the Soviet psychologist Vygotsky, Ilyenkov used the term *artifact* to refer to any created human object – or quasi-object like a sign – which is used in social practice and thus has activity embodied in it. Because artifacts play a mediating role in human activity they acquire meaning within the social group. They are not dumb objects but speak to us of our own activities and strivings which are inscribed in them. Artifacts are, then, extensions of bodily practices and the social contexts in which they function. There are many different kinds of things that can be regarded as artifacts; they could be tools – or any form of technology – or signs. Ilyenkov therefore reverses the argument often run in the social sciences, that objects take on meaning because of their inclusion in symbolic systems, thus giving primacy to signs, and instead, for him, signs are just one aspect of all humanly created, meaningful artifacts, rather than the primary base of all meaning (Bakhurst, 1991: 186). However, meaning does not just reside in those objects fashioned by humans, for once this process has begun, meaning infuses a large part of the environment so that even those objects not created by humans are given meaning. Human beings no longer live in a purely physical environment, but one saturated with meaning, in which we can recognize our own humanity, purposes and needs in even the most inert, non-human objects.

Ilyenkov is therefore very much against the transcendental position in philosophy that would posit deep a priori structures given in the 'mind', or mechanisms underlying the 'objective' world, through which we must achieve knowledge and intelligibility. Instead of this, he sees that the world we create is given structure through the forms of social practice in which people engage with it. Here we see what Bakhurst refers to as Ilyenkov's *radical realism*, 'that treats the thinking subject as located in material reality, in direct contact with its objects' (1991: 215). Furthermore, this thinking subject is not a Cartesian self, an isolated rational cogito fathoming the deep structures of an ontologically separate world: rather, thinking emerges in embodied social practices, in the socially formed nature of our corporeality. Ilyenkov says that 'thinking is not the product of an action but the action itself, considered at the moment of its performance, just as walking, for example, is the mode of action of the legs. . . . And that is that' (1977: 34–5).

However, it is not just the way that Ilyenkov unifies body and mind that is important, but the way in which he refuses to separate the thinking subject from social practice in material contexts, thereby maintaining a cohesive view of culture and nature. By concentrating on the role of artifacts in the mediation of activity, Ilyenkov has focused on the areas of human social life that are at one and the same time social, semiotic and natural. As Bruno Latour has commented on artifacts and quasi-objects, '[the] latter, as I have said, are simultaneously real, discursive, and social. They belong to nature, to the collective and to discourse' (1993: 64). Also, 'nature and society are not two opposite transcendences but one and the same growing out of the work of mediation' (Latour, 1993: 87–8). This means we can maintain a form of social constructionism without falling into the trap of reducing everything to the text, to signs, or to discourse: there can be understanding of the way knowledge is socially constructed in relationships and practices that does not ignore the natural aspect of much of our lives. This can be done without getting trapped in a philosophy that separates ontology and epistemology, material reality and knowledge, but only by concentrating on the way in which human life is simultaneously social, discursive and natural. And this can best be done by studying artifacts and quasi-objects which are a combination of all the different dimensions of human life, incorporating the human and non-human, the social, semiotic and material. Artifacts are created within relations of communication and relations that transform the real.

However, this brings us to another issue, which is the way relationships are simultaneously social, discursive and material, so that in relations of power there arises the question of the real conditions of people's lives – the issue that is often most hotly contested in political discourse, and a question on which constructionism is often accused of having little to say because of an inherent relativism. Yet as Gergen claims, in a critique of those who pursue an extreme discursive constructionism and who would admit to the existence of nothing beyond the text; 'As a unifying discourse the literary standpoint is also flawed. Its chief problem is its inability to exit from the self-created prison of the text. . . . As a human scientist one could scarcely take an interest in poverty, conflict, the economy, history, government, and so on, for these are but terms lodged within a textual-rhetorical history' (1994: 46). Human scientists, therefore, need to search for more satisfactory ways of explaining these things. Here we meet head on the issue of the politics of constructionism.

Relations of Power

As Bhaskar has claimed, relations of power also have a material dimension, which is important to remember when we reflect on the 'prevalence and impact of the phenomena of hunger, homelessness and war' (1989: 4). He has often accused constructionists such as Shotter of becoming trapped in a form of voluntarism where no binding objective structures or consequences limit the actions of individuals in relationships (Bhaskar, 1993). But once more, can we take Bhaskar's critique of constructionism seriously, incorporating more material aspects of relationships into our account, without being ensnared in his transcendentalism? Also, Bhaskar claims that a rational analysis of relationships can reveal aspects of the social structure, such as causes of inequality and exploitation, which provide grounds on which people can take effective action to eliminate these factors (an example would be Marx's analysis of capitalist social relations). However, the same problems arise as in Bhaskar's critical realism of the ontological realm: who can say that the realist account of power relations is the superior one and, even if this could be established, what about those who would regard the current social structure as the best form of human society?

As Shotter (1993) claims, in political discourse there are seldom, if ever, grounds for one rational way forward that can be established as the view that all reasonable people would take on examination of the facts. Indeed, politics is about the *persuasion* of people as to the reasonableness of one's views or plans. Social analysis will not help much either, as this is also an area of contested claims regarding the diagnosis of social problems and proposed remedies. Yet this need not lead us into an 'anything goes' type of relativism or nihilism. Being based in a relational and communicative view of the world, constructionism can argue for a broadly based polity where there is democratic access to debate and government (see Shotter, 1993: Ch. 10). Given what I have said above, constructionism can also argue for the material consequences of power relations to be taken into account in political debate so that there can be discussions of poverty, unemployment, homelessness, and exclusion of certain groups from the democratic process and from the use of political resources. While such factors may not prove a particular view, they do add moral weight to the argument.

Moreover, constructionism can also present a view of human life as necessarily composed of relations and interconnections, where society is not an amalgamation of isolated individuals but a collectivity of social selves (albeit a divided one). The views often put forward by Conservatives that relationships have only secondary importance in the lives of individuals (if they are seen to have importance at all), and that the social structure and its inequalities are determined by the innate attributes of individuals (as, for example, in arguments for the biological inheritance of intelligence levels) can be countered in constructionism. Here the view of individuals as social selves can be argued for, along with the idea that knowledge and morality are a communal achievement in which all people should fully participate. In pursuing relations of communication, relations that transform the real and relations of power, constructionists can show how knowledge is created in social contexts that also have a material dimension, but the validity of various viewpoints is inevitably based in the communities that generate them. However, it is possible from this standpoint to argue for opening up the channels of dialogue, and for the eradication of material and social inequalities that block people's access to cultural resources, restricting their ability to develop fully as social beings.

References

Bakhurst, D. (1991) *Consciousness and Revolution in Soviet Philosophy: From the Bolsheviks to Evald Ilyenkov*. Cambridge: Cambridge University Press.

Bhaskar, R. (1989) *Reclaiming Reality: A Critical Introduction to Contemporary Philosophy*. London: Verso.

Bhaskar, R. (1991) *Philosophy and the Idea of Freedom*. Oxford: Blackwell,.

Bhaskar, R. (1993) 'Afterword', in J. Shotter, *Conversational Realities: Constructing Life through Language*. London: Sage.

Burkitt, I. (1993) *Social Selves: Theories of the Social Formation of Personality*. London: Sage.

Elias, N. (1991) *The Society of Individuals*. Oxford: Blackwell.

Foucault, M. (1980) *Power/Knowledge*, ed. Colin Gordon. Brighton: Harvester.

Geras, N. (1983) *Marx and Human Nature: Refutation of a Legend*. London: Verso.

Gergen, K.J. (1994) *Realities and Relationships: Soundings in Social Construction*. Cambridge, MA: Harvard University Press.

Ilyenkov, E. (1977) *Dialectical Logic: Essays on its History and Theory*. Moscow: Progress Publishers.

Kitwood, T. (1996) 'A dialectical framework for dementia', in R. Woods (ed.), *Handbook of Clinical Psychology*. Chichester: Wiley.

Latour, B. (1987) *Science in Action: How to Follow Scientists and Engineers through Society*. Cambridge, MA: Harvard University Press.

Latour, B. (1993) *We Have Never Been Modern*. Hemel Hempstead: Harvester Wheatsheaf.

Murphy, R. (1994) 'The sociological construction of science without nature', *Sociology*, 28(4): 957–74.

Sève, L. (1978) *Man in Marxist Theory and the Psychology of Personality*. Brighton: Harvester.

Shotter, J. (1992) 'Is Bhaskar's critical realism only a theoretical realism?', *History of the Human Sciences*, 5(3): 157–73.

Shotter, J. (1993) *Conversational Realities: Constructing Life through Language*. London: Sage.

9

Social Constructionism and the New Technologies of Reproduction

Erica Haimes and Robin Williams

This chapter examines an issue that is central both to the disciplinary concerns of social constructionism and to the practical world of policy-making: the apparent dualism of the natural and the social. We explore this dualism through the substantive example of the 'new technologies of reproduction' – a phrase and a field of practice and debate that immediately conveys the complexity of the interweaving of domains that can appear, ontologically and pragmatically, to be separate. However, for both constructionists and policy-makers the extent of separateness and of mutual penetration of those two domains is the focus of concern. For both, the question is 'How far can we go?' For social constructionists, how far can we go in appropriating the natural to the social? For policy-makers, how far ought we to go in attempting to control events in the natural world?

Our intention in this chapter is not to answer these questions directly but to explore how others have attempted to answer them. In this exploration we identify the debates around this dualism within constructionism and argue that the key debate (between nature as a social artefact and nature as a residual reality) runs the risk of becoming sterile: irresolvable within the ontological parameters it has set itself. We suggest the need to turn to the pragmatic concerns of everyday actors (in this case, policy-makers) to see how the categories of the 'natural' and the 'social' are displayed and deployed. Whilst such a move is commonplace in some forms of constructionism, it is missing in others. In making this move ourselves we are arguing the case for prescriptive constructionism to be joined by, or indeed replaced by, a more widespread 'descriptive constructionism'.

The term 'new reproductive technologies' (NRTs) emerged in the mid-1980s to describe a range of clinical and scientific developments to help men and women with fertility problems to become parents. These technologies are described as 'new' in order to distinguish them from 'older' reproductive technologies in the field of childbirth, such as amniocentesis, induction and foetal monitoring.

A list of the procedures covered by the term 'new reproductive technologies' would include: donor insemination; egg donation; embryo donation; *in vitro* fertilization; embryo freezing; pre-conception sex selection techniques; gamete intra-fallopian transfer and other associated manipulative procedures, plus surrogacy if any of the above procedures are used. Other areas of scientific activity associated with NRTs are embryology (experiments on human embryos) and the later developments of genetic manipulation, gene therapy and indeed the Human Genome Project. We will pay particular attention to discussions concerning a possible future development: the use of foetal and cadaveric ovarian tissue as a source of donated eggs.

It is evident from this list that the term NRTs is itself a complex construction, covering as it does a variety of procedures with different degrees of technological interventions, different histories of development and different contexts of use. It has been used to cover a range of both scientific and clinical interests and activities. As a term it appeared in two different contexts in the 1980s: in the American Fertility Society's report 'Ethical considerations of the new reproductive technologies' (1986) and in the emerging radical feminist critiques of the technologies. It was seen by both as preferable to the previously popular term 'artificial reproduction'. It is, however, not a term much used (in Britain at least) by practitioners themselves, who tend instead to prefer the phrase 'assisted conception' or to refer to specific procedures.

What is clear about all these associated areas (which helps to explain the tendency to group them all together) is that they involve work with eggs, semen and embryos: work that is aimed at creating 'new life', a baby for the individual or couple involved. It is this intervention with what many see as the fundamental 'building blocks of life', that has aroused so much interest in the NRTs.

For clinical scientists, medical practitioners, theologians, policy-makers, infertile individuals, and those appointed to regulate such practices, the recurrent question has been: how far should such interventions be allowed to go? However, this practical question is of conceptual significance for social constructionists too since its discussion and use have the capacity to generate new incongruities and anomalies around one of the most basic themes of the human sciences: the distinction between natural and social events.

Throughout the short history of the human sciences, there has existed a recurrent debate concerning the relationship between the social and the natural – sometimes phrased as between society and nature, sometimes between culture and nature, sometimes between the social and the material. The parameters of this debate have been multiple and complex, depending as they have on the definitions and usages given to the overwhelmingly encompassing terms whose provenance is being contested. Of course the distinction between nature and culture, or nature and convention, has a much longer history than that inscribed in our own discipline. It was used by Aristotle to differentiate two forms of justice, and by both Hobbes and Locke to mark what was distinctive about political society and political obligation (see Horigan, 1988). Later, for many Enlightenment thinkers 'nature' was valorized as an alternative pure realm against which could be displayed the range of 'unnatural' practices of the social – 'forced and arranged marriages, celibacy, inheritance and bastardy laws, war and the inquisition' (Jordanova, 1986: 37).

The distinction played an important part in a variety of attempts to found sociology as a distinct discipline: for example, in the form of Durkheim's social realism in which biological explanations of human conduct are explicitly rejected even while the methodological unity of the sciences is preserved (see Durkheim, 1938). Or again, in the uncompromising assertions of some historians and sociologists of the late nineteenth and early twentieth centuries, there are clear though varying accounts of both ontological and methodological disjunctions that mark the boundary between the social and the natural. The *Geisteswissenschaften* have as a necessary feature of their constitution a concern with mental life, and an acknowledgement that attached to this there are specific methodological requirements for the study of such a domain. In Dilthey's words, 'We explain nature but we understand mental life . . . this means that the methods of studying mental life, history and society differ greatly from those used to acquire knowledge of nature' (Dilthey, 1976: 172). While the particulars of biology or a certain form of physicality might be a precondition for having such a mental life, any reduction of the mental to the physical was to be resisted. Again, Weber's distinction between action and behaviour, however compromised it might be, is evidence of his intention to exclude the biological from the domain of his sociology (Weber, 1948). The flesh and blood body can be safely left to other disciplines; for sociology, it can be treated as no more than an environmental constraint.

In the course of the twentieth century there have continued to be arguments about the exact nature and significance of the boundary between nature and culture, and more particularly between the cultural and the biological. We want to draw attention to some of the issues that social constructionism has raised, in its contributions to the ongoing debate and for our understanding of the difference between these predicated realms. Our sense of social constructionism is a broad one, defined as the assertion that 'objects are not given in the world but constructed, negotiated, formed, and fashioned by human beings in their effort to create and sustain a stable word of events and actions' (Best, 1989: ii).

In the classical text of the constructionist canon – Berger and Luckmann's *The Social Construction of Reality* (1971) – attention is given to what the authors describe as 'the organismic presuppositions and limitations of the social construction of reality'. The phrase itself suggests that they are aware of an analytic boundary to social constructionism, and it is relevant to this chapter that their formulation of this boundary provokes a discussion of biology. The presuppositions and limits they consider are those that are constitutive of human biology – of the human body. The organism, they assert, sets limits to what is socially possible. Biological factors limit the range of social possibilities, but at the same time the social world imposes limits on what is biologically possible.

For Berger and Luckmann, consideration of these two limits gives a clear sense of the effects of each domain on the other. The social realm influences the functioning of biological organisms (e.g. sexuality and nutrition are both biological givens grounded in natural drives but they are also sufficiently plastic to be moulded differently by different societies and social contexts). However, this plasticity is not without limits. The biological substrate can both resist social moulding (in primary socialization, the disciplining of the young within social organization can produce high levels of frustration) and it can also 'refuse' social moulding (social legislation that men should bear children would founder on the hard facts of biology).

Using ideas derived from Arnold Gehlen, who himself derived them from Nietzsche, Berger and Luckmann assert that man is a 'not yet determined animal', an unfinished biological creature not at home in nature, requiring instead the protection of social and cultural institutions during the process of socialization. Their descriptions of even such unfinished biological stuff remain imprecise – they are couched in the language of philosophical anthropology rather than in the language of contemporary biology, although reference is made from time to time to the idea of instinctual drives. Throughout, their examples are taken from the familiar trio of reproduction, nutrition and mortality.

Vague and diffuse as Berger and Luckmann are, however, their sense that there is some kind of material substrate (describable but not necessarily described in the vocabulary of another discipline, probably human biology, whose findings are not strictly relevant to our understanding of the social) fed into a good deal of the 'interactionist' social constructionist writings of the 1970s and 1980s. Since one of the other sources for this work was symbolic interactionism, Mead's (1938) views on the significance of the material were also important. It was Mead's intention, like Dewey, to attempt to understand the distinctiveness of human social existence while demonstrating our rootedness in nature. Mead sees the process of human experience as a natural process, and he stressed the importance of human manipulation of, and direct contact with, nature for our understanding of the world. He talks very enthusiastically about the direct experiential manipulatory realm: about our manual contact with the objects of our experience. Although we have elaborations and extensions of our hands in the form of mechanical devices of a variety of kinds, the ability to fashion such alternatives to direct manual contact would have been impossible if we did not have a central nervous system that could make use of the devices.

The following paraphrase of remarks by Rose et al. (1984: 13) would probably encompass most of what was assumed by the 'interactionist constructionists'. There are non-trivial features of human biology whose significance is difficult to contest: we walk upright on two legs, we have hands that manipulate and construct objects with some seeming success, we are capable of speech. We have a range of sizes, but that range is limited; we are sensitive to specific wavelengths of light but we are relatively insensitive to other wavelengths like that of radio. We do not have wings. Yet despite these limitations, we are able to modify our immediate environment in such a way that some of those powers, natural in other species, are available to us through our constructive capacities.

One area of social life in which the biological has traditionally been awarded some descriptive – and even sometimes explanatory – significance is that of the study of social problems: crime, mental illness, sexual deviance, drug use, etc. The interactionist constructionist approach to the study of such phenomena sidelined such a tendency very rapidly. Social problems were not to be treated as objective events requiring measurement and then explanation, but rather seen as consisting of the activities of those 'individuals or groups making assertions of grievances and claims with respect to some putative condition' (Spector and Kitsuse in Best, 1989: xviii), and secondly of the activities of those who respond to these claims. In stating the methodological injunction that such phenomena were not to 'be treated as objective events', Kitsuse and Schneider argued that there was no intention to imply that such conditions were not real or did not exist. Researchers were not to compete with everyday members of society as an arbiter of true and accurate knowledge, but rather study how claims are defined, lodged and pressed, how concerns are promulgated, how they are redefined and how one set of claims can be aligned with others (in Best, 1989: xii–xiii).

In the many interactionist constructionist studies of such phenomena as the family, kinship, racial categories, race, intelligence, illness, genius, the nature of emotions, sexuality, drunkenness, child abuse, rape, spouse abuse and elder abuse – to list a sample – biological attributes were rarely discussed or challenged directly. What was of interest to such analysts was the way in which claims about such attributes were mediated through language, as well as through the expression of attitudes, of ideas and social relations. Here, then, analysts were not denying the reality of a material biological substrate; it was simply not accorded any fixed causal role (but neither was it subject to erosion by the social).

However, even this residual autonomy of the natural can be seen to come under threat from the advance of other types of study which are relevant to this book.

First there were historians of ideas, often influenced by linguistics and literary studies, who were willing to characterize the nature/culture distinction as a cultural artefact, and as such, one with shifting denotations and connotations. Jordanova for example has written of 'the languages of nature' as constructed 'according to different rules, assumptions and aesthetic preferences for distinct purposes by various constituencies according to their context' (1986: 27). In her essay on the biomedical sciences in the late eighteenth century she is concerned to show the communality between medical, scientific and literary accounts of topics like sexuality and reproduction, and through doing so, to provide a sense of the wider cultural context in which biology developed during this period. Yet even here the status of the facts of biology is not directly the subject of her work, preferring as she does to speak of representations rather than constructions.

Secondly there was the more linguistically based constructionism of Gergen, Shotter and their colleagues who regularly contribute to the Sage 'Inquiries in Social Construction' series (e.g. Gergen, 1994; Sarbin and Kitsuse, 1994; Shotter, 1993; Shotter and Gergen, 1989). In comparison to the previously mentioned work, Gergen's vocabulary is more idealist and relativist. For Gergen, the language of social description cannot be mapped onto stable external realities: language is the only reality we can know. In that sense reality (and we assume he means all reality, natural and social) is the result of social processes.

Thirdly there is that large range of studies that is written about at greater length in Part 1 of this book: studies in the social construction of science. The claims of these kinds of studies seem to take us towards a social essentialism in which even the residual autonomy of the natural – or the biological – is further destabilized. The facts of nature – the facts of biology – the facts of any science are to be given the same status. As Knorr-Cetina (1993) has asserted: this known world is a cultural object, a world identified and embodied in our language and our practice. In Latour and Woolgar's 'Laboratory Life', there is as clear a statement of what is being asserted as may be found anywhere. Using the term 'inscription' to refer to any recorded symbols, including texts written by scientists, graphs drawn by computers, measures on scales and the rest, they say that

> Despite the fact that our scientists held the belief that our inscriptions could be representations or indicators of some entity with an independent existence 'out there', we have argued that such entities were constituted solely through the use of these inscriptions. . . . We do not conceive of scientists using various strategies as pulling back the curtain on pre-given, but hitherto concealed truths. Rather objects (in this case substances) are constituted through the artful creativity of scientists. (Latour and Woolgar, 1979: 128)

If the sciences of nature are cultural constructions, if there is nothing but the social, only socially constructed natural phenomena, then in what sense can we use established biological facts as even a stable background to our understanding of the activities of subjects within the social?

Such radical claims for the autonomy of the social and its appropriation of the biological for a time led to a certain unwillingness within sociology to think about flesh-and-blood bodies and their place within the space of an autonomous but non-reductionist biological sphere. The popularity of recent work on the 'sociology' of the body is testimony to a shift away from a previous disembodied sociology, and the corporeal character of the human subject has become a focus of interest in a number of related disciplines. Some earlier arguments are being revisited (e.g. Merleau-Ponty, 1962, 1968 on 'carnal sociology'; Nietzsche, 1977 on the organic instinctual body; and Mauss, 1973 on bodily discipline). Giddens (1984) has talked persuasively of the doubly enabling and constraining features of

the human body and its worldly location, and Turner (1984) has argued that
we cannot safely assert that there are no biologically based commonalities
that feature as causal backgrounds to cultural practices. The contribution of
both essentialist and constructionist feminisms is also significant in this
renewed interest. There are additional arguments concerning how best to
think of the relationship between the natural and the cultural in a number
of more general contexts. Timpanaro (1975) offers a weak biological determinism as an attempt to counter cultural and social relativism in sociology
but, more interestingly, Benton's (1991) argument for a new synthesis of
social and biological science includes the effort to transcend the network of
categorical oppositions within which we so easily move at present (including mind/body, culture/nature, society/biology, meaning/cause, human/
animal). For Benton these contingent dualisms are capable of dissolution
through the recognition of recent non-reductionist understandings of biological processes (e.g. advances in neurophysiology, in developmental
biology, in animal ethology and in modern ecology). A less detailed but
more politically significant contribution to this debate has been made by
Lord Runciman (1993) in his annual lecture to the Economic and Social
Research Council – the main source of government funding for the social
sciences in the United Kingdom. In this document, Runciman proclaims the
possibility of a new Darwinian sociology. For Runciman, the most interesting question concerns a consideration of what is 'selected for what' in the
transition from nature to culture.

Some may feel safe in the assertion that the discussion of the adequacy
and propriety of the distinction between the social and the biological will
continue to resist resolution. In this case, the developments alluded to
above can be ignored The boundary itself should perhaps be accorded the
status of an essentially contested boundary if we can borrow and modify
Gallie's (1964) original expression. In the world of social theory, essentially
contested boundaries are just part of what there is. We will continue to talk
around them, but accept them as simultaneously irresolvable and productive dualisms.

However, not everyone can take advantage of such a privilege. There are
individuals and social groups who encounter such dualism in the context of
pragmatic choices that have to be made, policy that has to be formulated,
scarce resources that have to be distributed. The UK Human Fertilisation
and Embryology Authority (HFEA) is one such group; we now turn to one
of their recent publications, to see how the dualism features in their concerns and to see how they deal with it.

The HFEA is the regulatory authority set up under the 1990 Human
Fertilisation and Embryology Act, to license clinics providing research and
treatment programmes which manipulate embryos created outside the
body and/or which use donated gametes (sperm and eggs) for treatment
purposes.

In January 1994 the HFEA published an important consultation document *Donated Ovarian Tissue in Embryo Research and Assisted Conception*

in response to widespread publicity in the British newspapers over the possibility that treatment for infertility would extend to using eggs obtained from foetuses and/or the cadavers of women and girls to enable infertile women to become pregnant. This possibility was set alongside two other developments that broke in the newspapers at the same time: one, that a post-menopausal 59-year-old woman had given birth to twins following treatment received in Italy; the second, that a black woman receiving egg donation as part of her treatment for overcoming infertility had asked for an egg from a white donor on the grounds that a child born from such an egg was likely to have a lighter skin colour and would therefore have a better chance in life overall. In 1993 there had been much adverse publicity about the opening of a baby sex selection clinic in London.

Individually any of these developments raises the question of what types of intervention should be allowed in reproduction; together they raised the spectre of ghoulish and even eugenic possibilities; of messing with the fundamentals of life, of trying to control things that should perhaps be left to chance, of choosing the types of parents and children we might want. In short, what type of intervention should there be in nature: how far should we go?

The purpose of publishing this document was to explain the HFEA's remit on this one issue of the use of ovarian tissue in embryo research and assisted conception and then to elicit responses from the public, to help the HFEA gauge the acceptability of the procedure. Precisely because it is a consultation document and therefore has a political context and purpose, the authors of the document have to be particularly conscious of the fears generally associated with the new reproductive technologies and assisted conception: that of going too far, intervening too much in nature, using unnatural procedures and techniques. These are not of course the only fears nor necessarily the most prominent; some might argue the potential or actual exploitation of women is the biggest risk associated with the NRTs; others might say the same about the exploitation of the foetus: however, both these fears themselves rest on an idea that the NRTs involve intervention in areas that previously were not amenable to intervention and manipulation and that the problems for women and foetuses are at the very least exacerbated, if not necessarily wholly created by, those interventions.

The consultation document contains an outline of the issues around the need for donated eggs in infertility treatment and research and notes that there is a shortage of such eggs. The shortage means that infertile women who need eggs have to wait a long time for treatment. It notes that the main source of eggs at the moment is adult women; however, other possible sources are the cadavers of adult women, the cadavers of girls and aborted female foetuses. These cadavers and foetuses can provide either ovarian tissue itself or eggs extracted from that tissue. The authors of the document note that there are 'legal, scientific, social, ethical and moral issues and implications' (1994:1) of using this tissue and call for responses from the public and interested parties, so that the Authority can then decide whether to license treatment and/or research using this tissue.

There is much that can be written about a document such as this: the authors, the audience, the framing of the questions and so on. However, given an interest in the standing of the dualism between the biological and the social we simply want to note some examples of the way that dualism is expressed by the authors of this document, as part of their practical and political activity of deciding what sort of help should be given to the infertile.

In reading the document it is possible to suggest that the authors express ideas about biological and social matters, and the boundaries between them, in four different ways. First, they express an understanding of certain unproblematically biological facts, processes and entities. Secondly, they express an understanding of matters that reside, unproblematically, in the social domain. Thirdly, they deliberately (since this is the purpose of the document) cite instances where biological facts/entities/processes encounter social activities and they explicitly question whether such encounters are problematic. Not surprisingly, perhaps, they conclude that some are problematic and some are not; that is, that some, but not all, incursions across the boundary between the two are legitimate. Fourthly, they use some phrases and concepts that express boundary entanglements between the biological and the social though the character of these entanglements remains unexplicated and even perhaps unnoticed by the authors, in so far as they do not comment on their usage of such phrases in the way that they comment on the encounters mentioned under the third example, above.

To illustrate these briefly. First, in the formulation of unproblematically biological facts/processes/entities: the authors refer to entities such as ovarian tissue, eggs, foetal tissue; they refer to biological processes, for example 'the ovary produces the hormones and eggs required for reproduction' (1994: 1). Secondly, in the formulation of the unproblematically social, the document refers to the activities of the Authority itself, the fact of existing legislation, the interest groups that might respond to the document, the public itself: all are discussed without any attempt to define precisely the meanings given to these terms. Thirdly, there are several examples of encounters between biological processes and social activities: for instance, paragraph 5 says, 'There is a valid aim for scientists to discover as much as possible about biological systems', which can be read as a claim for an unproblematic boundary incursion. However, problematic incursions are noted throughout the whole document (since that is its purpose). For example, paragraph 7: 'This document invites views about whether the use of ovarian tissue from adults, cadavers or foetuses may be considered necessary or desirable in the context of licensed fertility treatment or embryo research in the U.K.' Fourthly, the following may serve as an example of unexplicated boundary entanglements: paragraph 1: ovarian tissue can be obtained from 'mature women, from girls or women who have died (cadaveric tissue), or from aborted foetuses'. It is interesting for our purposes to note that the authors use these particular categories to describe the sources rather than simply say that eggs can be obtained from female bodies, dead or alive. In other words, the social categories of the sources of the biological material are considered to be significant. Further, those social identities are reinforced by the way each is categorized in relation to the other: for example, a foetus is not seen as the social equivalent of a cadaver. The social identity and status of the foetus is further specified by its having been aborted, either spontaneously or by intervention, rather than having been conceived specifically for the purpose of contributing ovarian tissue. Throughout the document, as elsewhere in discussions of NRTs, the foetus is not easily categorized as either biological material or social being. The fact that these sources do have social identities might be seen as the reason for the anxieties about these practices, except that these particular social identities are used apparently unreflexively by the authors and are not commented on as themselves presenting any problems.

Many more examples of each of these points can be found throughout the document but it might be more useful to look at a couple of paragraphs in some detail since this will show an additional important feature of this talk: the manner in which these four ways of seeing the relationship between the biological and the social intertwine:

> Paragraph 6: The subject of this consultation is a matter of considerable sensitivity and raises fundamental and complex issues. The HFEA is aware that while the public is generally willing to accept organ donation and the use of fetal tissue for therapeutic purposes generally, it may feel an instinctive repugnance to the use of ovarian tissue from these sources for research or fertility treatment. The HFE Act has resolved the earlier debate on research on human embryos, but the public may still be alarmed that the frontiers of medical science are being pushed forward too far and too fast. The Authority has a role in informing the public about these issues in a balanced way.

Whilst examples of all four boundary expressions can be found in this paragraph, the phrase 'instinctive repugnance' merits particular attention as an example of an unexplicated boundary entanglement. This phrase, translated in the wider public debate in the newspapers as the 'yuk factor', suggests a biologically based, fundamental, pre-rational, pre-explanatory rejection of using foetuses and cadavers as sources of eggs. But note that the rejection is seen as all the more authoritative for that. We have here a biologically derived but socially expressed form of rejection based on an assumption about the fundamental reality, and hence authority, of biology, which gives us instincts; but these instincts only make sense with reference to the specific social context of using these particular materials for treatment and research. So this small but important phrase depends on the interplay of the biological and the social, but in a way that the authors appear to take for granted.

> Paragraph 21: A potential difficulty might be thought to be that a generation of human development would be skipped if fetal ovarian tissue were used in fertility

treatment. Ovarian tissue or eggs from an aborted foetus have not been subjected to the pressures which govern survival and normal development to adulthood. This raises questions about the degree of risk of abnormality, at present unquantifiable, in embryos produced using such tissue. This might be seen as breaking a natural law of biology.

This paragraph is one of two listed under a heading 'Scientific Issues'. Our reading of it is that it reflects some of the four different features of boundary expressions just described, but in ways which raise more questions. For example, what does the first sentence mean? It suggests that the difficulty be read as a difficulty for science, because skipping 'a generation of human development' would mean that the biological system, hitherto uncovered by science, is now being manipulated or thwarted by science. But surely science is doing this all the time – uncovering in order to manipulate/control? Or does the raising of this difficulty in this way, by the authors, tell us something about the political dilemma of presenting science? That presenting science as uncovering the secrets of nature is acceptable, but playing about with nature, manipulating those secret processes is not acceptable? Or at least, it is only acceptable to a certain extent and that is what this document is for – to discover that extent. So is that what this first sentence does – construct the political context for the practice of reproductive science? Maybe it has that effect but note that the question is posed as a 'scientific issue' and not a 'social and moral question', which happens to be the subheading for the next section of the document.

The problem identified in the second and third sentences is that the intervention into normal biological processes might in fact constitute bad science since the effects of that intervention are unknowable. Again, the question is not presented as a moral point but as one of good and bad science.

The final sentence poses the real puzzle in this paragraph. After all, what would it mean to be able to break a 'natural law of biology'? The phrase 'natural law' suggests the fixed conditions or processes found in nature that give nature its foundational qualities. If however one can break those laws, this suggests that biology has no foundational properties, or at least that those foundations haven't yet been reached and that therefore the status of current knowledge should be one of contingency (as in fact one might expect from 'good' science), rather than law.

Paragraph 23: An important issue in considering these new sources of eggs for treatment is the psychological effect on a child of knowing that it was born from an egg derived from a cadaver or from an aborted foetus. Children born from current techniques using donated eggs or sperm, which are regulated by the HFEA, may have to come to terms with the circumstances of their conception. In the case of children born from cadaveric or fetal ovarian tissue, the particular implications of finding out that their genetic mother had died before they were conceived, or was an aborted foetus, are unknown. It would be necessary to consider further how to assess the likely effects on children and their wider family relationships of knowing they were born from donated material from these sources.

This might be seen as an example not just of where the biological and the social encounter one another but of where they collide. However, in raising this explicitly as an area of problematic boundary incursion the authors are also deploying less explicit understandings about the interplay and entanglement of the social and the biological. In talking about the problems of being born from this type of genetic material the authors are drawing an implicit distinction with being born from other types of genetic material. Thus the same biological material has a different social status according to its source. The range of socially differentiated sources of genetic material is quite extensive: it can come from a live woman who also carries the child (our conventional understanding of the term 'mother') or it can come from a donor. That donor can either be genetically related to the recipient and therefore to the child too, for example as the recipient's sister, or the donor can be a non-genetically related live woman; the non-genetically related donor can be either known or unknown to the recipient; the unknown donor can be either an adult woman or a girl (though the latter is illegal under UK law). Another social distinction is that the donor can be alive or dead; the donor could be someone who lived then died or 'someone' who had never lived (i.e. a foetus).

The use of the phrase 'genetic mother' in this paragraph entails a linguistic switch (again, not explicitly signposted) from what have previously been referred to as 'sources of genetic materials' (and thus as sociobiological entities) into social categories of parenthood and kinship. Not only does the concept of a 'genetic mother' reinforce the new vocabulary of parenting that the NRTs have introduced, it also introduces a semantic difficulty for the resultant child: explaining the circumstances of having a mother who had died (or never lived) before one was born entails providing details of the source of one's genes. If Oscar Wilde could create a social impropriety out of being a foundling, imagine what connotations of unseemliness are raised by one's origins being in a cadaver or a foetus. Perhaps this is where the instinctive repugnance, the yuk factor, has most force – in the connections between the child and the source of that child's genes.

This reading of the consultation document is deliberately open-ended and questioning: there seems little point in trying to make claims about what these authors really intended in writing the document, what they really mean. It seems much more fruitful to us to open up the analytical space and point to some interesting possibilities for the ways in which members handle the ideas about the natural and the social, about biological facts and social proprieties.

For these authors the boundaries between the biological and the social are clearly seen as politically sensitive, but they also use these domains in ways that allow the boundaries between them to be pragmatically and conceptually permeable. Whilst the political and the practical concerns are uppermost and thus demand the more explicit rendition, conceptual fluidity is needed in order even to be able to discuss those practical concerns.

Earlier in the chapter we wrote about the disciplinary politics embedded in debates concerning the boundary between the social and the natural. The contributions of social constructionists to these debates have been significant and powerful, and the slogans of constructionism have proved useful for those concerned to establish a distinctive voice for sociology. Along with more generic 'cognitivist' and 'linguistic' orientations, the constructionist impulse has proved capable of making significant contributions to a number of other disciplines within the human sciences, including psychology, philosophy, anthropology and archaeology.

At the same time, the rhetorical and political uses of the term 'social constructionism' are capable of overwhelming its analytical capacity. There are two obvious limits to the ambitions of constructionism. The first of these is phenomenological, the second disciplinary.

We have seen, from the example of the consultation document, that if constructionist assertions of the nature of physical being are placed alongside phenomenological intuitions concerning our selves and our bodies, those assertions fail to capture the full range of how actors display those intuitions. Notions of construction seem to fly in the face of the way that these actors (and the rest of us) talk about a number of ineradicable features of our lives. Our talk of how we reproduce ourselves, let alone how we live and die, eat and sleep, feel pleasure and pain, endure illness and violence all constitute examples of such features. It is difficult for us as individuals to dismiss facts like these as mere constructions; it is even more difficult to conceive how policy-makers might resolve their questions with a view that the source of donated eggs does not matter since those sources are mere constructions. That such questions do matter, and matter in a way that goes beyond simply establishing the ontological status of those eggs and their sources, is evidenced by the existence not only of the document, but of the whole Human Fertilisation and Embryology Authority itself. But as Butler (1993) has pointed out in a discussion of sex and gender, the irrefutability of such facts doesn't imply what it might mean to affirm them, nor does it encourage us to consider the discursive means through which they are confirmed.

In addition to phenomenological limitations to the ambitions of constructionism, there are disciplinary ones. Here we return to a basic question: how should we think of nature from within the disciplinary boundary of sociology? As a passive surface but necessary counterpart to the social? Or should we think of nature as an artefact of the social? Both of these positions run into problems. In the first version, our biology marks one limit of constructionism, a limit which constructionism had better do its best to discover. In the second, version, biology – or nature – is merely one of the range of such linguistic or practical artefacts that litter the social.

Within the human sciences, 'the autonomy of culture' is a useful slogan. It rallies our forces in opposition to those demanding that we march under the one banner of a universal science based on someone's version of what physicists are said to do. However, it may also be that for many forms of human and social behaviour we can safely leave nature – however described – to the role of a substantial but unchangeable material substrate – maybe a set of limited but extensive potentialities. The danger is that if constructionism seeks needlessly to assimilate that substrate into the social, then it has simply substituted for one version of the unity of the sciences another – more vulnerable – one. And such an effort would serve only to sacrifice the potential of the approach, a potential that lies in its ability to act as a device – to raise detailed questions about the organization of the social – rather than prescribe 'the answer' to general questions concerning the appropriate hierarchy of disciplinary ambitions.

The very idea of the construction of a shared reality seems to carry within it the idea of material outside 'stuff' from which constructions are made, an ontological thereness that lies outside the boundaries of discursive constructions. This pre-constructed is bounded by linguistic or practical activities that themselves presuppose a delimitation of the constructed object. Such a presumed separation seems a constitutive feature of the overwhelming majority of contemporary arguments about how to choose between what is true and false, real or imaginary. That these matters are given attention, rather than resolved in one or other hard and fast fashion, is what we think of as necessary and sufficient to constructionism. The strength of constructionism lies in its encouragement of the detailed study of the individual and collective work necessary to create and sustain a shared social and natural reality. This chapter has offered a glimpse of the negotiations that have accompanied one such effort – in the case of NRTs – but this has barely scraped the surface of a tiny part of such ongoing activity.

References

American Fertility Society (1986) 'Ethical considerations of the new reproductive technologies', *Fertility and Sterility*, 46 (3) Supplement 1.

Benton, T. (1991) 'Biology and social science: why the return of the repressed should be given a (cautious) welcome', *Sociology*, 25: 1–30.

Berger, P. and Luckmann, T. (1971) *The Social Construction of Reality*. London: Penguin.

Best, J. (ed.) (1989) *Images of Issues: The Construction of Social Problems*. New York: Aldine.

Dilthey, W. (1976) *Selected Writings*. Cambridge: Cambridge University Press.

Durkheim, E. (1938) *The Rules of Sociological Method*. New York: Free Press.

Gallie, W.B. (1964) *Philosophy and the Historical Understanding*. London: Chatto & Windus.

Gergen, K. (1994) *Realities and Relationships: Soundings in Social Construction*. Cambridge, MA: Harvard University Press.

Giddens, A. (1984) *The Constitution of Society*. Cambridge: Polity Press.

Horigan, S. (1988) *Nature and Culture in Western Discourses*. London: Routledge.

Human Fertilisation and Embryology Authority (1994) *Donated Ovarian Tissue in Embryo Research and Assisted Conception: Public Consultation Document*. London: HFEA.

Jordanova, L. (ed.) (1986) *Languages of Nature*. London: Free Association Books.

Knorr-Cetina, K. (1993) 'Strong constructionism – from a sociologist's point of view', *Social Studies in Science*, 23: 555–66.

Latour, B. and Woolgar, S. (1979) *Laboratory Life*. London: Sage.

Mauss, M. (1973) 'Techniques of the body', *Economy and Society*, 2: 70–88.

Mead, G.H. (1938) *Mind, Self and Society*. Chicago: University of Chicago Press.

Merleau-Ponty, M. (1962) *The Phenomenology of Perception*. London: Routledge.

Merleau-Ponty, M. (1968) *The Visible and the Invisible*. Evanston, IL: Northwestern University Press.

Nietzsche, F. (1977) *A Nietzsche Reader*. London: Penguin.

Rose, S., Lewontin, R. and Kamin, L. (1984) *Not in Our Genes: Biology, Ideology and Human Nature*. Harmondsworth: Penguin

Runciman, G. (1993) *Competition for What?* (ESRC Annual Lecture). Swindon: Economic and Social Research Council.

Sarbin, T. and Kitsuse, J. (eds) (1994) *Constructing the Social*. London: Sage.

Shotter, J. (1993) *Conversational Realities*. London: Sage.

Shotter, J. and Gergen, K. (eds) (1989) *Texts of Identity*. London: Sage.

Timpanaro, S. (1975) *On Materialism*. London: New Left Books.

Turner, B. (1984) *The Body and Society*. Oxford: Blackwell.

Weber, M. (1948) *Theory of Social and Economic Organization*. New York: Free Press.

10

The Social Construction of Outliers

Sandy Lovie and Pat Lovie

Real data are dirty.

(Velleman, 1993: 30)

We consider what is often referred to in statistical data analysis as 'the outlier problem' from three social constructionist perspectives.[1] Adopting such an eclectic approach to the analysis of our material, that is, by offering relativistic, ethnographic and political deconstructions, requires some explanation. Mathematics and its applications have traditionally been thought of as presenting special difficulties for deconstruction (see Bloor, 1976; also the commentary by Woolgar, 1988). Consequently, we did not know a priori what additional insights any one of the alternative social constructionist strategies might achieve. In the event, what we might have lost in methodological and theoretical purity, we believe that we have gained in a rounder and richer analysis. For instance, to argue (as we do) that outliers are contextually embedded does not *necessarily* help us to understand why they are also invariably morally evaluated, nor does it account for the origins of, or the reasons behind, such an evaluation.

The Outlier Problem

Outliers are observations which do not seem to follow the pattern of the other values in a sample of data. Suppose, for instance, that a survey finds that the wages of employees in a small firm are between £100 and £200 per week but their boss is paid £1,200 per week. The latter's salary appears to be an outlier viewed against the other amounts earned.

As an illustration of how an outlier might manifest itself in a more complex situation, we take data collected by the physicist James D. Forbes in the middle of the nineteenth century. Forbes's interest was in whether the relationship between the temperature at which water boiled and atmospheric pressure might be strong enough to allow altitude to be estimated by measuring the boiling point.[2] A scatterplot of $100 \times$ log pressure against boiling point, with a least squares fitted regression line superimposed (Figure 10.1a) shows a strong linear relationship between the two variables, although one observation does not seem to follow the general pattern quite

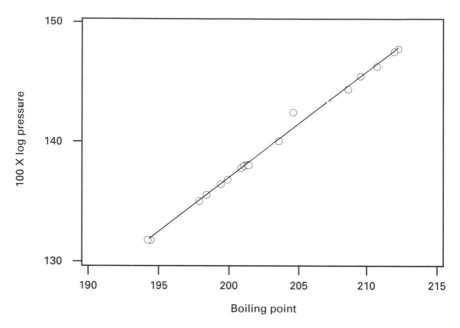

Figure 10.1a   *Forbes's data. Scatterplot of 100 × log pressure against boiling point (pressure measured in inches of mercury, boiling point in degrees Fahrenheit). (Data from S. Weisberg,* Applied Regression Analysis. 2nd edition. *Copyright © 1985, John Wiley & Sons Inc. Reprinted by permission of John Wiley & Sons Inc.)*

so well. Plotting the residuals (differences between the observed and fitted 100 × log pressure values) against boiling point (Figure 10.1b) emphasizes the separation of this single point from the mass of the data.

From the data analyst's standpoint, a separated data point, such as that visible in the above plots,[3] is generally unwelcome. In short, for the statistician, there are good observations and there are suspect ones. Some of the latter are said to be *blunders* whose causes are, in principle, immediately and unproblematically apparent; these include such contingent events as transcription errors and measurement instrument failures. There are, however, other outliers (*rogues*) which cannot be accounted for in this way and which require alternative, substantive explanations.

The Relativity of Outliers

As our first perspective on the social construction of outliers, we argue that outliers have invariably been defined in a fundamentally relativist and reflexive fashion. Thus, an outlier is pragmatically meaningful only within the context of the sample in which it is situated and against which it is contrasted. In particular, as Weisberg pointed out: 'Outlier identification is done relative to a specified model. If the form of the model is modified, the

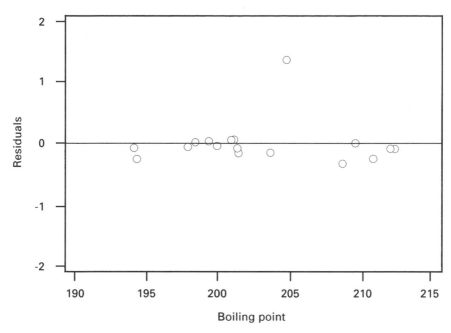

Figure 10.1b *Forbes's data. Residuals from least squares fit against boiling point.*

status of individual cases as outliers may change' (Weisberg, 1985: 115). This notion of the relativity of outliers is reinforced by the following quotation from what is regarded as the classic text on the outlier problem:

> Clearly, *the answer* [to the outlier problem] *depends on the form of the population*; techniques will be conditioned by, and specific to, any postulated (basic) model for that population. Thus, methods for the processing of outliers take on an entirely *relative* form: relative to the basic model. (Barnett and Lewis, 1994: 7)

To put these ideas in a slightly more concrete form: an individual observation identified as an outlier in a sample assumed to be drawn from a normal population would not necessarily be classified as such if the underlying distribution was now assumed to be longer tailed (for example, exponential) or heavier tailed (such as Student's *t*).

Similarly, if we are concerned with the relationship between two variables, the functional form we specify determines the status of any individual observation. For example, on the scatterplot in Figure 10.2a we see data for body weight versus brain weight of thirty-five mammals to which a simple linear least squares regression model is fitted to predict brain weight from body weight.[4] Notice the single observation well separated from the main data mass. On the other hand, when the relationship is assumed to be linear for the logarithms of the variables (Figure 10.2b), this observation no longer appears inconsistent.

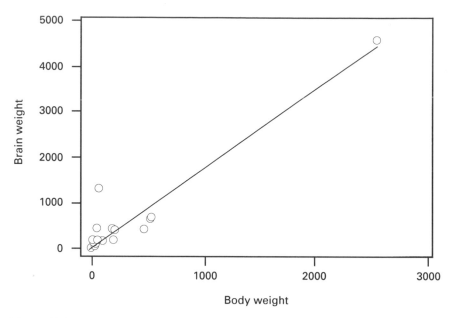

Figure 10.2a   *Scatterplot of brain weight (g) and body weight (kg) of mammals. (Data from S. Weisberg,* Applied Regression Analysis. 2nd edition. *Copyright © 1985, John Wiley & Sons Inc. Reprinted by permission of T. Allison and John Wiley & Sons Inc.)*

That outliers are constructed in relation to the particular model specified by the data analyst is only one aspect of their relativity. There are several other facets of outlier detection technology which undermine the notion that an outlier can be defined in an absolute fashion.

More precisely, as a number of authors have demonstrated,[5] whether an observation is detected as an outlier or not can crucially depend on which statistical hypothesis test (or even more simply which sample measure and rule of thumb)[6] is chosen by the data analyst. The test statistics may reflect different features of the assumed underlying population, such as its spread or its shape. Some tests in effect assess the candidate as if it were already foreign, while others embrace it.[7] Moreover, excluding a detected outlier from a sample (as is often the practice) will sometimes 'uncover' a further candidate on re-analysis. Of course, the basis on which the new candidate is assessed is now different because the initially discarded value no longer plays any part in the reduced sample.

When it is a small cluster of values that seems inconsistent, the notion of outlierness becomes even more slippery. For example, in a sequential procedure which tests one outlier candidate at a time, starting with the most extreme, and then terminates at the first non-significant result, the presence of the next most discrepant observation in the sample can 'mask' a candidate. Thus the data analyst might conclude that there are fewer outliers in the sample than would be the case of an alternative approach which tests

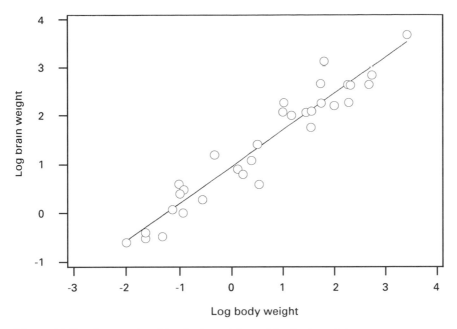

Figure 10.2b   *Scatterplot of log brain weight and log body weight*

'the least likely' candidate first were adopted. Yet another approach is a block procedure in which the perceived inconsistent values are examined together in a single test. The effectiveness of this method depends greatly on the analyst's ability to identify all candidates. If the number chosen for testing is too small, masking is a risk. On the other hand, if the analyst chooses too many candidates, perfectly reasonable values can be swept through on the tide and henceforth designated as outliers.[8]

Finally, we argue that how an outlier is defined is also relative to the data analyst's conceptually embedded work. In other words, we assume that the data analyst is operating within a knowledge context such that classificatory decisions as to the status of members of a sample can be made on plausible grounds. For instance, the following quotations suggest that the outlier is constructed according to professional expectation and judgement:

> What characterizes the 'outlier' is its impact on the observer (not only will it appear *extreme* but it will seem, in some sense, *surprisingly* extreme). (Barnett and Lewis, 1994: 7)

and

> The points that we are thinking of are those that would be removed as 'imposs-ible' by 99% of the technical experts in the field under study. (Daniel and Wood, 1971: 84)

Often the perceived need is also for scientific respectability:

> In practice, not infrequently, the researcher finds subjectively that a value is probably an outlier and then he looks for a rule to reject it, in order to make his opinion more 'objective'. (Hampel et al., 1986: 57) [9]

There is also a growing suspicion within the statistical profession that what constitutes an outlier is linguistically constructed, that is, as the outcome of some collective speech act:

> What is true is that 'outlier' is a Humpty-Dumpty word; it means just what the user chooses it to mean – neither more nor less. (Fieller, 1993)

In essence then, we find that an outlier is jointly constructed from the means whereby it is defined, and by the data analyst's own embedded work.

The Ethnography of Outliers

An article of faith in social constructionism is that behind any collective action and choice is the wish to impose a meaningful structure on the world. One way of achieving this order is through the differential evaluation of relevant elements of the world, thus separating them out according to their moral attributes. As we shall see, elements of a sample are indeed evaluated in this way by data analysts.

To investigate this evaluative dimension of outliers we draw on Mary Douglas's anthropological insights about the value of dirt and pollution for making (moral) sense of the world. According to Douglas: 'Dirt offends against order. Eliminating it is not a negative movement, but a positive effort to organise the environment', and 'I believe that ideas about separating, purifying, demarcating and punishing transgressions have as their main function to impose system on an inherently untidy experience' (Douglas, 1969: 2, 4).

That outliers are characterized in a moral or evaluative fashion can be seen from the following list of common epithets applied to them:

anomalous	blunders	contaminants
deviant	dirty data	discordant
discrepant	errors	extraordinary
extreme	far out	gross errors
mavericks	outside values	rogues
strays	unreasonable	weird
wild		

We observe here socially framed descriptions of outliers which imply that samples can be thought of as collectives with an in-group/out-group structure. In-group members, that is non-outliers, are termed 'acceptable', 'genuine' and 'ordinary', while out-group members are ascribed socially isolating and socially undesirable characteristics.[10] Some descriptors even offer a metaphysical categorization by seeming to undermine the reality of such readings since they have also been termed *spurious, impossible* or *non-missing* (the latter explained as values which should be missing but are not; see Velleman, 1993: 30, fn. 1).

Such morally charged elements invite morally figured action to achieve a form of purification. Thus, when detected, outliers are typically

cut	deleted	discarded
excised	rejected	suppressed
trimmed		

The primary emphasis on outliers as negatively glossed sources of social and moral order has provided a rationale to account for the language in which outliers are described and a justification for the ways in which they are subsequently treated. However, Douglas also points to the positive role that embracing dirt or pollution can play in hastening or empowering change. In this latter case, pollution is now represented as an anomaly to be accounted for and hence its unambiguous status as dangerous is undermined: 'Ambiguous symbols can be used in ritual for the same ends as they are used in poetry and mythology, to enrich meaning or to call attention to other levels of existence' (Douglas, 1969: 40).

Outliers may also assume a similarly ambiguous mantle. Although their usual fate is to be discarded, there are situations where the focus is on the outlier rather than the sample, for example detecting cancerous cells in cervical smears or identifying oil-bearing rock strata. More relevant to our thesis, however, is that the rescue or re-evaluation of an outlier can lead to an increase in knowledge. For instance, the acceptance that a hole exists in the ozone layer over the Antarctic was a direct result of a socially negotiated recategorization of the status, that is, the meaning, of unexpectedly low ozone readings. These figures had originally been suppressed because the computer analysing the data was programmed to 'assume that deviations so extreme must be errors' (see Gleick, 1986; also Moore and McCabe, 1993: 15).

A further instance of differing attitudes to outliers as harmful or creative phenomena can be seen in the different ways that the protagonists in the great electron controversy (1910–13), Robert Millikan and Felix Ehrenhaft, approached data (and outliers). Their bitter debate illustrates Douglas's notion of dirt as something whose control underpins the existing order, but whose acceptance can lead to new insights. In Gerald Holton's (1978) account of the controversy, it is the conservative physicist Millikan who maintained the received view of the size of the electron charge by either rejecting data he considered suspect,[11] or substituting summary values which by their very nature would conceal the amount of variation. On the other hand, Ehrenhaft presented his own data and also Millikan's in their entirety, thus opening up the possibility of more radical construals such as those which supported sub-electrons, or even questioned the existence of the electron itself.

The Political Challenge of the Outlier

The third and final theme explores the possible reasons for the data analyst's perception of outliers as generally unwelcome events. Specifically we
argue that outliers seriously challenge the power of the analyst to offer
politically correct and empirically grounded descriptions of data. The
dilemma facing a data analyst when outliers have been detected in a
sample is succinctly captured by Barnett and Lewis:

> Should *such* observations be foreign to the main population they may, by their
> very nature as contaminants, cause difficulties in the attempt to represent the
> population. (1994: 7)

For illustrative purposes, let us ring the changes on our first simple example:
suppose that the ten workers in our small firm are each paid £100 per week
and their boss earns £1,200 per week. Is it now credible to report that the
average weekly wage is £200 – a figure which is twice as much as ten out of
the eleven people earn? In other words, in the face of outliers, traditional
representations of data are compromised.

In further unpacking this theme, we touch first on the history of statistics
within social policy. In Daniel Defoe's book *Robinson Crusoe* (originally
published in 1719), Crusoe recounts his father's observation 'that the
middle station [of life] had the fewest disasters, and was not exposed to so
many vicissitudes as the higher or lower part of mankind' (pp. 2–3). This
bourgeois ideology was given quantitative expression in the mid-nineteenth
century by Adolphe Quetelet, one of the founders of modern statistics,
whose own immediate influence had been the political philosopher Victor
Cousin. In Quetelet's hands, measures of the average or mean value of any
variable were morally preferable as the basis for action and choice to any of
the extremes (see, for example, Hacking, 1990). His notion of *l'homme
moyen* added moral gloss to simple descriptive measures of a sample and
echoed uncannily Defoe's words (see Porter, 1986: 102–3; also Porter,
1985). Although Quetelet's middle-class vision of a world bereft of the
contribution of idiot or genius, beggar or millionaire, was challenged on
technical and political grounds (see Stigler, 1986: 171), his legacy of statistics as the search for representations of the typical or the norm remains to
this day.[12]

Thus, modern statistical practice is concerned with the degree to which
samples are representative of populations, with the result that the descriptions generated are congruent with the bulk of the population in terms of
non-extreme features such as location and spread. The reason for this is
clear: if the statistician were to offer advice or location based on values
assessed as atypical (for example outliers), then this would not be seen to
apply to the majority. And in a bourgeois political system, statisticians
would lose any power to influence events if their advice was obviously
based on, and hence might overly benefit, the minority.

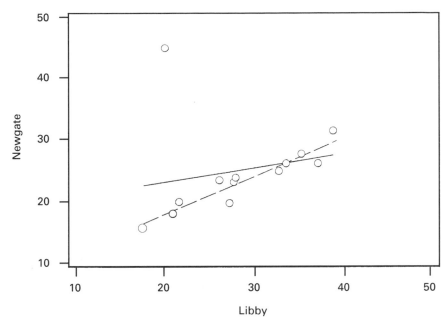

Figure 10.3   *Scatterplot of waterflow at two points on the Kootenay river in January, 1931–43, with least squares regression lines. The solid line was fitted using all the data, the dashed line with the single separated point omitted. (Data from F.R. Hampel et al.,* Robust Statistics, *Copyright © 1986, John Wiley & Sons Inc. Reprinted by permission of the Mordecai and Lucille F. Ezekiel Trust and John Wiley & Sons Inc.)*

The long-term interest in outliers can now be seen in political terms as attempts by data analysts to ward off serious challenges to their power as experts in dealing with (or even transcending) uncertainty.[13] Hence the joint interest in the detection *and* the treatment of extreme values.

The barely concealed political nature of the outlier problem may also be seen in the use of the term 'influence' in regression analysis to describe the contribution that each observed point makes to the fitting of a linear model to data. Ideally, each observation should contribute equally to model fit, again by analogy one of the prerequisites of a bourgeois or democratic political process. However, a small number of outliers may constitute points of high influence, that is, as a tiny minority they exercise *too much* control over the form of the final model, and hence violate this political ideal. Thus detecting and rejecting outliers now becomes part of the political imperative driving the ideologically embedded data analyst into maintaining the ideological status quo. It is no coincidence, we would argue, that the fitting of models to data is usually undertaken explicitly in order to predict and (by extension) control events and actions.

The data displayed in Figure 10.3 are waterflow readings at two points along the Kootenay river measured in January of each year between 1931 and 1943. The fitted least squares regression lines (for predicting the flow at

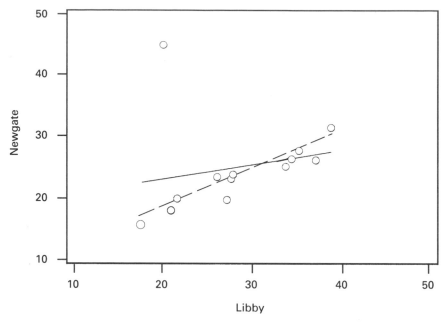

Figure 10.4   *Scatterplot of waterflow at two points on the Kootenay river in January, 1931–43, with fitted regression lines. The solid line was fitted using least squares, the dashed line by a robust method*

Newgate from that at Libby) show the influence of the single disparate value (in the upper left of the plot). When this value is included in the computation, the fitted line (solid) offers a poor representation of the data; its slope is too shallow, its intercept too high and thus it passes close to only a few points. However, when this single value has been removed, the fitted line (dashed) passes centrally through the point cloud. The data analyst would argue that since this single point is exerting too much influence on the model, so it has to disappear.

We argue further that ideological considerations may also have provided the *raison d'être* for the growing use of robust measures and models in data analysis in which outliers are now accommodated by mechanically reducing their influence, rather than being discarded. The grounds on which one chooses between the bewildering number of rules for effectively marginalizing the influence of errant values inevitably reflects differing political and personal construals of the world. However, the advantage of such methods for the data analyst is that they obviate the need to make decisions to exclude any data points, thus avoiding many of the conceptual contradictions and paradoxes in the conventional treatment of outliers discussed earlier.

We return to the Kootenay river data to illustrate the results of employing a robust regression method. The solid line in Figure 10.4 is the least squares regression line using all the data; the dashed line was fitted by the robust method, again using all data points. Notice that the robust fitted line is scarcely distinguishable from the least squares line with outlier removed (shown as a dashed line in Figure 10.3). The non-conforming observation has been equally effectively gagged by the downweighting in the robust procedure.

Cooking, Trimming and Preserving

As we mentioned in an earlier example, the physicist Robert Millikan pursued an informal and incomplete type of robust data analysis by discarding readings which he personally considered 'uncertain'. Such an approach could be criticized for breaking the scientific canon of objectivity since his strategy would have strengthened the coherence between data and theory *by subjective means*. However, a competing policy of systematically trimming a certain proportion of observations from each tail of an ordered sample 'without fear or favour' had been advocated long before Millikan. Although the explicit justification for this practice was that it maximized the chance of removing any outliers from a sample, politically it seems to have been driven by the early critics of a selective, 'experimenter-centred' rejection procedure.[14] We observe, therefore, that a mechanical 'hands-off' discard policy is promoted to ensure the theoretical and rhetorical separation between data analyst and data, thus preserving the necessary distance between scientific truth and its empirical grounding.

Notes

1 For an elementary discussion of the application of a social constructionist approach to the history of British thinking about statistical analysis, see MacKenzie (1981).

2 These data have been used by Weisberg (1985) and others to illustrate various aspects of regression analysis.

3 Residual plots of the type shown in Figure 10.1b embody a number of perceptual devices which are designed to reveal the presence of possible outliers. These include scaling with respect to the fitted line, rotating the line to the horizontal, etc.

4 These are selected points from a dataset used by Weisberg (1985) and others to illustrate certain aspects of regression analysis. The original data were collected by Professor Truett Allison of Yale University.

5 See for example, Barnett and Lewis (1994), Lovie (1986) and Wetherill (1986).

6 For instance, diagnostic measures in regression analysis, such as residuals, are usually 'tested' against informal cut-off values.

7 For example, a class of test statistics commonly used when the assumed initial model is normal has variants in which estimates for measures of location and spread are obtained either from the whole sample or from the observations remaining when the candidate has already been excluded.

8 See Lovie (1986) for an elementary discussion of the problems of detecting single and multiple outliers.

9 Notice the ironicized word 'objective' which implies that Hampel et al. believe that all decisions about discarding are in fact still subjective.

10 We believe it is significant that there are far fewer descriptive terms for non-outliers than for outliers.

11 Following Holton's analysis of an article by Millikan which appeared in 1910 and his notebooks for the years 1911 and 1912, 'suspect' appears to have two distinct meanings. First, it refers to readings which are heavily discrepant with respect to the average value, and secondly, to those which, although not unusual values, were obtained under less than ideal (that is, 'uncertain') experimental conditions.

12 See MacKenzie (1981) for a brief discussion of the slightly delayed influence of Quetelet on leading figures in British statistics, particularly Galton and Edgeworth.

13 By this we mean the statistician's claimed skill in turning the intrinsically probabilistic into the deterministic.

14 See, for example, Barnett and Lewis (1994: 27–31).

References

Barnett, V. and Lewis, T. (1994) *Outliers in Statistical Data*, 3rd edn. Chichester: Wiley.

Bloor, D. (1976) *Knowledge and Social Imagery*. London: Routledge & Kegan Paul.

Daniel, C. and Wood, F.S. (1971) *Fitting Equations to Data*. New York: Wiley.

Defoe, D. (n.d.) *Robinson Crusoe*. London: Nelson.

Douglas, M. (1969) *Purity and Danger: An Analysis of the Concept of Pollution and Taboo*. London: Routledge & Kegan Paul.

Fieller, N. (1993) Comment on 'The identification of multiple outliers' by L. Davies and U. Gather, *Journal of the American Statistical Association*, 88: 794–5.

Gleick, J. (1986) 'Hole in ozone over South Pole worries scientists', *New York Times*, 29 July: C1, C3.

Hacking, I. (1990) *The Taming of Chance*. Cambridge: Cambridge University Press.

Hampel, F.R., Ronchetti, E.M., Rousseeuw, P.J. and Stahel, W.A. (1986) *Robust Statistics*. New York: Wiley.

Holton, G. (1978) *The Scientific Imagination: Case Studies*. Cambridge: Cambridge University Press.

Lovie, P. (1986) 'Identifying outliers', in A.D. Lovie (ed.), *New Developments in Statistics for Psychology and the Social Sciences*. London: BPS and Methuen.

MacKenzie, D.A. (1981) *Statistics in Britain 1865–1930*. Edinburgh: Edinburgh University Press.

Moore, D.S. and McCabe, G.P. (1993) *Introduction to the Practice of Statistics*, 2nd edn. New York: Freeman.

Porter, T.M. (1985) 'The mathematics of society: variation and error in Quetelet's statistics', *British Journal for the History of Science*, 18: 51–69.

Porter, T.M. (1986) *The Rise of Statistical Thinking 1820–1900*. Princeton, NJ: Princeton University Press.

Stigler, S.M. (1986) *The History of Statistics*. Cambridge, MA: Belknap-Harvard University Press.

Velleman, P.F. (1993) *Learning Data Analysis with Data Desk*. New York: Freeman.

Weisberg, S. (1985) *Applied Linear Regression*, 2nd edn. New York: Wiley.

Wetherill, G.B. (1986) *Regression Analysis with Applications*. London: Chapman & Hill.

Woolgar, S. (1988) *Science: The Very Idea*. London: Sage.

11

Procedure, Reflexivity and Social Constructionism

Philip Manning

Those who remain to speak must claim some kind of intellectual authority in speaking; and however valid or invalid their claim to a specialized vocabulary, their speaking presupposes and supports the notion of intellectual authority in general: that through the statements of a lecturer we can be informed about the world. Give some thought to the possibility that this shared presupposition is only that, and that after a speech, the speaker and audience rightfully return to the flickering, cross-purposed, messy irresolution of their unknowable circumstances. (Goffman, 1981: 195)

The more I know about what really happened, the more I wonder if there is a 'what really happened'. (Hacking, 1991: 839)

There is probably no hope of ever containing the burgeoning debate about social constructionism. The label is now used to connote different ideas in different areas of social scientific inquiry, with the result that there is an exciting but nevertheless chaotic proliferation of both conceptual and substantive applications of social constructionist work. For many sociologists, social constructionism has its roots in the Schutzian-inspired phenomenology of Berger and Luckmann's *The Social Construction of Reality* (1966) in which social constructionism is virtually identical to the sociology of knowledge, the task of which is to analyse everything that passes for knowledge in society (1966: 26). This style of work has in some ways been incorporated into Garfinkel's (1984) programme of reflexive, ethnomethodological work, and recently developed by Pollner (1987; 1991) and others. However, there is also a rich heritage of social constructionist work in the literature concerning social problems, where it is used, initially by Malcolm Spector and John Kitsuse (1987 [1961]), to suggest that there are powerful interest groups that define and mould our understanding and vocabulary about a range of social problems. This perspective is clearly evident in research concerning the medicalization of deviance (Conrad and Schneider, 1981). Elsewhere, in the sociology of science, social constructionism has been used to refer to the strategic attempt to show that key scientific developments occurred through a combination of logical, experimental and normative elements. The presence of a normative component to scientific work suggests that scientific or technological discoveries 'could have been otherwise' (Fuller, 1994) without loss of logical rigour. For example, Trevor Pinch has shown that the development of the bicycle was not simply a problem of aerodynamics, but was also a normative problem concerning (often gendered) expectations about acceptable public displays by bicyclists.

Kenneth Gergen has defined social constructionism as the explication of the 'processes by which people come to describe, explain, or otherwise account for the world (including themselves) in which they live' (1985: 266). This definition encourages a hermeneutic view of social construction-ism as the way in which a person's understanding and interpretation of an activity is constitutive of the activity itself. From this perspective, to under-stand an activity is to recover the ways in which practitioners make sense of that activity. When viewed in this way, social constructionism can be seen as a warrant for various strands of interpretive sociology.

However, this social constructionist argument is not limited to the subject matter of sociology but can also be applied to sociology itself. This radical gesture introduces a reflexive component that is not evident in the defi-nition of social constructionism offered by Gergen. It threatens to relativize the findings of sociology by suggesting that they are not discoveries but instead merely ways of looking at the social world. John Shotter, for example, recently discussed the tension between realism and construction-ism in Harré's work, noting that social constructionism suggests that since no independent reality exists and social reality can only be understood from 'within', there cannot be any independent standards to which to appeal and hence sociology risks sliding into 'relativistic nihilism'. Similarly, Bruno Latour has noted that reflexive sociologists of science find themselves caught in self-contradictory positions, 'from which they cannot escape except by indefinite navel-gazing, dangerous solipsism, insanity and prob-ably death' (1988: 155). So the apparently simple sociological claim that what people think about what they do is a significant part of that activity, turns out to have important and potentially damaging reflexive implications for sociology itself.

For some versions of social constructionism, the key question concerns the extent to which the social world is able to serve as an adjudicator for competing empirical claims. The American sociologist Joel Best (1993) perhaps states this claim most persistently. It is clear from his work that he has become frustrated with sceptical, sometimes deconstructive, versions of social constructionism. For example, he ended one of his papers by asking: 'Isn't it time for constructionists to worry a little less about how we know what we know, and worry a little more about what, if anything, we do know about the construction of social problems?' (1993: 124). There is a degree of exasperation in this question. As I will argue shortly, Best is reiterating a theme of Goffman's (who was one of Best's former profes-sors). At one end of the continuum of opinion is an idealist position which suggests that social scientific research is not a representation of the social world, and at the other is the view that social theories are proven or disproven by empirical test. Somewhere midway lies the Quinean view (and also that of the neo-Kantians), that since all theories are 'undetermined' by the facts there is always the possibility that several theories are equally acceptable, equally plausible, representations of actual states of affairs. This block to cumulative social science accounts for its 'eternal youth', according to Max Weber.

However, for other social constructionists, perhaps most notably Steve Woolgar (1988), the key question concerns the substantive and methodological possibilities of a thoroughgoing reflexive, self-conscious programme of sociological research. What might a 'postmodern' sociology (Rosenau, 1992) that constantly interrogated its own knowledge claims look like? Under what conditions might it be successful? What might success look like?

I want to suggest that there are two versions of social constructionism, the first procedural, the second reflexive. The procedural version emphasizes that the ways in which we interpret activities are an important part of those activities; the reflexive version emphasizes that this is an all-embracing argument and hence can be applied to sociology and social constructionism themselves. For advocates of procedural social constructionism, such as Gergen, reflexivity deflects attention from the processes whereby people make sense of the social world. For advocates of reflexive social constructionism, reflexivity is a revelation about the limits and validity of sociological claims.

The project of procedural social constructionists is to explicate the signs, meanings and procedures by which we make sense of the social world, thereby revealing the intricate and subtle aspects of everyday interaction. Michael Lynch describes this process evocatively as a 'molecular sociology' (1993: Ch. 6), and he suggests that conversation analysis (CA) is an exemplary sub-disciplinary version of this practice. As initially envisaged by Harvey Sacks in the 1960s, conversation analysis employs a 'primitive science' based on observation, description and replication (Lynch, 1993: 208). By using electronic recording material and a formal transcriptional scheme, the findings of conversation analysis can be publicly scrutinized. The basic unit of social analysis is no longer an idealized or ideal-typical 'social actor', who is in some way a microsociological element of a macrosociological order. Instead,

> CA's molecular sociology begins with a conception of social order in which different combinations of heterogeneous techniques produce an endless variety of complex structures. . . . The basic unit of analysis is . . . a plurality of socially structured techniques through which orderly activities are assembled. The research agenda is to unpack these molecular sequences. (1993: 259)

The unpacking of these sequences turns out to be a normal scientific enterprise (in Kuhn's sense) with the result that conversation analysis becomes a technical and professional enterprise. Conversation analysts and ethnomethodologists, following implicitly or explicitly the Wittgenstein of the *Philosophical Investigations*, have produced molecular analyses of the ways in which the *in situ* production of social order generates our sense of living in a regulated and understandable world (Garfinkel, 1984; Maynard and Clayman, 1991). Studying this production involves a procedural social constructionism which generates detailed descriptions of naturally occurring interaction. The hope is that descriptions such as these produce sociological discoveries about the endogenous order exhibited in mundane interaction. These discoveries identify the sense-making devices through which the social world is routinely and unproblematically made understandable. Devices of this kind reveal the ways in which a hopelessly indexical world is 'remedied' and made intersubjectively understandable to participants.

Of course, procedural social constructionism is not limited to conversation analysis. Any attempt to understand the procedures by which people construct and maintain a sense of the social world is likely to raise these issues. For example, Martha Minow reveals a tacit procedural social constructionism in her discussion of issues underlying legal reasoning:

> I believe we make a mistake when we assume that the categories we use for analysis just exist and simply sort our experiences, perceptions, and problems through them. When we identify one thing as like the others, we are not merely classifying the world; we are investing particular classifications with consequences and positioning ourselves in relation to those meanings. When we identify one thing as unlike the others, we are dividing the world; we use our language to exclude, to distinguish – to discriminate. (1990: 3)

Minow develops her argument by discussing a paper by Harold Herzog about the curious moral status of mice in laboratory experiments, in an attempt to persuade us that mice exist for us only in the context of various categories. Our description of these mice is constitutive of their status and will also determine their life chances. A mouse officially engaged in an experiment has statutory rights, and its welfare is monitored by a division of the Department of Agriculture. However, should the mouse escape, either by accident or ingenuity, it is transformed into a 'pest' with no civil rights. Should it fall from the laboratory bench to the floor, it also loses all rights instantly. Finally, should the laboratory have a supply of snakes, then the mouse can at any time become transformed from a sentient being with moral and legal rights into something else's lunch (Herzog, 1988; Minow, 1990: 4–5).

The social world, even the precarious social world of laboratory mice, is 'saturated' in meaning, to use Gergen's (1991) apt expression. We live in, and in a sense we are, a compilation of semiotic systems that channel, exchange and constantly produce negotiated and negotiable meanings. As Goffman (1971) puts it, we are 'sign vehicles'. This can be shown by considering Heritage's (1984) analysis of the apparently simple comment: 'Why don't you come and see me sometime?' This can be heard in different ways: it can be taken as a complaint, a request, an invitation, a question and so on. If the speaker emphasizes the word 'you', as in 'Why don't *you* come and see me sometime?' then the utterance can be heard to be distinguishing the recipient from somebody else who may or may not have already responded to this query. The person responding to the utterance is then put in a delicate position, because any reply will be heard as an interpretation of this statement, and as such it commits the respondent to one (and possibly an unintended) version of it. To miss these subtle differences is to miss the constitutive elements of the interaction. It is extremely difficult to produce even an approximate description of this process, and even this limited claim does not do justice to the indeterminate character of many of these signs and meanings. Nor can they be eliminated from analysis on the grounds that they are merely incidental features of the social setting. Rather, the finely grained details of everyday interaction are constitutive of the interaction itself. Procedural social constructionism concerns itself with these important problems.

Goffman's work offers a sustained and compelling account of these intricate procedures as they unfold in face-to-face interaction. Although Goffman understood the reflexive possibilities available to sociologists, and although he could on occasion use them brilliantly, as in the preface to *Frame Analysis*, he typically avoided reflexivity for fear of reducing his analysis to the question of reflexivity itself:

> Methodological self-consciousness that is full, immediate, and persistent sets aside all study and analysis except that of the reflexive problem itself, thereby displacing fields of inquiry instead of contributing to them. (Goffman, 1974: 12)

By contrast, reflexive social constructionists, such as Woolgar (1988), view their non-reflexive colleagues as unwitting writers of realist fiction. They propose instead to be self-consciously literary so as to be able to use the range of narrative devices available to novelists. Critics of reflexive social constructionism point out that this way of doing sociology 'leads nowhere' and supporters reply that getting nowhere can itself be an accomplishment.

The question of the relationship between social constructionism and reflexivity can be understood as a question about how 'fuzzy' sociology ought to be. Reflexive social constructionists are willing, even enthusiastic, to reorder our general knowledge of the social world by blurring the differences between explanation, description, discovery, invention, fact, artefact, theory and evidence. The result is a version of sociology that must appeal to 'community standards' (which Rorty, 1991 thinks of as an appeal to ethnocentrism) to justify their 'findings'. Procedural social constructionists are happy to blur the difference between explanation and description, but they balk at the suggestion that they are inventing the social world rather than discovering its mechanisms or procedures.

Despite his own protestations, some of Goffman's critics have pointed out that his work can nevertheless be read reflexively, a reading that transforms his findings from discoveries about the social world to inventions or reinventions of it, created by the imposition of a vocabulary on to their subject matter. Reflexive readings suggest that the examples Goffman gives tell us about the usefulness of a schema rather than about an element of the social world. The literary critic, Fredric Jameson, stated this position in a review of *Frame Analysis*:

> it is hard to escape the impression that logical priorities have been reversed . . . and . . . the various examples and illustrations [are] useful merely to show how wide [is] the range of applicability of [his analysis]; and, as in a dictionary or grammar book, to furnish a range of different but acceptable syntactical exercises for the beginner to practice on. But this means that *Frame Analysis* is only apparently about social life; in reality, it is self-referential. (1976: 128)

Jameson is neither the first nor the last to discuss this problem in Goffman's work. Aaron Cicourel had earlier suggested that all of Goffman's work is 'prematurely coded' (1974: 24), that it is a set of schemata that demonstrates its range of application. Clearly this argument runs counter to the prevailing view that Goffman was a master of naturalistic observation and a successor to Simmel (see Smith, 1994 for an insightful investigation of the relationship between Goffman and Simmel).

Similarly, Anderson and Sharrock (1982) have suggested that Goffman's interpretations of face-to-face interaction produce the 'solution before the puzzle', since they precede any serious engagement with empirical data. They claim that Goffman's work begins with the result that it is meant to discover and then develops in what Watson (1992) calls a 'pattern-elaborative' manner, which means that it exploits the reader's willingness to become a 'pattern detector' who can extend the analysis into new settings. This suggestion is very similar to Jameson's observation that *Frame Analysis* contains 'syntactical exercises for the beginner to practice on'.

Schegloff has argued that it is a mistake to think of Goffman's work as 'densely empirical', a mistake that is commonly made because of Goffman's mastery of the 'darting observation' that generates an evocative 'sociology by epitome' (Schegloff, 1988: 101). Schegloff is also critical of Goffman's occasional comments about the inevitability of reflexive social constructionism, especially when they are used to challenge the empirical claims of conversation analysis. Schegloff's position is that Goffman avoids the pressing task of analysing naturally occurring interaction and offers us instead only fabricated and hence 'convenient' imagined examples of social interaction.

What is at stake here is more than a preferred way of working. Schegloff is suggesting that the data – the audiotape, videotape or transcript – when examined closely will contain a record of the molecular techniques out of which the social world is constituted. By contrast, Goffman suggests that these empirical records will not be sufficient indicators of these techniques, and that the analyst or reader has to draw upon tacit social knowledge to impose order on the materials. If this is the case, then procedural social constructionism has, so to speak, been infected by reflexive social constructionism.

Those researchers, who by my definition are procedural social constructionists, endeavour to uncover the complicated web of meanings which is activated in everyday interaction through 'indexical expressions', whose purpose is to express a complicated sentiment in a flexible way. They argue that to understand the social world is to understand the process of remedying indexicals. Michael Lynch (1991) explained this point by recalling an explanation given by Harvey Sacks of the description of someone as a 'fast driver'. Lynch recounts Sacks's argument that:

> 'You like to drive cars fast' can be preferred over any numerical account of miles per hour read off a speedometer. The standard against which 'fast' is measured is 'the traffic', where 'traffic' is produced *in situ* by drivers who drive so as to be 'with' the traffic; drivers who, in effect, constitute the very traffic they are 'with'. The expression 'fast' translates into no single numerical formulation, since the measurement device – 'fast/slow'/'with traffic' – is flexibly used in reference to the vicissitudes of traffic, local speed limits, and police surveillance. (1991: 92–3)

So, the apparently simple lay description of someone as a 'fast driver' turns out to be an extremely intricate assessment of an approach to driving that covers not simply speed, as one might suppose, but instead describes speed relative to the range of contingencies that drivers may encounter.

However, procedural social constructionists are themselves divided by the question of reflexivity, since considering its role in their own analysis directs attention away from the detailed description of social life. Sometimes questions about reflexivity have been suppressed. It is ironic that this charge has been levelled against conversation analysts and ethnomethodologists, who were very interested in this phenomenon in the pre-postmodern 1960s, when reflexivity was not a fashionable issue. However, in recent times, ethnomethodologists have, as shown by Pollner (1991), emphasized 'endogenous reflexivity' over 'referential reflexivity'. The former refers to 'how what members do in, to, and about social reality constitutes social reality'; the latter 'conceives of all analysis – ethnomethodology included – as a constitutive process' (1991: 372). In order to focus their efforts on the fine-grained description of everyday interaction, ethnomethodologists accentuate the importance of endogenous reflexivity and suppress referential reflexivity. This is because referential reflexivity runs the risk of turning the analysis in upon itself, at the expense of detailed, naturalistic observation. This debate is very familiar to contemporary sociologists of science (see Pickering, 1992; Woolgar, 1988). The question of whether the risks of referential reflexivity outweigh the gains remains unanswered. Gergen (1985) acknowledges that social constructionism is not immune from reflexive criticisms and hence it cannot offer 'truth through method'; nevertheless he holds on to the idea that a variety of research methods can still produce 'compelling' arguments (1985: 272–3). Reflexivity certainly has the role of unsettling inquiries whenever they begin to claim an objectivity or importance that is beyond the competence of any sociological theory; but whether referential reflexivity has a greater role remains to be seen.

In this chapter I have suggested that the social constructionist perspective can be understood in either procedural or reflexive terms. Each of these options introduces a degree of fuzziness into analysis. Procedural social constructionists acknowledge that the social world is saturated in meanings that are constitutive of the social world itself. The task of the social sciences is therefore, in part, an interpretive one. To use the evocative phrase employed by Lynch, procedural social constructionists are practising a 'molecular sociology', the task of which is to identify the interactional devices whereby everyday social interaction is contingently achieved. This project, as Lynch has shown, is clearest in the expansion and professionalization of conversation analysis, which was once an esoteric, extraordinary set of studies initiated by Harvey Sacks and is now an established, cumulative, 'normal' science, in Kuhn's sense. By contrast, reflexive social constructionists are critical of all attempts to establish normal science. Instead they endeavour to preserve the social sciences as permanent revolutionary sciences that are inherently unstable. Reflexive social constructionists are happy to live with extensive and irremediable fuzziness; they willingly blur the distinctions between description, explanation, discovery, invention, theory and evidence. Fuzzy, reflexive, social constructionists generate vocabularies which reorder our knowledge of the social world. They acknowledge the limitations of social theory and try to reconcile themselves to their new status, not as molecular biologists, physicists or zoologists but as literary critics with empirical ambitions.

Note

This chapter is an expanded version of my earlier paper, 'Fuzzy description: discovery and invention in sociology', *History of the Human Sciences*, 7(1): 117–23. A version of this paper was presented at the conference, Constructing the Social, at the University of Durham, 7–8 April 1994. I benefited from the comments of Irving Velody, Robin Williams, David Chaney, Michael Lynch and Steve Woolgar. I have also learned a lot from discussions with Joel Best, who organized an interesting panel discussion about social constructionism at the SSSI meetings in Los Angeles, August 1994.

References

Anderson, R. and Sharrock, W. (1982) 'Sociological work: some procedures sociologists use for organizing phenomena', *Social Analysis*, 11 (November).
Berger, P. and Luckmann, T. (1966) *The Social Construction of Reality*. Harmondsworth: Penguin.
Best, J. (1993) 'But seriously folks! The limitations of the strict constructionist interpretation of social problems', in G. Miller and J. Holstein (eds), *Constructionist Controversies: Issues in Social Problems Theory*. New York: Aldine Press.
Cicourel, A. (1974) *Cognitive Sociology*. New York: Free Press.
Conrad, P. and Schneider, J. (1992) *Deviance and Medicalization*. Philadelphia: Temple University Press.
Fuller, S. (1994) 'The reflexive politics of constructivism', *History of the Human Sciences*, 7(1): 87–84.
Garfinkel, H. (1984) *Studies in Ethnomethodology*. Cambridge: Polity Press.

Gergen, K. (1985) 'The Social constructionist movement in modern psychology', *American Psychologist*, 40: 266–75.

Gergen, K. (1991) *The Saturated Self: Dilemmas of Identity in Contemporary Life*. New York: Basic Books.

Goffman, E. (1971) *Relations in Public*. Harmondsworth: Penguin.

Goffman, E. (1974) *Frame Analysis: An Essay in the Organization of Experience*. New York: Harper & Row.

Goffman, E. (1981) *Forms of Talk*. Oxford: Basil Blackwell.

Hacking, I. (1991) 'Two souls in one body', *Critical Inquiry*.

Heritage, J. (1984) *Garfinkel and Ethnomethodology*. Cambridge: Polity Press.

Herzog, H. (1988) 'The moral status of mice', *American Psychologist*, 43 (June).

Jameson, F. (1976) 'Review of fame analysis', *Theory & Society*, 13: 119–33.

Latour, B. (1988) 'The politics of explanation: an alternative', in S. Woolgar (ed.) *Knowledge and Reflexivity: New Frontiers in the Sociology of Knowledge*. Newbury Park, CA: Sage.

Lynch, M. (1991) 'Method: measurement – ordinary and scientific measurement as ethno-methodological phenomena', in G. Button (ed.), *Ethnomethodology and the Human Sciences*. Cambridge: Cambridge University Press.

Lynch, M. (1993) *Scientific Practice and Ordinary Action*. Cambridge: Cambridge University Press.

Maynard, D. and Clayman, S. (1991) 'The diversity of ethnomethodology', *Annual Review of Sociology*, 17: 385–418.

Minow, M. (1990) *Making All the Difference: Inclusion, Exclusion, and American Law*. Ithaca, NY: Cornell University Press.

Pickering, A. (ed.) (1992) *Science as Practice and Culture*. Chicago: University of Chicago Press.

Pollner, M. (1987) *Mundane Reason*. Cambridge: Cambridge University Press.

Pollner, M. (1991) 'Left of ethnomethodology: the rise and decline of radical reflexivity', *American Sociological Review*, 56: 370–80.

Rorty, R. (1991) *Philosophical Papers, Volume 1*. Cambridge: Cambridge University Press.

Rosenau, P. (1992) *Post-Modernism and the Social Sciences*. Princeton, NJ: Princeton University Press.

Schegloff, E. (1988) 'Goffman and the analysis of conversation', in P. Drew and A. Wootton (eds), *Erving Goffman: Exploring the Interaction Order*. Cambridge: Polity Press.

Smith, G. (1994) 'Snapshots "sub specie aeternitatis": Simmel, Goffman and formal sociology', in D. Frisby (ed.), *Georg Simmel: Critical Assessments*, Vol. 3. London and New York: Routledge.

Spector, M. and Kitsuse, J. (1987 [1961]) *Constructing Social Problems*. New York: Aldine Press.

Watson, R. (1992) 'The understanding of language use in everyday life: is there a common ground?', in G. Watson and R. Seiler (eds), *Text in Context*. Newbury Park, CA: Sage.

Woolgar, S. (ed.) (1988) *Knowledge and Reflexivity: New Frontiers in the Sociology of Knowledge*. Newbury Park, CA: Sage.

12

Social Constructionism as a Political Strategy

Tom Shakespeare

This chapter develops a schematic historical and political analysis of the rhetorical usages of social constructionism within specific social movement contexts. It is therefore an attempt to illuminate the essentialism/social constructionism debate, rather than to explore the social theoretical issues around constructivism itself. It is concerned with the power of such arguments to mobilize public support, and as instrumental interventions in the political process.

It is my suggestion that this very power consists in the ability of such discourse to represent social reality in a way which individuals see as corresponding to personal experience, in the first instance, and to open up the space for dynamic social change, in the second. Social constructionism is a rhetorical strategy. Judgements are made by social actors in terms of their understanding of biographical experiences, the prospective political utility of the analysis offered, and the context in which they find themselves. Further, arguments appeal to two relevant constituencies: first, an indigenous community of interest, which I will explore further below, and second, the wider public including, critically, that section of the population with access to governmental power, notably legislators and other members of the ruling class.

My discussion will centre on three critical arenas of politics in the late twentieth century: the women's movement; the gay and lesbian liberation movement; and the disability movement. The absent term in this argument is the issue of 'race', which is excluded not because it is irrelevant, but because I am already making claims at the further reaches of my competence, and do not wish to do injustice to the debates around 'race' of which I know even less. As it is, I have spread my discussion wide, and will therefore be dealing with broad generality and superficial similarity: I hope readers will accept the benefits of a synthetic and heuristic approach, and forgive the limitations.

The three areas under discussion have clear parallels (as has the absent term). In each, issues of politics intermesh closely with issues of theory. As different forms of identity politics, each has an appeal to a specific constituency, and has involved campaigns for progressive social change. That

identity
*
progressive
social change

is to say, constituencies have been characterized as oppressed or marginalized within society, and restoration of full civil, social and economic rights has been a central strand of these arguments. Academic and theoretical investigation of these areas has therefore been closely linked, in the first instance, with political goals. The Marxian concept of praxis is clearly relevant.

These arenas have often been subsumed in the wider sociological discussion of new social movements, a distinction being drawn with previous politics based on class, nation and other cleavages. As politics, however, these arenas are distinct from other new social movements around issues of post-materialism, ecology, peace and so forth, because these arenas appeal to a personal interest based on identity. As I have argued elsewhere (Shakespeare, 1993), an indigenous political activism, together with an indigenous theoretical voice, has been central to this new politics. The identity focus, based on construction of a shared constituency around a common analysis of social experience, and consequently on mobilization of that constituency around injustice, is central to my present concerns: so also is the struggle over meaning and self-definition which lies at the heart of this process.

A necessary preliminary consists in pointing out that by social constructionism I am not referring to the phenomenological or post-structuralist perspective associated with sociology of knowledge approaches to reality ('strong' social constructionism), as much as to that approach which seeks to distinguish the causal role of social factors, as opposed to biological or 'natural' factors. The chapter is not concerned with the debates over the construction of categories or concepts, vital though these are, but with constructionist versus essentialist explanations of minority group experience. By saying that gender, for example, is socially constructed, I am following feminists who account for gender in terms of social relations and material processes (for example resource distribution or violence), rather than seeing it purely as a matter of social attitudes or definition. This is a more extensive distinction than the one drawn by Conrad and Schneider (1992: 21). I believe these two varieties of social constructionism have often been conflated. By separating and specifying my usage, I avoid the necessity of inventing a new term, such as Oliver's social creationism (Oliver, 1990: 82). However, I do not wish to imply a correspondence theory of truth, or a simplistic positivism. External reality and personal embodiment are clearly not accessible except via contingent language and concepts, and the crude dichotomy between biology and society which I rely on throughout this chapter should not be taken as a denial that the natural is already and always social. Therefore in maintaining the importance of lived experience, I am also engaging in the balancing act which Donna Haraway describes:

> how to have simultaneously an account of radical historical contingency for all knowledge claims and knowing subjects . . . and a non-nonsense commitment to faithful accounts of a 'real world'. (1988: 579)

Traditional Explanations

First, I will briefly explore the ways in which traditional discourses of
gender, sexuality and disability are characterized by reactionary formulations based on a notion of difference which usually can be reduced to
biological determinism. That is, there is a dominant history of the sub-
altern positions of women, gay and lesbian people and disabled people
being explained with reference to biological incapacity. Kate Millett has
written: 'Patriarchy has a tenacious or powerful hold through its successful
habit of passing itself off as nature' (1971: 58). Women and disabled
people form the strongest examples of this tendency, because these categories are more easily distinguishable in a historical context. While
accepting the importance of a deconstructive approach (Riley, 1988), it is
clear that for women and disabled people being named bodily as other is a
significant experience which does not generally allow for the possibility of
passing as normal.

    In the West, the dominant attitude to women has been in terms of 'the
weaker sex'. Women's abilities have been underplayed: women's physicality has been constructed as weak and flawed; women's intellectual capacities have been denigrated. This physical and intellectual deficiency has
also been often joined to psychological instability and moral deficiency.
Due to feminist work, there is now a considerable documentation of this
history, covering both literary and philosophical misogyny, and popular and
political opinion. It is important to point out that this reactionary construction of a female difference based on nature has persisted in the work of
contemporary sociobiologists (Sayer, 1982).

    While the use of biological determinist arguments to justify social sub-
ordination has been exposed and criticized in terms of gender, only recently
has comparable analysis been applied to the experience of disability. That
is, while it is now commonly (although not universally) accepted that
women are not substantively inferior to men, the notion of disabled people's incapacity is deeply rooted. The notion of 'natural difference', so
strong in the case of women, is even more incontrovertible evidence of
disabled people's inadequacy. Hence the stress on medical management of
disability; on the search for a cure for common impairments; on therapeutic
intervention and rehabilitation (Oliver, 1990).

    However, since the 1970s, a new view of disability has developed in
association with a vigorous political movement of disabled people (Davis,
1993). This *social model* reconceptualizes disability as a relationship
between people with impairment, and a society which discriminates on
that basis. The distinction between impairment and disability corresponds
to the feminist distinction between sex and gender (Oakley, 1972), and
enables us to situate disability in specific historical, cultural and social
contexts. Disability, that is, is about social arrangements; employment and
welfare patterns; architectural barriers; cultural representation and terminology. This new political approach, and the intellectual developments

associated with it, have exposed traditional models of disability as forms of biological determinism.

Since the identification of the modern homosexual as a category during the nineteenth century, this social experience has been characterized as that of a pathological species (Foucault, 1989; MacIntosh, 1968). The focus of social relations shifted from merely seeing homosexual behaviour as immoral (alongside various forms of heterosexual behaviour), to seeing homosexual people as physically and psychologically degenerate. The moral disapprobation continued, focused on a type rather than just a series of sexual acts, but it was allied to a medical discourse of sickness and inferiority, and often ludicrous attempts at cure. Whether viewed as evil, or sick, or eventually as inferior but acceptable, homosexuality was seen as an essential and innate element, whether physiological or psychological.

The Social Constructionist Strategy

In each of the cases under discussion, some form of essentialist argument has traditionally been used to underpin social subordination. That is, social discrimination and prejudice have been based on an appeal to natural attributes. It would be wrong to characterize these historical treatments as homologous. However, there is a fundamental continuity in these biological determinist positions which justifies the parallels I am drawing here.

The political tactics of what I will call liberationists can also be perceived to be analogous. But there are some subtle differences, and considerable internal debates, which render the situation more complicated. In general, however, progressive political interventions have been based on social constructionist arguments. The clear benefit of taking a social construction-ist approach is that it allows for social change: if an experience is not natural, then it is dynamic and open to social interventions based on progressive values.

However, there have also been more essentialist versions of progressive politics, which have sought to revalorize difference. I will attempt to sum-marize some of the issues, before going on to focus on the rhetorical implications of these different political and intellectual strategies, and conclude with a discussion of what I will call adequate materialism. There are as many differences as similarities between the experiences I am analys-ing. For example, sexual identity is capable of being concealed, whereas gender and many forms of impairment are immediately visible. Moreover, various identities may have different degrees of salience, and plural iden-tities may have different resonances entirely.

Gender

The analysis developed above is a generally accepted version of traditional approaches to gender. Much feminist scholarship has been devoted to the misogyny at the heart of mainstream (or malestream) intellectual activity, and to deconstructing notions of commonsense femininity. Important to this process was the work of Ann Oakley, who showed the distinction between sex and gender – the one biological, the other social – and indicated the cultural variation in the experience of gender roles (Oakley, 1972). The difficulty presented by difference has been the subject of continuing debate within feminism, with strategic political consequences. Cynthia Cockburn, whose recent work compares the experience of women, lesbians and gay men, and disabled people within the context of organization strategies for equal opportunities, quotes Ann Phillips:

> Once feminists admit the mildest degree of sexual difference, they open up a gap through which the currents of reaction will flow. Once let slip that pre-menstrual tension interfered with concentration, that pregnancy can be exhausting, that motherhood is absorbing, and you are off down the slope to separate spheres. (Cockburn, 1991: 161)

Subsequent work has focused on two areas, both suggesting that the debates are much more complicated than I have indicated. Political discussion has tended to characterize the distinction as one between difference and equality strategies (Bock and James, 1992). The latter, sometimes called emancipationism, argues for social equality of men and women on the basis of equivalence: that any biological or psychological differences are minimal and do not justify subordination. This position, central to early second wave feminism, gave way to a more nuanced version based on difference: that men and women were indeed different, but that this did not justify differential treatment. Variations of this position have been the arguments that the problem has stemmed from differential valuation of men and women's differences, or that women are different and in fact better, and that society should reflect feminine qualities rather than masculine faults.

This political debate runs into the theoretical arguments between essentialism and social constructionism, and to an extent the two debates are overlapping. Proponents of the former position have been accused of biologism, while the latter have failed adequately to account for the differences which seem to lie at the heart of gender experience. Particular nuances of these two debates, which are neither as separate as I have suggested (Fuss, 1989), nor as neatly confined to politics or to theory, have taken different cultural tones, dependent on whether they are based in Britain, America or France. Within each country there has also been considerable disagreement – for example, the clash between Christine Delphy and Annie Leclerc in France (Delphy, 1984).

Disability

The social constructionist approach to disability, coupled with the indigenous development of the disability movement, has revolutionized the status of disabled people in the last decade. While the arguments for better treatment were not new – there has been a tradition of reformist approaches to disability – the idea that disability was a product of social relations was a critical mobilizing factor.

> The 'big idea' which set the work in context was the social model of disability. It said something which on the surface sounds like the 'attitudes' idea so popular in IYDP [International Year of Disabled People] – that the problems disabled people face stem not from their physical or mental limitations, but from the inappropriate social responses to them. But the social model does not just challenge attitudes; it challenges the very assumption of 'normality'. It suggests that the problems disabled people face constitute a specific oppression, rooted in the systematic exclusion of disabled people from everyday life. (Hasler, 1993: 280)

In terms of developing an identity politics of disability, the concept that the problem of disability was the disabling society rather than the individual pathological body was crucial. Relocating the problem enabled disabled people to develop a positive self-identity based on shared resistance, anger and pride, instead of a negative self-identity based on self-pity and dependency.

In order to make the social constructionist argument effective, it was advanced in its most absolute form, particularly within political interventions. The role of impairment in the social experience of disability was denied, just as the role of difference in feminism had initially been underplayed. Disability was constructed exclusively on the basis of social relations, and it was suggested that reforming society would abolish disability. For example, according to Finkelstein, 'Once social barriers to the reintegration of people with physical impairments are removed, the disability itself is eliminated' (1980: 33). A similar claim is made in his famous article, 'To deny or not to deny disability' (1981), in which he postulates a fully accessible environment, in which wheelchair users are not disabled, but able-bodied people have become so (see French, 1993 for a discussion of this suggestion). Sally French has described this rhetorical strategy:

> It is no doubt the case that activists who have worked tirelessly within the disability movement for many years have found it necessary to present disability in a straightforward, uncomplicated manner in order to convince a very sceptical world that disability can be reduced or eliminated by changing society, rather than attempting to change disabled people themselves. . . . Any talk of difference, therefore, might threaten to weaken this united front. (French, 1993: 24)

The only attempt to deal with impairment within the disability studies perspective came from Paul Abberley, who argued:

> While in the case of sexual and racial oppression, biological difference serves only as a qualificatory condition of a wholly ideological oppression, for disabled people the biological difference, albeit as I shall argue itself is a consequence of social practices, is part of the oppression. It is crucial that a theory of disability as oppression comes to grips with this 'real' inferiority, since it forms a bedrock upon which justificatory oppressive theories are based and, psychologically, an immense impediment to the development of political consciousness amongst disabled people. (Abberley, 1987: 8)

I cannot support Abberley's denial of the importance of difference in the context of gender, and I find his attempt to solve the problem of impairment, by showing the massive element of social causation in the aetiology of impairment, to be ultimately unconvincing. However, the problem he poses is a significant one, and not just for disability activists.

More recently, and largely in the work of feminist disability theorists such as French, Morris and Crow, a more nuanced position has developed based on the recognition of impairment, and the incorporation of physical difference. Liz Crow summarizes this development:

> As individuals, most of us simply cannot pretend with any conviction that our impairments are irrelevant because they influence every aspect of our lives. We must find a way to integrate them into our whole experience and identity for the sake of our physical and emotional well-being, and, subsequently, for our capacity to work against Disability. (1992: 7)

This argument, paralleling earlier developments within feminism itself, enables accounts of disability to include the role of impairment, while not explaining disability by its physical dimension:

> This does not mean that impairment causes Disability, but that it is a 'biological precondition' for that particular oppression. However, impairment can also be triggered or compounded by Disability. (1992: 9)

While the failure of social model approaches to encompass the issue of impairment has certainly been perceived as a problem (Shakespeare, 1992), there is also an inherent contradiction within radical responses to disability which has thus far rarely been considered. Both academic and political developments have conflated two positions which are actually distinct claims. First there is the social model, arguing that disability is a social relationship, not a physical attribute, and focusing practical campaigns on barrier removal. Secondly, there is the social oppression approach, arguing that disabled people are a coherent minority group and demanding an end to discrimination and prejudice. While these positions obviously are inextricably linked, the arguments are different, and contradictory. This tension between celebrating difference, and removing exclusionary barriers and categorization has been discussed by Liggett (1988) and Shakespeare (1996).

Sexuality

Within the theory and politics of sexuality, issues are more complicated still. Distinctions have to be drawn between politics and theory, and between lesbian and gay versions of both, between progressive and reactionary positions, and between social constructionist progressivism, and essentialist progressivism. Moreover, in the last twenty years, both political strategies and theoretical approaches have varied between divergent analytical positions.

Theories of homosexuality, from the late 1960s onwards, have stressed its socially constructed nature. From Mary MacIntosh, the notion of the historical development of the homosexual role has provided the basis for research. The work of Michel Foucault is critical here. British authors such as Jeffrey Weeks and Ken Plummer developed independent and parallel analyses, often predating Foucault's published work. As in the case of disability and gender, there is a similar unity of theory and practice, in that theorists were both indigenous and politically active in the politics of Gay Liberation. Yet this praxis can be very precarious, as the openness and theoretical sophistication of the most radical moments of gay liberation give way to a renewed closure: the politics of Queer, for example, was very short lived.

Often the politics of homosexuality has evidenced a reluctance to be parted from essentialist notions of sexuality. As the gay and lesbian community, and the associated political movement, developed, the idea of a separate and distinct gay or lesbian identity became more attractive and deeply rooted. Diana Fuss has written: 'the notion of a gay essence is relied upon to mobilise and to legitimate gay activism' (1989: 97). As in the feminist movement, a dichotomy between equality and difference, based around choice and essence, becomes evident. Difference is revalorized, in order to develop a sense of distinctiveness and specialness. Nietzsche discussed the way in which adversity and persecution caused identities to strengthen and become more defined: 'A *species* arises, a type becomes fixed and strong, through protracted struggles against essentially constant *unfavourable* conditions' (Nietzsche, 1990: 199), while Foucault suggested: 'One should not be a homosexual, but one who clings passionately to the idea of being gay' (1990: xxiii).

Vance discusses the unhappiness of lesbian and gay communities with the tendency of social constructionist accounts (for example, that of Foucault himself) to deprive them of a continuous homosexual tradition or history (Vance, 1989: 27). This picture is further complicated, because personal accounts by gay men often stress a feeling of having been born different (evident as early as seven or eight years of age), while lesbians are more likely to explain their sexuality as a freely chosen identity and a political commitment to a broader woman-identified politics. In general, however, I think Girlin's comments are relevant:

> For all the talk about the social construction of knowledge, identity politics de facto seems to slide towards the premise that social groups have essential identities. (1990: 153)

Most recently, several theoretical accounts of homosexuality have been developed which explicitly return to biological and essentialist explanations. Rather than relying on freedom of choice arguments, such approaches seek legitimation through abnegation of choice in identity, sometimes using 'justification by birth' strategies in association with 'Creater intention' arguments. Simon LeVay's theory of the 'gay brain' (supposed differences in the hypothalamus between gay and straight men), and the discovery of the 'gay gene', have both purported to explain sexuality by virtue of innate difference (Conrad and Schneider, 1992: 284). This new determinism is not advocated against homosexuality, but in order to defend it. Nevertheless, it runs the risk of supporting the old reactionary positions.

Again, while many in the gay community would resist such arguments, an essentialist assumption is nevertheless evident in recent campaigns for lowering the age of consent, it being suggested that teenagers are not 'vulnerable to temptation', as the Right feared, because homosexual identity is congenital, or at least fixed at an early age. To quote Carole Vance from a different context:

> Within the lesbian and gay community's internal discussions and self-education, the failure to make a distinction between politically expedient ways of framing an argument and more complex descriptions of social relations promoted an increasingly rigid adherence to essentialism as an effective tool against persecution. (1989: 28)

A complex and dynamic political context, in which theorists and activists, lesbians and gays, and reactionaries and progressives are all adopting a variety of positions, often out of political expediency rather than ontological conviction, makes it difficult to arrive at agreement, and of course empirical evidence is highly contested (*pace* LeVay). As with disability, political strategies have varied between promoting sexual liberation for all (for example, in the early 1970s with Gay Liberation, and in the early 1990s with Queer), and promoting the emancipation of lesbian and gay groups.

Rhetorical Strategies

My interest in explanations of sexuality, as of gender and disability, is chiefly in the political resonance of various causal arguments. In general, it seems that biological determinism has been used to justify social inequality on the basis of natural difference. Social constructionism, in opening up the sphere of free will, choice and the potential for progressive social change, has been associated with positive political developments and liberation strategies. Rhetorically, social constructionism is a very powerful correlative to reactionary arguments. Demonstrate that some experience varies between cultures, and it becomes very difficult to justify the perpetuation of negative treatment on the basis of nature.

However, while social constructionism is good at breaking down reactionary attitudes (as emancipationism), it is less effective for developing positive positions. As Calhoun argues, 'Social constructionism was an ambiguous ally in the attempt to oppose the devaluing of various identities' (1994: 16). This is for two main reasons, one of which is shown in the example of disability, another in the example of sexuality, and both in the example of gender.

The problem with the strong constructionist account of disability was that it failed adequately to deal with lived experience. Rhetorically, it is a very potent argument for social change: if society creates disability, society can rectify disability. But where people identify on the basis of impairment, then an account of disability which almost totally ignores impairment ultimately fails to reflect personal experience.

On the one hand, activists began to doubt the validity of the social model; on the other hand, sceptical disabled people refused to identify with the new politics, because it did not adequately cover their physical experiences of pain, limitation and so forth. An implicit threat in this development, which could be called 'The Emperor's New Clothes', was that statutory authorities and others would see the divisions within the disability community, and the flaws in the radical argument, and reduce their commitment to social improvement. Recent media commentaries on the campaign for anti-discrimination legislation have started this backlash against the social model.

If the problem with the social constructionist view of disability was about adequacy and relevance, the issue with the social constructionist account of sexuality was a failure to give space to difference, and to validate a notion of gay and lesbian identity as distinctive, positive and natural. Showing sexuality to be socially constructed, chosen and variable potentially undermines any attempts to build a solid and coherent gay or lesbian cultural identity. An example of the difficulties in this social constructionist strategy is evidenced by the short-lived appeal of Queer politics: based on a radical deconstruction of heterosexuality, and an appeal to fluidity and commonality; it nonetheless failed to appeal to the entrenched lesbian or gay communities and a strong sense of difference and identity. (Other theorists of sexuality have also criticized social constructionism's disembodied nature: Vance, 1989: 23.)

In the case of gender, the problem was therefore twofold: on the one hand, a failure of strong social constructionism to account for the differences women perceived in their physical and psychological experience, and on the other hand, a failure of social constructionist arguments to underpin a strong and radical identity of woman-ness. Thus Birke argues:

> Pure social constructionism of the kind advanced by the Left in the 1960s and 1970s did not appeal to popular 'common sense', a failure which contributed to its demise. Into the breach stepped the appeals to commonsense notions of human nature made by the New Right, appeals which have found a willing audience. (1986: x)

Difference strategies, often employing essentialist arguments, were developed in order to give a more adequate account of women's experience, and to bolster a sense of self-worth and the valuation of feminine qualities and activities. Of course, especially in the latter case, social constructionist feminists (often from Marxist or socialist feminist camps) attacked the essentialist implications of difference feminists (usually radical feminists) for opening up space for all the old reactionary discourses of difference and inferiority to be readmitted.

There are many benefits to be gained from exploring the role of social constructionism as a rhetorical strategy. It enables us to identify the ways in which theoretical arguments can be instrumentally employed to develop progressive politics, either by challenging existing hierarchies, or by promoting positive identities (both imperatives having different implications in terms of rhetorical strategies). It might be argued that both biological determinism and social constructionism can be made to mean whatever their proponents want them to mean, but I suggest that a more empirical examination of recent political history is necessary to indicate the very specific articulations of theoretical positions for strategic effects.

Conclusion

These are deep-seated theoretical and political debates, to which a brief chapter can hardly begin to do justice. The work of Foucault in particular will offer opportunities for exploring these dichotomies and tensions, many of which centre around the role of categorization, and what Riley has called 'the dangerous intimacy between subjectification and subjection' (1988: 17). Hacking's concept of 'making up people' is clearly also relevant (Hacking, 1986). In this sense, this chapter may raise more questions than it answers, but here I have tried to limit my coverage to causal explanation rather than category formation, which I accept may well be putting the cart before the horse. I want to conclude by proposing a political and pragmatic strategy which may be more useful, adequate and effective in promoting liberationist identity politics, while bracketing the need for theoretical developments drawing on post-structuralist approaches, which I have attempted elsewhere (Shakespeare, 1996).

This 'third position' strategy, coming between biological determinism and social constructionism, is hardly new. It picks up on the work of Linda Birke and Janet Sayer in theoretical feminism; of Peter Freund in the sociology of the body; and the empirical account of the effects of menstruation on social experience which have been developed by Shirley Prendegast (1993); as well as the critiques of the social model of disability by Liz Crow, among others.

Earlier I referred to a strategy of 'adequate materialism': now I wish to suggest that the work of the Italian Marxist Sebastiano Timpanaro offers some pointers to the development of such a strategy, which is both progressive and realistic. While avoiding the rhetorical absolutism of some social constructionist arguments, it also avoids the dangers of biological determinism, and hence reactionary counter-arguments. It speaks to personal experiences of impairment, sex and so forth, while exploring the way that social implications of these personal attributes are sociohistorical and hence challengeable. It is, in effect, a compromise, and one which is able to deal with the specific nuances of various experiences, as well as the parallels between them. In one sense, it is so obvious as not to need stating, yet it has not often been advanced as a theoretical or political strategy, so it certainly needs representing.

Timpanaro rejects both biological determinism:

> For too long the ruling classes have attributed to 'nature' (i.e. to a secular version of the 'inscrutable decrees of Divine Providence') the iniquities and sufferings for which the organization of society is responsible. (Timpanaro, 1975: 17)

and also social constructionism:

> To maintain that, since the 'biological' is always presented to us as mediated by the 'social', the 'biological' is nothing and the 'social' is everything, would once again be idealist sophistry. (Timpanaro, 1975: 45)

Timpanaro's approach allows us to develop a materialism which can incorporate the role of nature (external and human), without being determined by it: a position which is of most use in the exploration of the disability experience, but which also has relevance to these wider debates. Freund has continued this materialism, as well as exploring the way that biology and society in practice interact and interpenetrate (Freund, 1988). Birke argues: 'Feminist theory needs to take into account not only the ways in which our biology is interpreted, but also the very real ways in which our biology does in practice affect our lives' (1986: 47).

One of the areas in which a renewed engagement with biological difference has become critical is genetic research, and particularly pre-natal diagnosis and screening. Several points are relevant. First, the massive explosion of human genome research has been associated, especially in the media, with a 'back to basics biology' which is reminiscent of the crude biological determinism of the 1970s. Secondly, technological developments are again occurring in contexts where social relations lead to the marginalization of particular groups. For example, amniocentesis has led to termination of female foetuses in India, and impaired foetuses in China. In the improbable event of the 'gay gene' hypothesis being accepted, it would be unsurprising if screening on the basis of sexuality was not prioritized in some societies. Thirdly, movements which have sought to deny or ignore biological difference risk abandoning the debate to those forces who would seek to employ difference as a criterion for selection. Specifically, the disability movement needs urgently to confront those who argue against the viability of impaired life forms, and it can only do this by engaging with the issue of impairment. As Morris (1991) has argued, none of this is to undermine the principle of a woman's right to choose. The argument is not about individual decision (which must be respected), but about societal judgements of quality of life and a medical profession which prioritizes eugenics.

This example indicates the importance of an approach which can reconcile biological difference with social constructionist analysis. This adequate materialism is devoid of great rhetorical flourishes, and it also avoids the epistemological fireworks of alternative ways of resolving the contradictions of essentialism and social constructionism: Diana Fuss, for example, uses feminist post-structuralist arguments to show that this dichotomy is less pronounced than it seems, and to demonstrate the interreliance of the two positions. However, unlike this and other approaches based on post-structuralism or postmodernism, an adequate materialist approach maintains a grounding in everyday life and social experience, and is an accessible social theory, as well as a useful political strategy. Rhetoric which is simplistic is ultimately ineffective. As Einstein said, 'Make everything as simple as possible. But not simpler.' In this chapter, which has explored the connections between radical theory and radical practice, I hope the importance of arguments which are immediate and engaged has become self-evident.

Note

Thanks to Lynda Birke, Hilary Rose, and especially Mark Erickson, for their constructive criticisms of this chapter. Any errors which remain are my own.

References

Abberley, P. (1987) 'The concept of oppression and the development of a social theory of disability', *Disability, Handicap & Society*, 2(1): 5–21.

Birke, L. (1986) *Women, Feminism and Biology*. Brighton: Harvester Wheatsheaf.

Bock, G. and James, S. (1992) *Beyond Equality and Difference*. London: Routledge.

Calhoun, C. (ed.) (1994) *Social Theory and the Politics of Identity*. Oxford: Blackwell.

Cockburn, C. (1991) *In the Way of Women*. London: Macmillan.

Conrad, P. and Schneider, J.W. (1992) *Deviance and Medicalization*. Philadelphia: Temple University Press.

Crow, L. (1992) 'Renewing the social model of disability', *Coalition*, July: 5–9.

Davis, K. (1993) 'On the movement', in J. Swain, V. Finkelstein, S. French and M. Oliver (eds), *Disabling Barriers, Enabling Environments*. London: Sage, pp. 285–92.

Delphy, C. (1984) *Close to Home*. London: Hutchinson.

Finkelstein, V. (1980) *Attitudes and Disabled People*. New York: World Rehabilitation Fund.

Finkelstein, V. (1981) 'To deny or not to deny disability', in A. Brechin, P. Liddiard and J. Swain (eds), *Handicap in a Social World*. Sevenoaks: Open University Press/Hodder & Stoughton.

Foucault, M. (1989) *The History of Sexuality, Volume 1*. Harmondsworth, Penguin.

Foucault, M. (1990) *Politics, Philosophy, Culture*. London: Routledge.

French, S. (1993) 'Disability, impairment or something in between', in J. Swain, V. Finkelstein, S. French and M. Oliver (eds), *Disabling Barriers, Enabling Environments*. London: Sage, pp. 17–25.

Freund, P.E.S. (1988) 'Bringing society into the body: understanding socialized human nature', *Theory & Society*, 17: 839–64.

Fuss, D. (1989) *Essentially Speaking*. New York: Routledge.

Girlin, T. (1990) 'From universality to difference', in C. Calhoun (ed.), *Social Theory and the Politics of Identity*. Cambridge, MA: Blackwell.

Hacking, I. (1986) 'Making up people', in T.C. Heller, M. Sosna and D.E. Wellbery, *Reconstructing Individualism*. Stanford, CA: Stanford University Press. pp. 222–36.
Haraway, D. (1988) 'Situated knowledges: the science question in feminism and the privilege of partial perspective', *Feminist Studies*, 14(3): 575–99.
Hasler, F. (1993) 'Developments in the disabled people's movement', in J. Swain, V. Finkelstein, S. French and M. Oliver (eds), *Disabling Barriers, Enabling Environments*. London: Sage. pp. 278–84.
Liggett, H. (1988) 'Stars are not born: an interpretive approach to the politics of disability', *Disability, Handicap & Society*, 3(3): 263–76.
MacIntosh, M. (1968) 'The homosexual role', *Social Problems*, 16: 182–91.
Millett, K. (1971) *Sexual Politics*. New York: Avon Books.
Morris, J. (1991) *Pride against Prejudice*. London: The Women's Press.
Nietzsche, F. (1990) *Beyond Good and Evil*. Harmondsworth: Penguin.
Oakley, A. (1972) *Sex, Gender and Society*. Aldershot: Gower.
Oliver, M. (1990) *The Politics of Disablement*. London: Macmillan.
Prendegast, S. (1993) *This Is the Time to Grow Up*. Cambridge: Health Promotion Research Trust.
Riley, D. (1988) *Am I That Name?* Basingstoke: Macmillan.
Sayer, J. (1982) *Biological Politics*. London: Tavistock.
Shakespeare, T. (1992) 'A response to Liz Crow', *Coalition*, September: 40–2.
Shakespeare, T. (1993) 'Disabled people's self-organisation: a new social movement?', *Disability, Handicap & Society*, 8(3); 249–64.
Shakespeare, T. (1996) 'Disability, identity, difference', in C. Barnes and G. Mercer (eds), *Exploring the Divide: Illness and Disability*. Leeds: Disability Press.
Timpanaro, S. (1975) *On Materialism*. London: New Left Books.
Vance, C.S. (1989) 'Social construction theory; problems in the history of sexuality', in D. Altman, C. Vance, M. Vicinus and J. Weeks (eds), *Homosexuality, Which Homosexuality*. London: GMP. pp. 13–35.

PART IV

THE POLITICS OF CONSTRUCTIONISM

13

Questions of Method

Mitchell Dean

This chapter takes as its topic, 'Foucault and constructionism'. This is a difficult, if not impossible, task. The reason for this is an elementary one, but not the one that I suspect first occurs to many of us. It is perhaps true, or at least so it seems to those of us outside studies of science and technology (e.g. Latour and Woolgar, 1979; Law, 1991) or certain currents in social psychology (e.g. Gergen and Davis, 1985), that there is no clear delineation of what we are talking about when we speak of 'constructionism' or 'constructivism'. This should not, however, cause too many problems. We can always take the licence provided by the phrase 'for present purposes', and define constructionism, within certain limits, to please ourselves. A harder task is demanded by the proper name in our equation: Foucault. By saying this, I do not mean to invoke the well-worn theme, no doubt Foucauldian, of the 'death of the author'. Rather, I want to notice the birth of the many Foucaults since his death over a decade ago. 'Foucault' has become less a part of the established canon of social theory and more the name for a site of continued contestation, struggle and appropriation. It would be tiresome to give names to this new generation of Foucaults. It is sufficient to say that, in our present case, it would be just as easy to make him a constructionist as an anti-constructionist, 'a phenomenology to end all phenomenologies' (Dreyfus and Rabinow, 1982) or a failed positivist haunted by the ghosts of critical grounds past (Habermas, 1987).[1] Indeed, one could invoke his own description of the genealogical mood as *un positivisme heureux* to play the game either way: a casual constructivist who banishes the constructing subject with uncertain consequences for his critical intent; or a fortunate positivist able to deal with truth, meaning and values as 'socio-discursive' constructions. It would seem that he is an altogether too paradoxical a fellow – or perhaps, just too multiple – to help us sort out this constructionist problem.

There are good reasons to play such games. They are intellectually stimulating. They are surely helpful to our various pedagogies. They show that 'there is nothing new under the sun'; they disabuse us of the 'genius' of the author. But, in the search for theoretical neatness, and in the polite cynicism affected by the learned to claims of novelty, it is possible that the unpolished, unrefined, rough grain and edge of thought is left untouched. The sense in which our work 'takes place between unfinished abutments and anticipatory strings of dots', as Foucault put it (1991: 73–4), is lost. This chapter does not claim to play out this game of philosophical location but engages it with a light-hearted seriousness, making at most an opening move that might prove stimulating to others. That move takes the form of the following proposition: if we are to grasp this relation between Foucault and constructionism we must try to grasp the specific character of Foucault's methods, even if these were never stable and their enunciation usually occurred *after* his analyses. Rather than engage Foucault in an ethos that is fundamentally alien to his work – the ethos of philosophical classification that leads ultimately to the kind of polemics that he himself disliked – I want to try to get a purchase on what he thought he was doing, the methodological maxims, if you like, he invented for himself, and which he would never have thought of 'applying'.

In this respect, I shall argue that Foucault does not present us with an epistemology, or at least anything resembling the philosophical definition of the term as the adequacy of knowing to being, or knowledge to reality. In this regard, he might appear close to Berger and Luckmann's (1967) classic social constructionist 'bracketing' of epistemology. However, the latter suspend epistemology to separate questions of the philosophy of methodology from their own project within sociological theory. This project seeks to reorient the sociology of knowledge towards an account of how actors construct social reality by means of commonsense knowledge. If they bracket epistemology, it is to investigate, not to evacuate, the problem of the general relations between the two ontologically separate domains of 'knowledge' and 'reality'. Foucault, by contrast, remains indifferent to problems of epistemology, to the question of the *general* relation between domains conceived in this way. His investigations are never so philosophically (or indeed, sociologically) grand. Given that, it is not possible to characterize him as offering an account of how knowledge is or can be attained, or of the nature of the reality to be known. To say this, then, is to say that Foucault does not fit easily within the topography of epistemology, one that maps out positivisms, constructionisms, realisms, empiricisms, rationalisms, and so on. To situate Foucault, it is not only necessary to discard these epistemological maps, but also to discover the type of map he has drawn up and to learn how to read it.

As one knows, this map has abundant, extraordinary features attached to the name Foucault: from *Histoire de la folie* and *The Order of Things* to the volumes on sexuality. If the proper name were erased from the covers of these books I suspect we would never guess they were all 'by' the same author. In the space of a brief chapter, a careful description of this topography would be impossible. Foucault, however, left us with many maps, diagrams and legends that make our cartography much easier. I want here to ignore all but one of them, having spent considerable time on virtually all of them elsewhere (Dean, 1994a). For if one little text were allowed to stand as a legend to all Foucault's work, it is one whose title is quite exact, at least in this English version. It is called 'Questions of method' (Foucault, 1991). On the basis of this one, perhaps minor, text, I hope to suggest both what Foucault was up to and why, ultimately, his position is *not* that of a constructionist, while aspects of his method are certainly describable as constructionist and his position shares some fundamental affinities with constructionism. Constructionism should be approached, with Foucault, less as an epistemology, or a sociological substitute for epistemology, and more as a technique or a mode of analysis that can be used with more or less subtlety, and for distinctive and variable ends.

Questions of Method

'Questions of method' is a strange text. It is based on a 'round-table' debate between Foucault and a group of French historians conducted (I guess) in 1976. The discussion was later reworked. Foucault revised his own contributions and the questions and comments of the historians are collated into a series of questions by a 'collective Historian'. Many of the French historians are now well known to English readers, and their questions display a certain perspicacity. The text mainly addresses the recently published *Discipline and Punish*, and it is clearly dated before Foucault's now justly famous excursions into questions of 'governmentality' (Burchell et al., 1991) and also before the volumes on sexuality and their deliberations on the analysis of ethical and ascetic practices, practices of the *rapport à soi* (of the relation of 'self to self') (Foucault, 1985; 1986a). After publication in the *Annales historiques de la révolution française* in 1977, it was republished in a volume edited by Michelle Perrot called *L'Impossible Prison* in 1980. The first English translation by Colin Gordon appeared in that important short-lived journal, *Ideology and Consciousness* (later, *I & C*) in what I believe was to be its second-last issue.[2] Here I shall cite the more widely available revised translation of the *I & C* piece in Burchell et al. (1991).

This unguarded and later cleaned-up text can, I believe, serve us in this meeting of Foucault and constructionism. Let us then go to a passage in which Foucault is trying to explicate his analytical domain:

> In this piece of research on the prisons, as in my other earlier work, the target of analysis wasn't 'institutions', 'theories', or 'ideology', but *practices* – with the aim of grasping the conditions which make these acceptable at a given moment; the hypothesis being that these types of practice are not just governed by institutions, prescribed by ideologies, guided by pragmatic circumstances – whatever role these elements may actually play – but possess up to a point their own specific

regularities, logic, strategy, self-evidence and 'reason'. It is a question of analyzing a 'regime of practices' – practices being understood here as places where what is said and what is done, rules imposed and reasons given, the planned and the taken for granted meet and interconnect. (Foucault, 1991: 75)

I think it is worth dwelling on this quotation if we are to come to terms with Foucault's relation to constructionism. What should we notice about the above paragraph? Certainly it exemplifies what I think can only be called Foucault's evident *materialism*. The objects of analysis are practices, or rather 'regimes of practices', the more or less organized or routinized ways of doing things that manifest an immanent logic or reason of their own. What a shock! The 'theorist' of power-knowledge or the archaeologist of knowledge is interested in practices. At the very least, then, we can say that Foucault proposes a kind of positivity for practices, one that does not reduce them to another level: whether that be the level of institutions, ideologies, circumstances and contexts, or, we should add at this point, the subject of any kind. This conception of practices raises then a primary and unremovable barrier to any species of constructionism in so far as the existence of an irreducible domain of 'regimes of practices' would present a limit to what any constructing agent or actor, human or non-human, individual or collective, could accomplish.

In regard to this notion of practices, it is worth taking up Stephen Turner's (1994) suggestion that constructionism depends on a notion of 'shared practices' to do the work of the construction of facts in the sociology of science. If I understand him, Turner (1994: 112–14) finds this notion of shared practices problematic in at least two ways. It assumes, first, that practices can be both shared and tacit, and, secondly, that constructionism depends on the notion of the successful performance of such practices. This characterization of the notion of 'shared practices' is helpful here in that it allows us to distinguish quite sharply Foucault's conception of 'regimes of practices'. The dimension of these 'regimes of practices' that Foucault wishes to analyse is one in which we find all the more or less explicit, programmatic attempts to organize institutional spaces, their adminis- trative routines and rituals and the conduct of human actors in specified ways. The question is thus not of a rationality that is implicit within the *reality* of a prison, a laboratory, a factory or a school, but all the attempts to codify, regulate, reform, organize, programme and improve what occurs in such locales in the name of all sorts of variable ends articulated with differ- ent degrees of explicitness and cogency. It is not therefore a question of a tacit practice but of the more or less explicit and calculated attempts to make a difference to particular spaces and the actors that inhabit them. Moreover, such a notion of practice does not assume successful perform- ance. The analysis of all these plans, diagrams and programmes of the reformation of practices proceeds from an analysis of, if not their congeni- tally failing character, their local and particular instances of problematiza- tion and reproblematization.[3]

If the analysis of the 'conditions of acceptability of practices' was all there were to Foucault's methods, however, his position would amount to nothing more than a repetition of the *doxa* found in French anthropology from Mauss to Bourdieu, and indeed in the French historical materialism of the 1960s. We should note, however – and this further distinguishes Foucault's 'regimes of practices' from a notion of shared practices – that practices do not form the basis of the intelligibility that Foucault is after. They are what is to be explained rather than the basis of explanation. Moreover, to echo Deleuze and Guattari (1981), it is not first principles that matter but second, third and fourth. Consider the sentence immediately following the above paragraph:

> To analyze 'regimes of practices' means to analyze programmes of conduct which have both prescriptive effects regarding what is to be done (effects of 'jurisdiction') and codifying effects regarding what is to be known (effects of 'veridiction'). (Foucault, 1991: 75)

Programmes of conduct? If we skip ahead a few pages we find something like a definition of such programmes: 'sets of calculated, reasoned, prescriptions in terms of which institutions are meant to be reorganized, spaces arranged, behaviours regulated' (1991: 80). Unlike a Weberian ideal type, which is an abstraction from empirically given instances, the programme is a rational schema of the hospital, of the prison, of the factory, of the enterprise, or even the person, that exists as a way of planning and projecting the formation and reformation of these spaces and agents.[4] As Nikolas Rose has put it, it functions as a kind of abstract machine at the heart of all the concrete machines.[5] For Foucault, I think, one can say that if the object is practice, or better 'regimes of practices', it is not a mute, deaf, practice, immune to the dimension of ideas. On the contrary, every regime of practices evinces at least a minimal quotient of 'thought', or 'ideality'. It is penetrated by all sorts of schemas, programmes, diagrams, maps and plans and marked by degrees of systematization and calculation. Foucault thus chides his interlocutors that to miss this dimension of practices one would have to have 'a very impoverished notion of the real' (1991: 81). The history of prisons and the history of schemas for prison reform are two quite different things. This does not stop us, however, from seeking to understand the relations between the two. For example we could ask how far the programme of conduct realized in Bentham's Panopticon (or in the countless other schemas and diagrams) came to have a whole series of effects: on conceptions of prison architecture, on the explicit purposes and reasons given for confinement, on the delineation of the functions of prison governors and warders, on the understanding of the prison as an integrated technology of punishment and reformation, on the forms of visibility held necessary to the effective management of inmates by various authorities. This is the case even if these effects depart from those claimed and projected by those who invented these schemas and even if, in their failure, such programmes help bring new objects of knowledge into being (e.g.

patterns of recidivism), and new grids of perception and evaluation of individuals (the incorrigible delinquent) and populations (the criminal races or dangerous classes).

Does this not illustrate that Foucault is the constructionist we suspected he was or perhaps we would like him to have been? In reply, I counsel patience. There is a kind of prima facie case for Foucault as a constructionist already evident in the above. These programmes of conduct he speaks of here have two types of effect: *jurisdictional*, those regarding what is to be done, and what he calls – following the work of French historian of science, Georges Canguilhem (1991) – *veridical* (Foucault, 1980), those concerning what is taken as true knowledge. And, while there is no exact correspondence between knowing and acting, there is a certain interconnection and intertwining of the two. One way of understanding Foucault's methodological project, at least at this point, might be to suggest that he sought to grasp the interpenetration, mutual support and conditioning of these regimes of practices with what he calls 'regimes of rationality' (1991: 79). I understand a 'regime of rationality' to be the particular ways in which domains and objects of knowledge are made verifiable and falsifiable, in which it is possible to affirm or deny statements and propositions about such domains. If we were to follow this schematization, the 'programmes of conduct' would be a kind of intermediate set of relations between the two regimes: here knowledge does not simply take the form of that which is produced under experimental, theoretical or scientific protocols, or in locale and by agents authorized as institutions for the production of truth, but from the points of contact of such forms of knowledge and the always incomplete task of the organization and ordering of conduct and bodies within spaces and temporalities. 'Practices' in this sense are not simply the empirical ways in which different groups go about doing things, such as might be discussed by a sociology of organizations, but the locus of problematizations that seek to reorganize, reform and improve them. If I might put it this way, practices are of interest here to the extent that they exist in the medium of thought, given that thought is conceived as a non-subjective technical and practical domain.

At first sight, then, Foucault qualifies as a 'constructivist'. These programmes of conduct could be said to 'construct' particular objects and means of knowledge that are attached to particular forms of action and means of intervention. Moreover, if we further examine his own account of his methodological procedures we find that his conception of these 'regimes of practices' is indeed a constructivist one. Foucault describes this method as one of 'eventalization', the delineation and attempted understanding of an event, such as the emergence of the prison as a general punitive practice or regarding madness as a mental illness, in its singularity. Here the event is invoked to create a 'breach of self-evidence', and, if one likes, to puncture the taken-for-granted necessities of anthropological universals, historical constants, or determinative global social processes. Eventalization, then, performs a kind of historical *époque* or 'bracketing' of the naturalness, necessity or self-evidence of an event to rediscover all the elements, relations and strategies that constitute it. Foucault speaks (1991: 76–7) of a ' "polyhedron" of intelligibility' and a method that proceeds by progressive, necessarily incomplete, saturation. According to this method, the more one breaks down the givenness of an event into the multiple processes that constitute it, the more 'one is enabled and indeed obliged to construct their external relations of intelligibility' (ibid.: 77).

Foucault goes on to describe the elements, relations and forces that compose the 'carceralization of the penal process'. Here we find multiple 'elements' (drawn from domains as diverse as educational practice to philosophy), heteromorphic relations (of the transposition of diagrams, of the use of tactics, of application) and several 'domains of reference' (from the history of detail to the emergence of a capitalist economy). Foucault's method – or at least his account of this method – moves from the taken-for-granted (say, the necessity of the prison), to its conditions of emergence as an event, through the processes that constitute that event, to the multiple elements, relations and domains of reference that incompletely make this event intelligible. It would seem that Foucault views these 'regimes of practices' as constructed from discursive, technical, social and institutional elements, relations and forces, as 'assemblages' of heterogeneous bits and pieces. In this sense the 'regimes of practices' share a striking similarity to the notion of 'technological systems' in the recent history of technology (Hughes, 1983), with the clear difference that the former emphasizes the relative instability of its assemblage of heterogeneous dimensions and does not assume a tendency toward a stable integration of parts (cf. Miller and O'Leary, 1994).

In one sense, we might want to regard Foucault as a constructionist who radically historicizes phenomenology. Here Foucault's approach can be characterized as a 'bracketing' of the naturalness, givenness or necessity of ways of seeing (e.g. the practice of medical examination, an anonymous panoptic power that sees everything), ways of doing (e.g. punishing by means of prisons), ways of knowing others (e.g. regarding madness as mental illness) and ways of understanding ourselves (e.g. taking sexuality for the truth of our identity). A 'regime of practices', then, or what he was later to call a *dispositif*, could be understood as a complex assemblage or, indeed, a construction, of these visibilities, statements, forces, actions and identities (Deleuze, 1992).[6]

The methods for revealing the constructed nature of these regimes of practices are historical, but the intent is far from that of the various uses of history Foucault had earlier found analysed in Nietzsche (Foucault, 1977b). In our text Foucault avers that his 'books aren't treatises in philosophy or studies of history: at most, they are philosophical fragments put to work in a historical field of problems' (1991: 74). Discussing the apparent indispensability of the prison today, Foucault says: '[i]t's a matter of shaking this false self-evidence, of demonstrating its precariousness, of making visible not its arbitrariness, but its complex interconnection with a multiplicity of historical processes, many of them of recent date' (1991: 75). Historical study has this specific purpose: to demonstrate that many of the things we take for granted (e.g. the prison) or natural (e.g. sexuality) have a history, are part of a trajectory (a genealogy, a lineage), and are, in this sense, artefacts of previous events, discourses, practices, so that we might engage in a kind of *diagnostic* of where we stand in relation to these assemblages today (Deleuze, 1992).

If one wants to continue to use Foucault's own terms, 'genealogy' and 'archaeology', for what he was doing, it is possible to consider them as aspects of this methodological programme. Both are framed in a project concerned to analyse those entities (the prison, sexuality, mental illness) that are problematized in the course of contemporary social and political struggles, a project encapsulated in the notions of a 'history of the present' (Foucault, 1977a) or a 'critical ontology of ourselves and our present' (Foucault, 1986b). I shall return to this feature of his work below. Within this framework, archaeology is a kind of strategy of distantiation and denaturalization. It is a kind of historicized version of Kantian critique: it attempts to analyse the conditions of existence of what is taken to be true knowledge, and the forms of categorization on which it depends. Without assuming that discursive forms partake of an ideal unity, it is a technique for the analysis of discourse such that discursive forms or 'regimes of truth' are neither read anachronistically through present concerns, norms and concepts nor viewed as components in the evolution of knowledge to necessary or inevitable outcomes. Its dictum is not that we should try to understand discourses *in* their own terms for, even if we succeeded in that impossible task, how would we communicate such an understanding? Its dictum is, rather, that we should try to make intelligible discourses *by means of* their own terms, of how such terms operate in concert, their system of discursive *formation*, not of how they are interpreted through other forms of understanding and explanation. Genealogy, on the other hand, might be understood as a kind of methodical problematization of these key, taken-for-granted, aspects of our 'present'. It constructs complex and multiple lineages of the events, processes, forms of knowledge and action, that render these entities intelligible as regimes of practices, i.e. as assemblages of diverse elements, forces and relations. Genealogy, if one likes, places the contents released by archaeology in heterogeneous and complexly interwoven continuities without definite origin or necessary end and punctuated by events and ruptures. Archaeology should be understood as a technique of distantiation from familiar ways of forming statements about and within particular regimes of practices, and genealogy as a technique of denaturalization of these regimes of practices that leads to the construction of intelligible trajectories of the events, knowledges, processes, relations and forces that compose them. As I shall show in the final section, however, both these techniques of distantiation and problematization grow out of a diagnostic set of concerns that binds Foucault's scholarly endeavours with present struggles and aspirations.

On Constructionism

These few pages from Foucault strike me as exceptionally relevant to our problem. I try to force them to give up some understanding of Foucault's work not because I believe the whole is found in the part but because understanding a part is a condition for understanding anything at all. Before proceeding with our exegesis, let's put off no longer the question of what we mean by constructionism.

Constructionism, as I understand it, entered sociology by a primary route in the 1960s with Peter Berger and Thomas Luckmann's *The Social Construction of Reality* (1967). As is becoming increasingly apparent to those of us not in science and technology studies, it also entered without quite so much fanfare by way of the mutation in epistemology occasioned by Thomas Kuhn's *The Structure of Scientific Revolutions* (1962). In many ways, the research programmes (phenomenological sociology, ethnomethodology, symbolic interactionism) associated with the first entrance of constructionism have quietly fallen out of fashion, or been restricted to small and dedicated bands of researchers, or been incorporated into mainstream sociological pedagogy as theory or methods. It is of note that it is in the area of personal and intersubjective relations, particularly in social psychology, that this form of social constructionism has exercised a significant – if never hegemonic – degree of continuing influence (Gergen and Davis, 1985). On the other hand, the surprising entrance of constructionism through a mutation in epistemology has spawned a form of research starting with Latour and Woolgar's *Laboratory Life* (1979) and a growing literature (e.g. the articles in Law, 1986, 1991) that has proved increasingly compelling to mainstream social science.

At the risk of grossly caricaturing these two massively complex lines of development within sociology and related disciplines, permit me to suggest what unites all this. I think we can seek to distinguish between the agent of construction, the means of construction, and what is constructed. At the starting point along the first line what is constructed is *reality* understood as the 'fabric of meanings' essential to the existence of a society, the means of construction is the 'commonsense knowledge' of social actors engaged in the routines of everyday life, and the agents of construction are human actors with their (inter)subjective capacities. 'Knowledge' here refers specifically to the pre-theoretical, pre-scientific knowledge actors have of their everyday lives, the often tacit repertoires by which actors deal with and negotiate their worlds and other actors.[7] What is being constructed are, indeed, complex but relatively stable social bonds, the bonds that tie actors together into the intersubjective life-world. Along the second line, the starting point is the construction of *facts*. The means of construction move from the generalized 'social context' to an increasingly detailed web of cultural and material artefacts, procedures, inscriptions and technologies (laboratories, experiments, computers, texts, tables, articles, etc.) and networks of human and non-human actors. However, this line of development moves from knowledge to reality, or at least to what it now appears as a 'sociotechnical reality'. This line unites with the first because the emphasis is again on the 'typifications' of experience given by actors (this time, scientists) and the ways in which an ordered account of both research and 'the facts' is produced from the disorder of the everyday micro-processes (here, of work in the laboratory, of the writing up and publishing of research).[8]

If I might put it this way, constructionism varies correlatively along two distinct axes: a kind of idealist–materialist axis in which the virtue of the sociology of science has been its increasingly detailed account of the technical and material means of construction; and a human–non-human one, in which constructing humans are increasingly made into effective agents of construction because they form networks with constructing non-humans. The further constructionism moves toward the materialist end of the first axis, the more it calls into question the supposedly universal constructing capacities of human (inter)subjectivity and regards human actors as mutual constructed/constructing amid other actors, including texts, graphs, buildings, money and machines, all pursuing programmes and anti-programmes (Callon, 1991). Given these variations, we can conclude then that neither the humanist–idealist nor ahumanist–materialist dimension defines what is essential about constructionism.

What is essential, or at least so it seems to me, are two things. First, both reject an absolutist account of knowledge to understand how knowledge comes to depend on certain actors, institutions, techniques, practices, inscriptions, and so on. In this regard, I think both lie on the terrain occupied by Foucault. Secondly – and this is what I think is the most surprising aspect of constructionism – both variants are species of realism.[9] Thus, no matter the means, the agents and the ends of construction, what is constructed is ultimately the reality in which actors live, operate, connect and form networks. Latour and Woolgar might be concerned with the micro-processes of the laboratory, the working activities of scientists, the production of facts and the construction of order out of disorder. Yet ultimately they are concerned with the construction of reality. 'Scientific activity,' they state (Latour and Woolgar, 1979: 242; original emphasis), 'is not "about nature": it is a fierce fight to *construct* reality.' Berger and Luckmann (1967: 13, 15; original emphasis) may regard reality as a 'a quality appertaining to phenomena that we recognize as having a being independent of our volition' that is woven from the fabric of our everyday lives; yet they still contend that *'the sociology of knowledge is concerned with the analysis of the social construction of reality'*. Here is the heart of what is at issue with Foucault and constructionism. While he rejects an absolutist account of knowledge to understand it as formed, first, within particular regimes of truth and rationality, then within regimes of practices, and finally in relation to what might be called 'regimes of identity', his methodology and, more importantly, his purposes, depart dramatically from such a realism.

A Nominalist Critique

Let us return to Foucault's text, armed, if ever so lightly, with the above typification of constructionism. The very last sentence of our text gives us a clue to what distinguishes his approach from that of either of the realist constructionisms outlined above. He states (Foucault, 1991: 86): 'Paul Veyne saw this very clearly: it's a matter of the effect on historical knowledge of a nominalist critique itself arrived at by way of historical analysis.' What is meant by this? The upshot of our excursus on constructionism was to show that neither the constructing agent nor the means of construction is sufficient to distinguish Foucault from constructionism. He also shares with constructionism the rejection of an absolutist account of knowledge and truth. Moreover, on both axes identified above, he comes down rather closer to the materialist and ahumanist account, perhaps unsurprisingly sharing many of the assumptions revealed in the work of thinkers like Latour and Callon. His account of the agents and means of construction is materialist and pluralist, and directed against the presupposition of a universal human (inter)subjectivity. However, it is *what* is constructed that reveals the force of his 'nominalism' (this term should be understood loosely) and the rejection of realism. His concern is not with the construction of social reality, whether conceived as an intersubjective life-world or a sociotechnical network:

> My general theme isn't society but the discourse of true and false, by which I mean the correlative formation of domains and objects and the verifiable, falsifiable discourses that bear on them; and it's not just their formation that interests me, but the effects in the real to which they are linked. (Foucault, 1991: 14)

In other texts he uses the terms, a 'history of truth', a 'critical history of rationality', or a 'history of problematizations', to describe the domain of his studies. What is being attempted, then, requires that Foucault be nominalist about 'truth'. It is truth, not reality or knowledge-becoming-reality, that is his domain. Foucault is concerned with the way in which the mechanisms, rituals and techniques of the production of truth (and falsity) vary historically. Regimes of rationality – or what he elsewhere called regimes of truth – might be considered to be the distinctive ways in which truth is formulated, involving the construction of domains of objects, strategies and procedures, concepts and vocabularies, and specific forms of knowledgeable or authoritative actors or subjects. These regimes of rationality traverse not only our human, social, natural and technical sciences, but our humanities and our political and moral philosophies. Regimes of rationality are already at work in specific forms of practice, what might be called 'veridical practices', practices concerned with the production of truth.

Yet Foucault avows that he is interested not only in such veridical practices but also in their effects in the real. Indeed, as we saw above, it is one dimension of these 'regimes of rationality' that particularly concerns Foucault: the 'programmes of conduct', the attempt to govern human conduct on the basis of the truth produced by such veridical practices. He is interested in effects of 'jurisdiction' as much as effects of 'veridiction'. These effects, however, are multiple and diverse and a matter of empirical inquiry. There is no general way in which we can account for the effects in the real of our truths conceived nominalistically. At the most one might want to say that veridical practices and regimes of rationality are one component or dimension of, or intersect with, the 'regimes of practices', the programmes of conduct defining the matrix of intersection. The realm of effects cannot be read off the realm of truth.

In order to make this point clear let me introduce a distinction made by Colin Gordon (1980) between *realization* and *effectivity*. Gordon (1980: 246) makes the point that many of Foucault's critics have elided these two terms. Thus the programme of conduct realized in the Panopticon is immediately mistaken for an account of the relations of power in a particular society – a disciplinary society. Such an account then collapses effectivity into realization. On the other hand, one might wish to say that it is impossible to study the realm of effectivity, the domain of effects in the real. Such a position would amount to saying that Foucault's studies are limited to the ways in which schemas of prison reform, the deinstitutionalization of the insane, diagrams of rational economic and social action, etc., become realized as programmes of conduct or, if one likes, formulae of government. This, however, is not Foucault's position. Such programmes of conduct have diverse effects in the real: they promote forms of visibility and grids of evaluation, they guide the way we understand ourselves and others, they allow us to conceive objects of government in specific ways, they make possible various forms of expertise and solidify into particular institutions, they allow certain forms of persuasive argument, and so on. They have a diverse effectivity. They have a range of intended, unintended, semi-intended and perverse effects that are never mapped out in advance and are never reducible to the explicit or implicit goals of particular programmes of conduct. On the basis of these effects, something like a 'strategy' might be discerned, a minimal and non-subjective form of rationality whereby particular unstable assemblages or 'regimes of practices' are invested with a set of functions in regard to a dynamic and variable set of objectives. There is, however, no master strategist at work here, no grand programmer (Gordon, 1980: 251). The realm of effectivity is always plural, and only ever partially legible from the discourse of true and false statements and the programmes of conduct constructed on the basis of them. What is constructed is never reality (a general, ontologically given sphere independent of subjective volition) but ways of knowing the truth about ourselves and others, and about human conduct, and the diverse effects of such regimes of truth. What is at issue is not the social construction of reality but the realm of effectivity of the construction of truth.

This domain of the critical history of truth is a thorny one. I shall dwell on it here for there is one memorable paragraph from this text I must quote in conclusion to illustrate the full force of Foucault's nominalism:

> The question which I won't succeed in answering here that I have been asking myself since the beginning is roughly the following: 'What is history, given there is continually being produced within it a separation of true and false?' By that I mean four things. Firstly, in what sense is the production and transformation of the true/false division characteristic and decisive for our historicity? Secondly, in what specific ways has this relation operated in 'Western' societies which produce scientific knowledge whose forms are perpetually changing and whose values are posited as universal? Thirdly, what historical knowledge is possible of a history which itself produces the true/false distinction on which such knowledge depends? Fourthly, isn't the most general of political problems the problem of truth? How can one analyse the connection between ways of distinguishing true and false and ways of governing oneself and others? The search for a new foundation for each of these practices, in itself and relative to the other, the will to discover a different way of governing oneself through a different way of dividing up true and false – this is what I would call 'political *spiritualité*'. (Foucault, 1991: 82)

This series of four questions is hardly one of a social constructionist, although there are certain overlaps. It is a series pertaining to the history of truth and its diverse effects. The first question is a question of *culture*. It is one of our insertion in a particular cultural ensemble. It asks: in what sense is the organized and institutionally sanctioned production of discourses based on the division between truth and falsity a feature of a particular intellectual and political culture? The second question might be regarded as a *Kuhnian* one. It is a question of the empirical examination of 'regimes of truth', their formation and transformation, their rise and fall, and their relation to the universalist claims of scientific reason. The third question is of the *aporia* that follows from this: how can we 'ground' historical knowledge in truth if we recognize the changing forms of the division between truth and falsity – how, if one likes, can we undertake a history of truth from the moment we realize that truth has a history? These are all questions that can, indeed, be posed within the framework of social constructionism: they concern the cultural and paradigmatic relativity of truth and its consequences for methodology.

It is at this point that Foucault's constructivist methods become inflected with something quite different: a concern to redeploy such questions that has, I think, two stages. The first is what I call an *analytic of conduct*. This is the final question. It is properly one of government, defined generally as the 'conduct of conduct', as the more or less deliberate attempts to act on the actions of self and others. It virtually condenses not only the entire Foucauldian *oeuvre* but the direction that his work was to take in the years following this interview. The question of relations between truth and the

government of self and others opens up both the exploration of the genealogy of ethics conceived as a practice of the action of 'self on self', with its
emphasis on techniques of the cultivation of identity in relation to specific
domains of knowledge, and the genealogy of the arts and mentalities of
government, of a government that is both individualizing and totalizing,
characteristic of liberal polities. I have suggested elsewhere that Foucault's
later work can be read as an analytic of these two autonomous yet reciprocally conditioning domains of 'practices of government' and 'practices of
the self' and their relation to a critical history of truth (Dean, 1994b).

If Foucault is indeed a nominalist, his method does not require us to
impugn truth. Quite the contrary: he insists, in a sense, that truth is multiple
(there are various forms of its production) but rare (it is produced in specific
domains, institutions, and with specific agents constituted as authorities of
truth). His methods arise once we examine the full consequences of what
we might call 'the social construction of knowledge' while abstaining from
providing an alternative account of reality (the reality of subjects, of
society, of humanity). Yet his nominalism is not so much a philosophical
position as a form of historical criticism, or a way of examining critically the
production and circulation of truth by authorities within institutions. But
this is also the limit of his nominalism: he refrains from the inference that
everything is thereby a construction. The real remains too indecipherable
ever to be able to be summed up into a formula (a theory of the subject, of
power, of a constructed object, a realm of facts, a network, a social reality).
The effects of truth in the real are multiple, partial and heterogeneous. This
is Foucault's irrealism, his agnosticism toward Reality.

Foucault (1985) came to understand his work as philosophy – or at least
as a form of philosophical practice, a form of asceticism. But this practice
was conducted within historical domains precisely because it was history,
the history of 'systems of thought' as the self-chosen title of his chair at the
Collège de France put it, that allowed him to pose fundamental philosophical questions and puzzles. Yet ultimately neither 'philosopher' nor 'historian' quite suits. I think this is finally the reason why we should not
assimilate Foucault with social construction despite the presence of constructivist methods within, if one likes, an irrealist framework. His work is
not ultimately directed toward scholarly ends but toward a *diagnostic* of our
present (Deleuze, 1992). This is the second stage of his displacement of
constructionism. If archaeology is the discussion of the systems formed by
rare statements, and genealogy the emplacement of such statements within
the trajectories of practices of the government of self and others, then
ultimately they are subsumed by a more fundamental concern. This is one
of the present, of a diagnostic of how we have come to understand, and act
upon, ourselves and others, today. Genealogy and archaeology can only be
tools that demonstrate what is necessary and what is contingent within our
present and its regimes of practices. Ultimately, however, and especially in
his interviews, Foucault demonstrates that his concern is with what might be
called the 'political ontology of ourselves', of how we have come to govern

ourselves and others through the truths about who we are, and with the potential for establishing new relations between forms of power, truth and identity. This, then, is what I take him to mean by his concern with 'political *spiritualité*'.

Irving Velody (1994: 82–3) has quite properly raised the problem that is the daemon of all forms of constructionism in relation to the work of Ian Hacking. Permit me to rephrase his problem for myself. It is all very well to demonstrate that entities like 'mental illness' and 'child abuse' are constructed from particular social, political and discursive practices and amid contending forces. However, this neither removes the problems of the real pain and suffering experienced by those designated as mentally ill or as victims of abuse nor absolves us of ethical responsibility on these matters. Foucault's response has always seemed to me particularly clear. If what is under analysis are the practices by which we come to know ourselves in a certain way, by which we seek to direct our conduct and that of others, then such an analysis does not claim for itself a position of authority in relation to the realities of the pain, suffering and anguish experienced by, say, victims of abuse, or by those designated as schizophrenic. It does not either deny or authoritatively encode these realities. In fact, it is by being 'nominalist' in Foucault's sense that we can show our respect for them. There is always another side to what is constructed in these 'regimes of practices'. We deal with 'suffering' in particular forms of discourse and have particular ways of 'treating' it, and these regimes of practice and truth may augment or diminish, or transform in some other way, that suffering, but they are never its totality, and they never construct it. The ethical responsibility that falls to us is to analyse the limits of the necessity of these 'regimes of practices' and the possibilities of their transformation, within a fundamental orientation towards what Foucault called the 'rights of the governed' and towards creating a clearing for the undefined work of freedom (Eribon, 1991: 279). The latter, I would suggest, is fundamentally different from strategies of empowerment and their emphasis on 'maximum feasible participation' (Cruikshank, 1994) in that such rights must include the right to dissent from all authoritative attempts at the construction of participation. All this comprises what I meant by using the term 'diagnostic'. Foucault's 'constructivist' techniques are oriented toward an engagement in the limits and possibilities of the present, not toward a general explanation of reality.

Once, however, we have dropped the realist stance with Foucault, we gain a greater respect for the 'regimes of practices' themselves. They might be constructed. They might be made up of elements with multiple trajectories. These elements might form themselves into assemblages held together by multiform relations and forces. The history of regimes of practices is in this sense fully contingent. However, that they came together to form an ensemble at a particular time and place that possessed a self-evidence it was difficult to challenge suggests equally some sense of the necessity of such regimes of practices. The fact that we are now able to problematize these regimes does not indicate that, being constructed, these are entities that can be scattered like a handful of dust thrown into the winds. Rather it suggests that they are in some way already problematic, that the conditions that sustained such regimes have changed, that rather than representing the totality of our contemporary experience they are now both 'unfinished abutments' and 'anticipatory strings of dots'.

Notes

1 I am aware, of course, that this phrase does not sum up Dreyfus and Rabinow's useful clarification of Foucault's position in relation to various forms of phenomenology and structuralism in philosophy and the social sciences. However, their use of this phrase does emphasize the sense in which Foucault can be read as an extension of the phenomenological project of 'bracketing'. They argue that Foucault not only brackets the truth claims of a statement (as does Husserl) but also its meaning claims, i.e. its claims to make a sense and a truth that is more than context specific (Dreyfus and Rabinow, 1982: 49). By contrast, I would claim that these eleven words sum up Habermas's sixty-page excursus on Foucault (but see Dean, 1994a: 120–40).

2 This journal proved an inspiration to its readers, myself included, I suspect, not only because of the exemplary 'histories of the present' it contained but also because it embodied the critical style of a 'studied casualness' and mood of 'felicitous positivism' that Foucault had already spoken about in his inaugural *leçon* at the Collège de France in 1970 (1971: 27).

3 Compare this from the introduction to *The Use of Pleasure* (Foucault, 1985: 11): 'It was a matter of analyzing, not behaviors or ideas, nor societies and their "ideologies", but the problematizations through which being offers itself to be, necessarily, thought – and the practices on the basis of which these problematizations are formed.' The study of 'governmentality' too, does not proceed from a general theory of politics, but from the local, domain-specific, problematizations of how the conduct of self and others is to be governed (see Dean, forthcoming).

4 The terms 'rational' and 'rationality' are used agnostically by Foucault. There is no standard of Reason against which empirical instances are judged or process of rationalization under which such instances are subsumed (Dean, 1994a). A rationality may be thought of simply as a regular way of producing statements, defined by the set of concepts it employs, the procedures and themes it characteristically uses, the objects is typically addresses, and the modes of address it adopts.

5 Written personal communication, 1994.

6 The emphasis here on the production of visibilities through inscription devices as a condition of knowledge brings this concept of 'regimes of practices' very close to the recent 'constructivist' aspects of the sociology of science (Latour, 1986).

7 It should be clear that the form of 'knowledge' at issue here is quite different from Foucault's analysis of 'veridical' practices. The tacit knowledge of everyday life is a very different object to the 'serious discourses' (Dreyfus and Rabinow, 1982) of the human sciences that are Foucault's concern, even if we concede the constructivist point that the latter are constructed out of the micro-processes of the everyday life of scientists.

8 While these roughly correspond to the two types of constructivism discerned by Fuller (1994), I am reluctant to assign political values ('left' and 'right') to them. For a discussion of the relation of constructivism in the sociology of science to more conventional critical sociological concerns with inequality and distribution see John Law's excellent introduction to Law (1991).

9 I realize I am using the term 'realism' in a broader sense than allowed within certain social constructionist typifications (Shweder and Miller, 1985). The latter distinguish between realist, innatist, and social constructionist theories of category formation. Realism here is a kind of an objectivism: 'people categorize the world the way they do because that's the way the world is'

(1985: 41). If realism, however, is defined as a concern for how things really work then social constructionism with its emphasis on the participation of 'people' in 'social practices, institutions, and other forms of symbolic action' (ibid.) is also a realism.

References

Berger, P. and Luckmann, T. (1967) *The Social Construction of Reality: A Treatise in the Sociology of Knowledge*. Harmondsworth: Penguin.
Burchell, G., Gordon, C. and Miller, P. (eds) (1991) *The Foucault Effect*. Hemel Hempstead: Harvester/Wheatsheaf.
Callon, M. (1991) 'Techno-economic networks and irreversibility', in J. Law (ed.), *A Sociology of Monsters: Essays on Power, Technology and Domination*. Sociological Review Monograph 38. London: Routledge.
Canguilhem, G. (1991) *The Normal and the Pathological*, trans. C.R. Fawcett. New York: Zone Books.
Cruikshank, B. (1994) 'The will to empower: technologies of citizenship and the war on poverty', *Socialist Review*, 23(4): 29–55.
Dean, M. (1994a) *Critical and Effective Histories: Foucault's Methods and Historical Sociology*. London: Routledge.
Dean, M. (1994b) ' "A social structure of many souls": moral regulation, self-formation and government', *Canadian Journal of Sociology*, 19(2): 145–68.
Dean, M. (forthcoming) *Governmentality*. London: Sage.
Deleuze, G. (1992) 'What is a *dispositif*?', in T.J. Armstrong (ed.), *Michel Foucault Philosopher*. New York: Harvester/Wheatsheaf.
Deleuze, G. and Guattari, F. (1981) 'Rhizome', *I & C*, 8: 49–71.
Dreyfus, H. and Rabinow, P. (1982) *Michel Foucault: Beyond Structuralism and Hermeneutics*. Brighton: Harvester.
Eribon, D. (1991) *Michel Foucault*, trans. B. Wing. Cambridge, MA: Harvard University Press.
Foucault, M. (1971) 'Orders of discourse', *Social Science Information*, 10(2): 7–30.
Foucault, M. (1977a) *Discipline and Punish: The Birth of the Prison*, trans. A.M. Sheridan. Harmondsworth: Penguin.
Foucault, M. (1977b) 'Nietzsche, genealogy, history', in D.B. Bouchard (ed.), *Language, Counter-Memory, Practice*. Oxford: Basil Blackwell.
Foucault, M. (1980) 'Georges Canguilhem: philosopher of error', *I & C*, 7: 513–62.
Foucault, M. (1985) *The History of Sexuality, Vol. 2: The Use of Pleasure*, trans. R. Hurley. New York: Pantheon.
Foucault, M. (1986a) *The History of Sexuality, Vol. 3: The Care of the Self*, trans. R. Hurley. New York: Pantheon.
Foucault, M. (1986b) 'Kant on revolution and enlightenment', *Economy and Society*, 15(1): 88–96.
Foucault, M. (1991) 'Questions of method', in G. Burchell, C. Gordon and P. Miller (eds), *The Foucault Effect: Studies in Governmentality*. Hemel Hempstead: Harvester/Wheatsheaf.
Fuller, S. (1994) 'The reflexive politics of constructivism', *History of the Human Sciences*, 7(1): 87–93.
Gergen, K.J. and Davis, K.E. (eds) (1985) *The Social Construction of the Person*. New York: Springer-Verlag.
Gordon, C. (1980) 'Afterword', to M. Foucault, *Power/Knowledge*. Brighton: Harvester.
Habermas, J. (1987) *The Philosophical Discourse of Modernity*, trans. F.G. Lawrence. Cambridge, MA: MIT Press.
Hughes, T. (1983) *Networks of Power: Electrification in Western Society 1880–1930*. Baltimore, MD: Johns Hopkins University Press.
Kuhn, T. (1962) *The Structure of Scientific Revolutions*. Chicago: University of Chicago Press.

Latour, B. (1986) 'Visualisation and cognition: thinking with eyes and hands', *Knowledge and Society*, 6: 1–40.

Latour, B. and Woolgar, S. (1979) *Laboratory Life: The Social Construction of Scientific Facts.* Beverly Hills, CA: Sage.

Law, J. (ed.) (1986) *Power, Action and Belief: A New Sociology of Knowledge*, Sociological Review Monograph 32. London: Routledge & Kegan Paul.

Law, J. (ed.) (1991) *A Sociology of Monsters: Essays on Power, Technology and Domination.* Sociological Review Monograph 38. London: Routledge.

Miller, P. and O'Leary, T. (1994) 'The factory as laboratory', *Science in Context*, 7(3): 469–96.

Shweder, R.A. and Miller, J.G. (1985) 'The social construction of the person: how is it possible?', in K.J. Gergen and K.E. Davis (eds), *The Social Construction of the Person.* New York: Springer-Verlag.

Turner, S. (1994) 'Relativism hot and cold', *History of the Human Sciences*, 7(1): 109–15.

Velody, I. (1994) 'Constructing the social', *History of the Human Sciences*, 7(1): 81–5.

14

Social Constructionist Political Theory

Craig Mackenzie

In his paper 'The making and molding of child abuse' (1991a), Ian Hacking argues that child abuse is both an intrinsically moral topic (259) and that it is socially constructed (254). In another paper he recommends that the social constructionist approaches developed in science studies be turned to 'conduct, ethics, morality' (1990: 358), and indicates that his work on child abuse is an example of this turn. In these papers I take Hacking to be recommending a social constructionist programme in moral inquiry, and offering a demonstration of it. Hacking's work on child abuse is impressive. His recommendations deserve to be widely implemented. Turning social constructionism to morality could be at least as productive and interesting as social constructionism has been in science studies. In order to encourage this programme, this chapter is devoted to interpreting the recommendation I am attributing to Hacking, and giving an example of an area of moral inquiry in which it could be applied. The area concerned is the liberal/communitarian debate in political theory, and in particular the 'interpretive turn' (Warnke, 1993: vii) taken by a number of prominent members of this debate. The liberal/communitarian debate may seem an odd context of *moral* inquiry to use, it is usually understood as a debate in political theory. However, one central characteristic of contemporary liberal and communitarian political theory is the importance it places on morality. Indeed some of the central texts in the liberal/communitarian debate – Rawls's *Theory of Justice* (1972), MacIntyre's *After Virtue* (1984) – are also canonical works in contemporary Anglo-American moral philosophy.

Hacking's Recommendation of a Constructionist Turn in Ethics

Hacking's recommendation of a social constructionist version of moral inquiry is most explicit in his paper 'Two kinds of new historicism for philosophers'. In this paper, Hacking's concern is to draw out the possibility of an approach to philosophical problems inspired by what Foucault called the 'history of the present' (Hacking, 1990: 343). He is particularly interested in the problems of moral philosophy. Hacking argues that the present tradition in Anglo-American philosophy is profoundly anti-historical, and that this is severely limiting. He offers two alternative ways of historicizing philosophy. The first kind is Richard Rorty's use of history to 'undo' foundationalist philosophy (Hacking, 1990: 351), the second is an empirical, social constructionist historicism. Hacking prefers the second kind. While he says Rorty's work, particularly *Philosophy and the Mirror of Nature* (1979), is 'profoundly original', he thinks that there is much more that history can give us than Rorty's 'fly-by-night encounter with the past' (1990: 345). The central problem Hacking has with Rorty's use of history is that as soon as Rorty moves from 'undoing' philosophical traditions to discussing philosophical problems, he stops historicizing and returns to more conventional, anti-historicist, philosophical argument. A consequence of this is that Rorty, despite his repeated advice that we insouciantly drop these problems, finds himself engaged in debates that perpetuate them.

Hacking recommends a different approach. He wants to go on with history where Rorty stops: he wants to historicize *philosophical problems*. The way he wants to do this is by 'taking a look' at the local, empirical facts that surround their emergence as problems. This is 'a local historicism, attending to particular and disparate fields of reflection and action' that 'discourages grand unified accounts' and demands 'taking a look at lots of little facts' (1990: 345). He illustrates this local historicism by describing the work of 'a generation of post-Kuhnian students of science . . . [that] takes social construction as its motto' (ibid.: 356). Here he mentions the work of Latour and Woolgar (1979), Pickering (1984) and Shapin and Schaffer (1985). Hacking says that these writers show how the ideas, categories and concepts which we use to talk about the world are social constructions. He emphasizes that this does not mean that what is socially constructed is not ' "really" a fact (now) only that the unthought world doesn't come in facts. The factization of the world is a human activity' (1990: 356). On this account social constructionists reject, as in another context Rorty puts it, 'the claim that the world splits itself up, on its own initiative, into sentence-shaped chunks called "facts" ' (Rorty, 1989: 5), and accept instead the idea that facts emerge in the context of webs of human beliefs and desires and the practices of which they form a part. The achievement of social constructionists in science studies is to give a history to these beliefs, desires and practices, and so to the activities by which facts are produced and made visible. Inasmuch as these categories, ideas, classifications and 'facts' constitute our contemporary attitudes to the world these social constructionist histories may be called, after Foucault, histories of the present (Hacking, 1990: 357).

In this paper, the main collection of philosophical problems which Hacking wants to historicize are problems in moral philosophy. Hacking believes that the concepts and problems in this area of philosophy are ripe for the kind of local historicism he is advocating. In fact he says that morality is an arena where we would be even more likely to find concepts 'molded by history' (1990: 358) than the arena of science. Hacking observes that just as philosophy of science has dealt with abstract concepts, like truth, reality and fact, moral philosophy has dealt with abstract topics like right, good and justice. Social constructionists have challenged the abstractions produced by philosophers of science by investigating 'not truth, reality and fact, but truths, real things and facts' (ibid.). Hacking urges us to follow post-Kuhnian science studies and to do the same to the abstractions of moral philosophy:[1] by turning away from abstract concepts to concrete ideas of the good, particular rights, and varieties of justice and to what Bernard Williams has called 'thicker . . . more specific ethical notions' (Williams, 1985: 129) like treachery, brutality, promise and courage. It is to Williams's (admittedly still somewhat abstract) list of 'thick' moral concepts, that Hacking adds child abuse (1990: 360).

Child Abuse

Hacking is explicit in linking his work on child abuse to his programmatic recommendation of turning constructionism to morality. Concerning the social constructionist approach to ethical concepts he advocates, Hacking says, 'The example of this sort on which I have done the most work is child abuse' (1990: 360). In his papers on child abuse (1988a; 1991a), Hacking reports 'lots of little facts' that collectively demonstrate how our beliefs about the harm adults do to children have changed in the last thirty years. He shows how 'new methods, new agencies, new laws, new education of children, new information for parents, new therapies, and above all new and growing knowledge [have] transform[-ed] the world' (1991a: 258). An important part of the world that has been transformed is the moral world; the domain which specifies the rights and wrongs of the relations between adults and children. As Hacking says,

> People do many of the same vile things to children, for sure, that they did a century ago. But we've been almost unwittingly changing the very definitions of abuse and revising our values and moral codes accordingly. (1991a: 253)

Hacking is very positive about the emergence (or construction) of the concept of child abuse in the last thirty years. He says that, in contributing to the social construction of child abuse, 'the child abuse movement may have effected the most valuable, albeit the most discouraging, heightening of awareness that has taken place in my lifetime' (1991a: 257).[2] However, Hacking has certain ambivalences. He worries, for example, about the way a wide variety of very different kinds of harm perpetrated on children by adults are lumped together into a single, all-embracing category. He is particularly concerned because he thinks that we may have constructed this umbrella category in an unfortunate manner. Though we use the single, blanket concept 'child abuse' to talk about these different kinds of harm, we are quite able to separate them out into different categories. Hacking quotes some research that shows how Californians are readily able to distinguish many varieties of harm: 'Physical Abuse, Sexual Abuse, Fostering Delinquency, Supervision, Emotional Mistreatment, Drugs/

Alcohol, Failure to Provide, Educational Neglect, Parental Sexual Mores' (1991a: 283).[3] Despite our ability to separate them, these forms of harm are persistently lumped together.

If this lumping was merely a matter of mere descriptive convenience it would not matter much. However, Hacking demonstrates that subsuming many kinds of harm under this one concept has many significant repercussions. In particular, it has powerful consequences for our moral beliefs about harm to children. Hacking presents these consequences by disclosing certain features of the local, historical origins of our concept of child abuse. He reports that the concept first gained wide public usage following the publication of a paper, by some doctors, which announced the existence of 'battered-baby syndrome'.[4] Hacking argues that, ever since, the development of child abuse has been controlled by the medical profession. Consequently it has become a strongly medicalized concept. One key feature of this medicalization is that child abuse has been constructed as a kind of *disease* (1991a: 280ff.). This has certain implications. One is that all cases of child abuse have a common cause, as it is a general feature of our ideas about diseases that they have common causes. (The cause of AIDS, for example, is a virus – though the presence of HIV may not exhaust the causal requirements for full-blown AIDS.) Another consequence of identifying child abuse as a kind of disease is that, like a disease, the evil of child abuse can be communicated. Parents can be infected by, say, violent pornography and, later on, in the course of abusing their children, they can pass on the disease to them. Another implication is that a mild case can develop into a serious one, if left untreated. Smack a child in anger today, and, unless you receive therapy, some time in the future you may be at risk of succumbing to the full-blown disease: sexual assault.

If Hacking is right that child abuse has been socially constructed on a disease model, and if he is right that we make certain assumptions based on this model, then there are several implications for our beliefs about child abuse as a social problem and, of particular significance here, as a moral problem. The assumption that all the kinds of harm adults inflict on children share a common cause may encourage the idea that all these different kinds of harm should be tackled by rooting out and eliminating this single cause; rather than by searching for a wide variety of potential causes, and developing a range of policies to address them. It also changes our moral beliefs. One possible example concerns our moral beliefs about parents smacking children.[5] If the same causal processes are present both in the most vicious sexual assault and in a parent's disciplinary smack, parents who smack their children risk succumbing to the full-blown disease of child abuse. And, worse still, they risk infecting their children with the disease, and so making them more likely to, later, abuse their own offspring. This confers on smacking a grave status in our inventory of moral evils, a status which the Victorians might have found ridiculous. The point here is not to defend smacking, but to illustrate the critical power of Hacking's history of the emergence of our concept 'child abuse'.

Hacking's work indicates that our ideas about child abuse rest, at least in part, on a disease model. This makes possible the hypothesis that the idea of a common causal link, operating subconsciously like a hidden psychological disease, may have been a powerful motor in the 'revision of our values' concerning corporal punishment. If, as seems likely, little evidence emerges for thinking that there is in fact a common cause of the forms of harm currently characterized as child abuse, then lumping them together, while rhetorically powerful,[6] is empirically dubious. Consequently, those moral beliefs and public policies that employ the disease model of child abuse begin to look unjustified. In assembling the historical case which points to this conclusion, Hacking's social constructionist moral inquiry serves as a 'critique of moral values'.[7] If it proves durable, Hacking's case offers a set of strong reasons to revise our moral judgements and social policies concerning certain aspects of child abuse.

The Methodology of Social Constructionism

The foregoing account is an attempt to give some indication of the kind of rewards to be gained by adopting Hacking's recommendation to take a local, empirical look at the particular history of the emergence and transformation of our moral concepts. His work provides a reasonably detailed account of the dynamics of a particular set of moral concepts. This account has strong critical implications for the moral beliefs that surround our concepts and practices. However, my brief sketch does not provide details of the methodology that Hacking is suggesting we use. In the preparation of a programme of research, this is an important practical issue. If you want to follow Hacking's recommendation, how do you *do* social constructionist research into morality?

Hacking's own constructionist work on morality is fairly brief. There are two papers on child abuse (1988a; 1991a), and some partly related papers on multiple personality and memory (1991b; 1992; 1994). In these papers he makes few remarks about methodology. There are also a few more theoretical papers that address constructionism (1986; 1988b), as well as the important paper already discussed above (1990). These are richer sources of ideas about what Hacking means by suggesting turning social constructionism to morality. One possible resource for interpreting Hacking on this point is the social constructionist work he specifically mentions: that of Pickering, Latour and Woolgar, and Shapin and Schaffer. However, these writers are themselves methodologically (not to mention epistemologically)[8] very diverse. Shapin and Schaffer use historical literature to reconstruct the emergence, in Britain in the 1650s, of the experimental method as a way of doing science. Latour and Woolgar use an ethnography of laboratory science to produce an account of the social construction of a scientific fact, in this case about the chemical structure of thyrotropin releasing hormone. Pickering offers a detailed 'sociological history' of the emergence of high energy physics, at various scientific institutions, since the 1950s.

This diversity provides an 'embarrassment of riches' problem for those who would follow Hacking's recommendation and turn social constructionism to morality: which model should they choose? The problem of excess is compounded because, in addition to recommending the work of social constructionists, in the same paper Hacking mentions, as examples of ' "Moral" enquiries not far removed from what I have in mind' (1990: 358), the social problems school of sociology 'stemming from Garfinkel, and responsible for labelling theory',[9] and the 'Agenda-Setting school, pioneered by Gusfield's study [Gusfield, 1981] of how "drunken driving" became firmly fixed on the political agenda' (1990: 359). In addition Hacking says that he knows of 'only one sustained model for this sort of enquiry, namely some of the work of Michael Foucault', and acknowledges that 'My work has been seriously influenced by Foucault (or by successive Foucaults) for exactly twenty years. Books I have written and books I am writing reek of his effect on me' (ibid.: 361).

I make no general complaints about the diversity of resources Hacking offers. The launch of a new avenue of research is an appropriate occasion for the presentation of an inclusive range of materials. It is to Hacking's credit that he draws attention to the many rich resemblances between these various important works. However, one specific problem of such inclusivity is that it is difficult to know how to begin formulating such diverse research strategies into a coherent method. But perhaps searching for a coherent constructionist methodology is an inappropriate response? In any case it is difficult to find evidence of such an attempt in Hacking's own work on child abuse. Indeed this work does not closely follow any of the writers he mentions. There are many similarities to be sure, but it is rarely possible to say whose methodology Hacking has employed in the production of his texts. For example, though Hacking, following Latour and Woolgar, urges the study of workplaces (1988b: 61), there is no evidence that he has done any ethnography in the course of his social constructionist work. Indeed there are hints that often the methodological tools that Hacking finds most suitable are those that are available to a good investigative journalist. This is no criticism. The more elaborate methodologies of the social sciences do not always supply the lucrative returns they promise.

One possibility is that Hacking might be happy with Michael Lynch's suggestion that constructionists (or at least ethnomethodologists) adopt the methodology of 'normal science'. This is not a reference to Kuhn but to a remark by Chomsky.[10] Chomsky gave a conference address about his political work on the US media. Afterwards a sociologist asked whether he followed the appropriate methodological canons. Chomsky replied that no special knowledge of sociology was necessary for his purposes, he practised 'normal science'. Lynch interprets Chomsky's use of 'normal science' to imply a methodological commitment to 'nothing fancy', which means:

> juxtaposing (arguably) comparable cases, citing testimonies and reports, drawing out common themes, noting relevant discrepancies and trends, and appealing to common intuitions and judgements. 'Normal science' in this sense uses ordinary

modes of observing, describing, comparing, reading and questioning, and its constituent activities are expressed in vernacular terms. (1993: 304–5)

Lynch finds this approach attractive, partly because 'it does not equate science with . . . methodological restriction' (1993: 304, n.80), and partly because 'The reference point for this primitive natural science is not a universal consciousness of a specialised community of experts but an immense and varied set of competencies that "we" already have available but that are amenable to further instruction and explication' (ibid.: 305). Lynch is writing about science studies here, but this last remark applies equally well to our 'moral competencies'. For Lynch, and possibly for Hacking, the point of constructionist studies is not to add further pieces to a unified scientific representation of the world, but, in the manner of Wittgenstein, to assemble 'perspicuous representations' (1993: 305) of our concepts and practices, that help us to get a clearer view, and perhaps heal us from some misconceptions.[11]

However, this kind of 'normal science' does not quite do justice to Hacking's method. It captures the style of his work, it may even reflect his epistemological perspective, but it leaves out his predilection for history. While Hacking can be read as practising 'normal science', he does so by collecting 'a lot of little' historical facts. And he does so with the pervasive historicist suspicion that that which seems most secure and eternal is not, but instead emerges at particular junctures and undergoes incessant transformations. Hacking's favoured way of producing perspicuous representations is to use detailed, historical accounts of the emergence and transformation of our concepts and practices. Hacking names this the 'Lockean imperative: to understand our thoughts and our beliefs through an account of their origins' (1990: 355). If Hacking finds this kind of reading of his work tolerable, then his recommendation of a social constructionist turn in ethics is not a recommendation of a turn to a specific canonical 'social constructionist' methodology, but instead a general recommendation of a local, historicist perspective that allows for considerable methodological pluralism.

The Interpretive Turn in Political Theory

There are many possible ways that Hacking's local, historicist, social constructionist approach can be applied to the study of morality. Here is one example. One of the most commonly reported events in narrative reconstructions of Anglo-American political theory over the last fifteen years is a debate between liberal and communitarian theorists about the nature of justice, and in particular about the best method for inquiring into justice. For the purposes of this chapter, the most relevant feature of this debate is a dramatic transformation in the nature of the foundational resources appealed to, particularly by communitarians, but also by some liberals.

Instead of making foundational appeals to metaphysical entities such as 'human nature', 'transcendental human reason', or some abstract conception of 'utility', a number of prominent political theorists have begun to appeal to the moral judgements of specific historical communities. More specifically they have appealed to, variously, the 'shared understandings' (Walzer, 1983), 'settled convictions' (Rawls, 1985), 'intersubjective meanings' (Taylor, 1971), inherited 'moral ideals' (Taylor, 1992), 'traditions' and 'social practices' (MacIntyre, 1984; 1988),[12] of 'our' community.[13] Rorty has summarized this move by saying that for these writers the 'moral justification of the institutions and practices of one's group . . . is mostly a matter of historical narratives . . . rather than of philosophical metanarratives' (1991a: 200). One crucial feature of this shift from metaphysics to shared understandings is a shift from abstract metaphysical speculation to the *interpretation* of the deeply held convictions of particular historical communities.

Rather than basing their theories of justice on philosophical items, interpretive political theorists base them on interpretations of the convictions and understandings that they claim we share. Their theories, therefore, rest heavily on the empirical adequacy of these interpretations. They must be able to convince us that their interpretations capture the actual moral practices of a particular historical community. Unfortunately, critics have found it easy to challenge the empirical adequacy of a number of the key interpretive claims of these political theorists. One negative response to such criticisms is the rejection of the interpretive approach. Another more positive alternative is to find ways to strengthen the interpretive method. Hacking's recommendation of turning social constructionism to morality offers a way of achieving this. In order to support these claims, I turn to two exemplary cases.

Walzer's Appeal to Shared Understandings

Michael Walzer claims that the theory of justice he outlines in his *Spheres of Justice* is different to the theories that preceded it because it is based, not on abstract, metaphysical ideas with universal application, but on interpretations of '*Our* shared understandings' (1983: xiv). He says:

> My argument is radically particularist. I don't claim to have achieved great distance from the social world in which I live. One way to begin the philosophical enterprise – perhaps the original way – is to walk out of the cave, leave the city, climb the mountain, fashion for oneself (what can never be fashioned by ordinary men and women) an objective and universal standpoint. Then one describes the terrain of everyday life from far away so that it loses its particular contours and takes on a general shape. But I mean to stand in the cave, in the city, on the ground. Another way of doing political philosophy is to interpret to one's fellow citizens the world of meanings that we share. (1983: xiv)

Walzer's statement here is a terse and much-quoted example of the communitarian rejection of the abstract universalism of much political theory.

Instead of seeking to ground their theory on general philosophical concepts, communitarians attempt to ground it on 'the world of meaning that we share', 'shared understandings', 'social meanings', 'social goods' (Walzer, 1983: 7–9). For Walzer, this shift is based on the idea that 'justice is a human construction, and it is doubtful that it can be made in only one way' (ibid.: 5). He argues that it is unlikely that we are well served by adopting a single universal conception of distributive justice that applies generally to all societies and to all aspects of our society because, he claims, distributions take place in a variety of contexts for a variety of different reasons. Chief among the reasons are the fact that the goods that are distributed have contextually defined meanings; goods are not abstract but 'social' goods. They 'come into people's minds before they come into their hands; distributions are patterned in accordance with shared conceptions of what the goods are and what they are for' (ibid.: 7). Because of this pluralism, Walzer divides his theory of justice into a number of different 'spheres', with different principles of justice for each. What counts as just for one sphere, may not necessarily count as just for another. In the same way he claims, even more controversially, that what counts as just in one culture may not for another. Walzer summarizes this by saying that:

> the principles of justice are themselves pluralistic in form; that different social goods ought to be distributed for different reasons, in accordance with different procedures, by different agents; and that all these differences derive from the different understandings of social goods themselves – the inevitable product of historical and cultural particularism. (1983: 6)

Walzer's approach to justice is to interpret the social meanings as a result of which goods have their sense for the communities in which they find their use. He seeks, in particular, to interpret what 'our' various goods 'mean to us' (1983: xvi). A first step in this interpretive process is to realize that 'Social meanings are historical in character' (ibid.: 9). He urges us to attend to 'conception and creation: the naming of goods, and the giving of meaning, and the collective making' (ibid.: 7).

Rawls's Appeal to Settled Convictions

My second example is the recent work of John Rawls, collected in his *Political Liberalism* (1993).[14] Rawls is often credited with the revival of universalist, deontological, liberal political thought. So he is often considered a classic case of a political philosopher offering a view from the mountain, and the opposite of particularists like Walzer.[15] However, in his work since his 1985 paper 'Justice as fairness: political not metaphysical', Rawls demonstrates a strong particularist, anti-universalist shift. This, he says, is not because of communitarian criticisms of abstraction and universalism, but because he noticed a practical problem with his theory (1993: xvii). The problem is that he considers his earlier foundationalist approach to be inconsistent with certain facts about modern liberal democracies. Rawls's project, in *A Theory of Justice* (1972) and since, has been to unearth the principles of justice which can serve as the basis for a stable, well-ordered society. He had thought that the philosophically grounded principles of justice set out in *A Theory of Justice* could serve as such a basis. He now sees a fatal flaw in this plan. He claims that there are, as a matter of empirical fact, a diversity of incompatible, yet reasonable, philosophical doctrines affirmed by the members of modern liberal democracies, and that it is a feature of liberal democracy to perpetuate such diversity. This he calls 'the fact of reasonable pluralism' (1993: 36). Rawls thinks that, in the light of this fact, it is unrealistic to expect that these diverse, reasonable doctrines be dropped in favour of the foundational philosophical doctrine contained in his earlier work. People, he thinks, already affirm their own doctrines; pragmatically, he does not think he can expect them to drop their cherished beliefs in favour of the philosophical theory outlined in his earlier work. Because of the 'fact of reasonable pluralism' Rawls now thinks that 'philosophy as the search for truth about an independent metaphysical and moral order cannot provide a workable and shared basis for a political conception of justice in a democratic society' (1985: 230). He therefore believes that any principles of justice should be capable of achieving principled endorsement by an 'overlapping consensus' (1993: 133ff.) from the variety of reasonable philosophical doctrines affirmed in modern societies, and not endorsement on the basis of the single philosophical doctrine he articulated in his earlier work. Rawls believes an overlapping consensus might be possible because, fortunately, despite the fact of reasonable pluralism,

> the political culture of a democratic society, which has worked reasonably well over a considerable period of time, normally contains, at least implicitly, certain fundamental intuitive ideas from which it is possible to work up a political conception of justice suitable for a constitutional regime. (1993: 38, n.41)

These intuitive ideas are to be found in 'our public political culture itself, including its main institutions and the historical traditions of their interpretation'. They take the form of 'settled convictions [such] as the belief in religious toleration and the rejection of slavery' (ibid.: 8). Rawls thinks the way to proceed is to collect these settled convictions and

> try to organise the basic ideas and principles implicit in these convictions into a coherent conception of political justice. . . . We hope to formulate these ideas and principles clearly enough to be combined into a political conception of justice congenial to our most firmly held convictions. (ibid.)

Rawls's idea is not that these shared and settled convictions have any metaphysical privilege, but that because they are widely shared and have a long pedigree they are the best chance we have to find some basic principles that can be used to 'construct' a concept of political justice that can achieve principled endorsement by the range of incompatible moral and philosophical doctrines that he assumes are a fundamental political fact of modern societies.[16] This kind of foundation for political theory is a pragmatic one rather than a metaphysical one.[17] Principles of justice constructed from it are 'securely founded in public political and social attitudes' (1985: 230), not in a philosophical theory grounded in metaphysics. A final feature of Rawls's approach is that not only is the basis of his theory of justice built up from the settled moral convictions of the community, but the recommendations that arise from the theory are constrained by these convictions. This is Rawls's idea of 'reflective equilibrium' (1972: 48ff.). While it allows that a Rawlsian theory of justice, built from our settled convictions, might then challenge some of those convictions, it may also, reciprocally, be contested by them.

Interpreting Shared Understandings

Borh Rawls and Walzer start with the idea that justice is a human construction, not an entity with some kind of metaphysical essence. The foundations of a theory of justice, they both argue, can most reasonably be built, not from philosophical conceptions of rationality or human nature, but from the shared understandings and settled convictions of particular historical communities. Their interpretive political theorizing, then, depends not so much on being right about philosophy as on being right about shared understandings and settled convictions. Being right about such things is a matter of good interpretation, of building a good interpretive case from convincing evidence.

Walzer's Interpretive Method

In the space of some 300 pages Walzer considers issues concerning the welfare state, health care, charity and dependency, money, markets, conscription, public office, dangerous and dirty work, free time, education, kinship and love, religion and the state, public honours, political power, and citizenship. Even this long list doesn't fully convey the enormous breadth of Walzer's work. Walzer interprets our social meanings with respect to the various goods in the domains listed by means of fifty case studies embedded in an argument peppered with instructive references to various significant figures in the history of political and social thought, and to the work of some of his contemporaries. Only a few of the case studies Walzer uses directly interpret the shared understandings of contemporary Americans; the majority are drawn from other, often distant, times and places. Examples from contemporary America include a refuse collectors' co-operative in San Francisco, and the idea of 'dating'. More distant examples are the classical Chinese meritocracy, the Israeli kibbutz, Aztec education, and Athenian ostracism. These studies vary quite considerably in texture; some are more historically detailed than others. But none are very detailed, most relying on rather venerable, secondary literature. Neither the lack of historical detail nor the reliance on secondary sources is a criticism in itself. Walzer has won considerable praise for including the wide and fascinating historical data that he uses. However, he does claim to be 'radically particularist': he has said that he means to 'stand in the cave, in the city, on the ground' (1983: xiv), so he needs to demonstrate conclusively that this is where he does stand; that his interpretations are interpretations of the particular shared understandings of contemporary Americans. If this ambition is taken seriously, (and it should be: he is, after all, claiming to base his theory of justice on these interpretive claims) then the historical materials he actually uses are placed under considerable strain; a weakness of which his critics have been able to make much.

Susan Moller Okin asks (parodying MacIntyre), 'Whose traditions? Which understandings?' (1989: 41). She criticizes MacIntyre and Walzer for paying insufficient attention to the fact that the appeals they are making are to the shared understandings of certain dominant classes, rather than to the shared understandings held by *all* their contemporaries. She claims that the understandings they appeal to do not represent the shared understandings of, say, the feminist tradition.[18] This criticism is partly one concerning the empirical claim that where MacIntyre and Walzer see single shared understandings, there is in fact a plurality of competing shared understandings;[19] and partly a criticism about the uncritical, conservative nature of the communitarian appeals to the shared understandings of an existing order. In particular she claims that, 'The appeal to "our traditions" and the "shared understandings" approach are both incapable of dealing with the problem of the effects of *social domination* on beliefs and understandings' (1989: 42–3). I will return to the latter criticism below. The use of the former criticism is not limited to feminists. Ronald Dworkin has criticized Walzer in much the same way (Dworkin, 1983). Dworkin says that where Walzer argues that there are single shared understandings implicit in the social meanings of various goods, in fact there are plural understandings. Taking the example of health care, he says that Walzer argues that there is one shared understanding operating: health care should be distributed on the basis of need. Dworkin denies that this is so. He says that 'the brutal fact is that we do not provide anything like the same medical care for the poor as the middle classes can provide for themselves, and surely this also counts in deciding what the "social meaning" of medicine is for our society' (1983: 6). More generally Dworkin argues that the various spheres of justice are characterized by disagreement between different kinds of shared understandings. Dworkin's criticisms, in part, rest on the common liberal claim that modern societies are characterized by a deep-seated moral pluralism, which Dworkin indicates that Walzer, despite his claims to particularity, ignores.

Rawls's Interpretive Method

Rawls can hardly be accused of this particular oversight. His 'Political liberalist starts by taking to heart the absolute depth of that irreconcilable latent conflict' (1993: xxvi). Rawls's later work places a lot of emphasis on this empirical claim about the profound nature of modern pluralism. However, as we have seen, while Rawls starts with moral pluralism, he makes another empirical claim that there are, in stable democracies, certain settled convictions and implicit, intuitive ideas about the basic political structure of society (1993: 38, n.41). By making such claims and putting much weight on them Rawls is, like Walzer, vulnerable to questions about the empirical validity of his interpretive claims. Rawls provides far less even than Walzer in the way of concrete historical evidence for the particular settled convictions he constructs his theory upon. For example, one of the central settled convictions he draws on is belief in 'religious toleration'. In *Political Liberalism*, he provides only three or four pages that deal with history of the emergence of this conviction. In these pages Rawls sketches the 'historical context' for the emergence of the modern democratic political culture. He notes 'three historical developments that deeply influenced the nature of its moral and political philosophy' (1993: xxii): the Reformation, the development of the modern state, and the emergence of modern sciences. Religious tolerance, he implies, emerged as a way of coping with the fallout from the Reformation. In contrast to religion in the 'classical world', medieval Christianity was authoritarian, central, credal and expansionist and

> When an authoritative, salvationist, and expansionist religion like medieval Christianity divides, this inevitably means the appearance within the same society of a rival authoritative and salvationist religion . . . Luther and Calvin were as dogmatic and intolerant as the Roman Church had been. (ibid.: xxiii)

The division of Christendom into two factions, each 'in no doubt about the nature of the highest good, or the basis of moral obligation in divine law' (ibid.: xxiv), led to the wars of religion, the resolution of which involved the widespread acceptance of the idea of religious toleration:

> Thus the historical origin of political liberalism (and of liberalism more generally) is the Reformation and its aftermath, with the long controversies over religious toleration in the sixteenth and seventeenth centuries. Something like the modern understanding of liberty of conscience and freedom of thought began then. (ibid.)

Apart from this very brief history Rawls pays little specific historical attention to the concrete historical nature of the settled convictions he works up into the basic principles of his theory. It is instructive that when he sets out the key components of his theory, namely the idea of 'society as a fair system of co-operation' (ibid.: 15), Rawls offers much interpretation of certain key ideas which he takes to be 'implicit in the public culture of democratic society' but offers no historical or empirical details of this public culture that demonstrate just how and where they are implicit. Though Rawls claims to be basing his theory on the interpretation of settled convictions, he does very little to show how his interpretations are specifically related to the historically specific understandings of the American people over the relevant period. He does not, for example, show how to move from the abolitionist movements, conflicts and legislation to the settled conviction that slavery is wrong, nor from this conviction to his abstract ideas of 'society as a fair system of co-operation'. As Bernard Williams has put it, Rawls lacks

> the dimension of what might be called sociological imagination, a sense that the peculiarities ... of American constitutionalism may depend on features of American society which are grounded neither in its political organisation nor in its ideas, but in such things as the history of its immigration and its dedication to the aims of commercial society. (Williams, 1993: 7)

This doesn't show that Rawls's interpretations are wrong, only that they leave many empirical questions unanswered. Rawls could offer the defence 'I'm a theorist and not a historian so leave me alone', but he does explicitly acknowledge the empirical nature of his claims. Rawls says, 'Any political conception of justice presupposes a view of the political and social world and recognises certain general facts of political sociology and human psychology' (1989: 34). He then proceeds to list four 'general facts', including the facts (mentioned above) that there are certain settled convictions and implicit intuitive ideas present in stable modern democracies that can serve as the basis of a theory of justice, and the stark fact of reasonable pluralism. Rawls says

> What justifies a conception of justice is not its being true to an order antecedent and given to us, but its compliance with our deeper understanding of ourselves and our aspirations, and our realisation that given our history and traditions embedded in our public life, it is the most reasonable doctrine for us. (1980: 519)

I have no criticisms here of this idea, but is Rawls's interpretation of deeper understanding of ourselves, our aspirations, our history and our public traditions empirically adequate? Rawls doesn't work very hard to prove it.

Social Constructionist Political Interpretation

Rhetorical Requirements

The criticisms of Rawls and Walzer's recent work that I have discussed put pressure on these theorists to justify their empirical claims. The failure of Walzer and, particularly, Rawls to provide sufficient empirical resources to make good their interpretive assertions is a serious weakness for their theories. This vulnerability is particularly acute because their theories place so much weight on their interpretive claims. This kind of weakness is a new problem in political theory. It is new, not because political theories in the past were well grounded in empirical evidence, but because the problem for previous foundationalist political theories was not to provide empirical justifications, but metaphysical ones. In making an interpretive turn, political theorists are exposing themselves to a new set of standards against which they may be judged. Rawls's and Walzer's interpretive claims no longer need to be adequate to standards supplied by the philosophical tradition, but they must be adequate according to more quotidian standards of empirical evidence.

While new in political theory, empirical adequacy is not alien to other fields in the human sciences. It is especially strong among the many kinds of human scientists who would be 'interpreters of culture'. As Clifford Geertz has put it, such writers face the rhetorical task of convincing their readers that they have 'been there' (1988: 5) and reported faithfully the shared understandings of the natives. If Rawls and Walzer, or MacIntyre, Taylor and Rorty, for that matter, are to persuade us that they are faithfully interpreting our shared understandings they must 'convince us that what they say is a result of their having actually penetrated (or, if you prefer, been penetrated by) another form of life, of having, one way or another, truly "been there" (Geertz, 1988: 4–5). The challenge interpretive political theorists face is to persuade us that they have been penetrated by 'our' form of life as it is actually, mundanely lived. The trouble is that, for the most part, interpretive political theorists give the impression that they have never left their libraries. The failure to demonstrate that they have 'been there' is a significant weakness of their work. Their critics are readily able to raise doubts about the fidelity of their interpretations to the facts, to question their reliability as witnesses. Okin criticizes MacIntyre and Walzer for failing to faithfully include the different shared understandings of women in their interpretations. Dworkin argues that Walzer fails to interpret authentically the plurality of shared understandings *within* his spheres of justice. Williams notes an inadequacy in Rawls's work that emerges in his failure to include in his interpretations large aspects of American social history.

The interpretive turn in political theory needs to find better ways to achieve the new rhetorical demands it has exposed itself to. One of the best resources available to interpretive political theorists for this purpose is, I believe, the local, empirical, social constructionist historicism that Ian Hacking has recommended. Hacking's work on child abuse can be read, in the light of the above discussion, as an interpretation of our 'shared understandings' about child abuse; as an account of the 'social meaning' of child abuse; or as a study of the emergence of our 'settled convictions' (in this case, unsettled convictions) about child abuse. Hacking's attention to specific historical details – dates, names, institutions, newspapers, empirical studies, contemporary social movements, jury decisions and legislation – offers much rich evidence that his interpretations provide a relatively faithful account of the emergence of child abuse in the last thirty years. His attention to local, historical details carries off the rhetorical task of convincing readers that Hacking has 'been there'; better at least than Walzer's and Rawls's more theoretical work is able to do. This rhetorical achievement is even more forceful in the social constructionist work Hacking cites as exemplary. Latour and Woolgar, Pickering, Garfinkel and Gusfield have all done detailed empirical studies of the practices they seek to interpret. Their work presents a very strong case that these writers have 'been there'. It does so partly because it displays detailed evidence that these theorists have witnessed with their own eyes what people do in science labs, astronomical observatories or law courts. But partly because it reveals (or claims to reveal) the detailed, often prosaic, processes by which 'shared understandings' about, say, the structure of thyrotropin releasing hormone, actually emerge.

Constructionist Method

Were intrepretive theorists to embrace the kind of local historicist, social constructionism to which Hacking has drawn attention, they would be doing much more than merely appropriating a form of rhetoric from the human sciences. The rhetorical advantages of social constructionist texts are not purchased cheaply; they are tightly bound to certain methodological and epistemological commitments. The central methodological commitment is to the collection of empirical evidence. Adopting such a methodological commitment would involve political theorists in a substantial methodological shift. Rather than looking at justice, equality, liberty, need or utility in the abstract, they would have to collect empirical data. Just as Shapin and Schaffer look at the historical details surrounding the birth of experimental method in Britain in the 1650s, so constructionist political theorists could refer to empirical data concerning the emergence of the belief that slavery is wrong. This might involve paying as much attention to the popularity of Harriet Beecher Stowe's *Uncle Tom's Cabin*, as to ideas in political philosophy.[20] Just as Latour and Woolgar do laboratory ethnography, constructionist political theorists could do ethnographies of ethics committees, constructionist political theorists could do ethnographies of ethics committees, legislatures and political pressure groups. Just as Pickering writes a history of the emergence of particle physics, constructionist political theorists could write the history of the emergence of, say, the concept of 'welfare', and the institutions that underpin it. This would require political theorists, at least part of the time, to leave their libraries and immerse themselves in the complex practical contexts in which shared understandings have emerged, evolved and been maintained.

The central epistemological commitment of a putative social constructionist interpretive political theory is to the idea of social construction itself. The shared understandings that interpretive political theorists interpret are, from this perspective, considered to be constructed during a social process, rather than emerging from some mysterious singularity complete with essence and necessity. Instead they are considered to be the contingent products of the shifting practices of historical communities. Those committed to Foucault's 'history of the present' believe that accounts of the particular contingencies surrounding the social construction of our 'shared understandings' reveals highly significant knowledge about them.

Constructionism as Social Criticism

One important respect in which such knowledge is significant is that it offers a way of countering the charge that interpretive political theory is bound to be conservative, and unable to serve as a basis for social criticism. I mention above that Okin criticizes Walzer and MacIntyre for paying insufficient attention to the 'social domination' expressed by 'our' shared understandings. In Walzer's case this is particularly notable when he argues that 'A given society is just if its substantive life is lived . . . in a way that is faithful to the shared understandings of the members' (1983: 313). The example of Walzer's work Okin mentions in particular is his discussion of caste society. In such a society the shared understandings about justice support dramatic and rigid inequalities in favour of the dominant castes. Okin argues that if the shared understandings of a society are to some extent determined by a 'dominant class' then, on Walzer's view, what counts as just in that society will be determined by the understandings of that dominant class. Any interpretations Walzer produces of these understandings will therefore serve to buttress the existing systems of domination. Whatever the challenges to this class-based model of power, it is clear that there is a significant problem here.[21] This problem emerges partly, I suggest, from the empirical thinness of Walzer's interpretation of shared understandings. As his critics have complained, his interpretations tend to offer singular, stable and unequivocal shared understandings on which to base his theories of justice for each sphere. If Walzer's interpretations were more empirical and historicist he might find, instead, a plurality of shifting and ambiguous shared understandings. If so, the critical resources available to him would expand dramatically. He would no longer be obliged to offer an interpretive restatement of the dominant shared understandings, but could opt, instead, to expose inconsistencies within this dominant understanding, or to promote one of the more marginal shared understandings he reveals.

In any case, this is the lesson offered by Hacking's constructionist interpretation of our shared understandings about child abuse. Hacking's account of the social construction of child abuse over the last thirty years indicates that these understandings have been socially constructed in a messy and contingent fashion from a diversity of other shared understandings, social movements and institutional practices. Specifically, he notes the roles played by feminism, jury decisions, children's rights, multiple personality disorder, the welfare state (1991a: 260ff.), the medical profession, the media (266ff.), definitional practices, political commitments to certain kinds of explanation of social problems (270ff.), ideas about incest (274ff.), the grammar of the word 'abuse' (277ff.), and the role of normality in modern knowledge (286ff.). Hacking also notes that causal processes by which our shared understandings about child abuse have been socially constructed are extremely convoluted; they are rarely one-way, and are often involved in reflexive, feedback relationships with each other.[22] Consequently, Hacking's work demonstrates that, rather than being singular, stable and unequivocal, our shared understandings about child abuse are complex, ambiguous and shifting; containing gaps, contradictions, and diverse kinds of reasoning. In revealing this complexity, Hacking's work is not conservative, but profoundly critical. It opens up a large new discursive space in which to investigate and debate our shared understandings about child abuse. Though Hacking is generally positive about these understandings, he does not simply defend them as they stand. In exposing their origins, he reveals at least one specific problem: the disease model of abuse. He also exposes a number of other historical oddities, which encourage us to feel less certain in the rightness of our convictions; making way for their criticism and revision.

It is possible that similar local, empirical, historicist and social constructionist interpretations of shared understandings in politics and morals could make visible a similar degree of complexity, inconsistency and impermanence. It may be that if one took a detailed look at the shared understandings of, say, a caste society, one would find, not univocal shared understandings about justice that buttress the position of the dominant caste, but a complex, shifting, ambiguous, and not always consistent network of shared understandings. If this turns out to be the case in caste societies, or in our society, such social constructionist interpretations could serve to expand the discursive space for moral criticism, offering new resources for self-understanding and the revision of moral and political values. This is the considerable opportunity which, I suggest, emerges in Hacking's social constructionist programme in moral inquiry.

Notes

1 Hacking is not the first to recommend this move. In the late 1960s, J.B. Schneewind wrote: 'If the study of the history of science is still at a comparatively early stage of development, the study of the history of moral systems has hardly even begun. At this point it can only be proposing a hypothesis to say that the pattern of thought revealed in [Kuhn's] studies of "scientific revolutions" may be useful as a guide in investigating the development of norms and values' (1970: 124).

2 Hacking's effusiveness on this point, perhaps, has something to do with the rhetorical problems of saying that child abuse is socially constructed. Saying this sounds, at least to some people, like saying it's not a real problem. This is a position which Hacking flatly denies. In a more recent paper he says 'I do believe that in at least one popular sense of the words, the idea of child abuse is what is called a social construction. That does not make it any less real, objective or awful' (Hacking, 1994).

3 See Giovannoni and Becerra (1979).

4 Kempe et al. (1962).

5 Hacking doesn't use this example, though he does mention our shifting attitudes to corporal punishment (1991a: 284).

6 See ibid. on this.

7 The phrase is Nietzsche's (1967: Preface, section 6). I believe that the social constructionist moral inquiry that Hacking is advocating resembles Nietzsche's 'genealogical' approach to morality, both in its methodological interest in empirical, historical data, and in its critical intent (though Hacking's moral commitments are starkly different). Nietzsche believed that if

we are to make progress with moral inquiry a new kind of knowledge of moral values is needed, 'a knowledge of the conditions and circumstances in which they grew, under which they evolved and changed (morality as consequence, as symptom, as mask, as tartufferie, as illness, as misunderstanding; but also morality as cause, as remedy as stimulant, as restraint, as poison), a knowledge of a kind that has never yet existed or even been desired' (1967: Preface, section 6). It is this kind of knowledge which I believe Hacking's social constructionist programme offers. This should be no surprise. Hacking has said that his own work in this area 'reeks' of Foucault's influence (Hacking, 1990: 361), and Foucault's work, it is well known, reeks of Nietzsche's.

8 There isn't space here to discuss the large epistemological differences that separate social constructionists, or to speculate on Hacking's position relative to them. I can only note that the history of science studies in the last decade has been characterized by vigorous epistemological disagreement between the various factions represented by the writers Hacking cites. But see Hacking (1983) for his lengthy survey of the epistemological issues at stake in the study of science, and see Pickering (1992) for a representative collection of epistemological arguments between constructionists.

9 Though Hacking doesn't mention it, in addition to any influence Garfinkel's work may have had on social problems sociology and on labelling theory, Garfinkel also contributed to the first ethnomethodological studies of work. This research approach has made strong contributions to the post-Kuhnian studies of science that Hacking refers to. See, for example, Lynch (1985) and (1993). Hacking also makes no mention of ethnomethodologists who have worked specifically on morality. See, particularly, Jayyusi (1984; 1991).

10 Lynch reports that Chomsky used this term in an offhand remark to a sociologist at the 1990 meeting of the Eastern Sociological Association in Boston. See Lynch (1993: 304, n.79).

11 See Lynch's excellent paper 'Extending Wittgenstein: the pivotal move from epistemology to social science' (1992), reproduced in altered form in Lynch (1993).

12 Though MacIntyre believes that one of the most serious malaises of modernity is that we no longer have any genuinely shared understandings, and therefore proclaims the need to revive a much older Thomist ethical tradition.

13 And though he is not usually characterized as a communitarian, these appeals have been compared to Bernard Williams's appeals to 'thick concepts' (Warnke, 1993: 3). I have already mentioned that Hacking claims child abuse is one of Williams's thick concepts.

14 Though *Political Liberalism* is a collection of earlier papers, Rawls has altered some papers significantly, changing their titles, and merging them into single chapters. This makes referencing difficult. On the assumption that the book is more widely available than the papers, I cite it rather than the papers. Occasionally, I have been unable to find a passage in the book that corresponds to one in the papers, so the paper is cited instead.

15 Though it is increasingly argued that this characterization of Rawls, though warranted, is not entirely accurate. See for example, Plant (1991: 354ff.).

16 Interestingly, in the present context, a central idea in Rawls's work in the last decade is his idea of 'Political Constructivism' (1993: 89–125). How does Rawls's constructivism relate to social constructionism? This is not a simple question. Rawls's constructivism is a way of doing political theory, which he claims to borrow from Kant. First he takes our settled convictions and formalizes them into certain idealized basic conceptions (a conception of moral personhood, a conception of a well-ordered society). He takes these basic ideas and models them using a representational device: 'the original position'. The principles of justice that arise from this model are counted as constructed (1993: 103). These principles are, on the face of it, likely to receive support because they are built from (it is claimed) our deepest settled convictions. However, the construction process for Rawls is an abstract one, taking place in a model, not *social* construction carried out by real, historical people.

17 A point on which Rorty has placed much emphasis (Rorty, 1991b).

18 Okin argues that there is a recognizable feminist tradition (1989: 60), that could well be appealed to as an alternative source of shared understandings.

19 While I am claiming that Okin is arguing that there a plurality of shared understandings, she in fact claims that there are '*no shared understandings*, even amongst women' (1989: 67).

This apparent contradiction rests on differing interpretations of the meaning of 'shared'. When Okin claims there are no shared understandings, she is discussing the plurality of different understandings about gender held by the members of our society. Because there is a plurality of different understandings there are no understandings shared by *everyone*, so in this wide sense there are no 'shared' understandings. But this doesn't mean there are no shared understandings of any kind. One might assume that understandings can be shared to different degrees. There are, I think, various factions in the feminist movement that do share understandings about gender. So, while one can readily concede that there are no universally shared understandings about gender, one can say that there are many different shared understandings of gender; shared, that is, by various groups of people.

20 Richard Rorty has made an interesting (if not very empirical) argument on this point. See Rorty (1993).

21 Walzer is aware of this problem. He accepts that he has to counter the argument that the appeal to shared understandings 'binds us irrevocably to the status quo . . . and so undercuts the very possibility of social criticism' (1987: 3).

22 This reflexive concern is captured in statements like: 'People act and decide under descriptions, and as new possibilities for description emerge, so do new kinds of action. This is a two way street. Because people behave differently in the light of how we classify them . . . the descriptions and classifications must in turn be modified' (1991a: 254–5).

References

Dworkin, R. (1983) 'To each his own', *New York Review of Books*, 14 April: 6.

Geertz, C. (1988) *Works and Lives: The Anthropologist as Author*. Cambridge: Polity Press.

Giovannoni, J. and Becerra, R. (1979) *Defining Child Abuse*. New York: Basic Books.

Gusfield, J. (1981) *Drink-Driving and the Symbolic Order*. Chicago: University of Chicago Press.

Hacking, I. (1983) *Representing and Intervening*. Cambridge: Cambridge University Press.

Hacking, I. (1986) 'Making up people', in T. Heller, M. Sosna and D. Welbery (eds), *Reconstructing Individualism*. Stanford, CA: Stanford University Press. pp. 222–36.

Hacking, I. (1988a) 'The sociology of knowledge about child abuse', *Nous*, 2: 53–63.

Hacking, I. (1988b) 'The participant irrealist at large in the laboratory', *British Journal for the Philosophy of Science*, 39: 277–94.

Hacking, I. (1990) 'Two kinds of new historicism for philosophers', *New Literary History*, 21(2): 343–64.

Hacking, I. (1991a) 'The making and molding of child abuse', *Critical Inquiry*, 17 (Winter): 253–88.

Hacking, I. (1991b) 'Two souls in one body', *Critical Inquiry*, 17 (Summer).

Hacking, I. (1992) 'Multiple personality disorder and its hosts', *History of the Human Sciences*, 5(2): 3–31.

Hacking, I. (1994) 'Memoro-politics, trauma, and the soul', *History of the Human Sciences*, 7(2): 1–32.

Jayyusi, L. (1984) *Categorization and the Moral Order*. London: Routledge.

Jayyusi, L. (1991) 'Values and moral judgements: communicative praxis and moral order', in G. Button (ed.), *Ethnomethodology and the Human Sciences*. Cambridge: Cambridge University Press. pp. 227–51.

Kempe, C.H. et al. (1962) 'The battered-child syndrome', *Journal of the American Medical Association*, 181 (July): 17–24.

Latour, B. and Woolgar, S. (1979) *Laboratory Life*. Princeton, NJ: Princeton University Press.

Lynch, M. (1985) *Art and Artifact in Laboratory Science*. London: Routledge & Kegan Paul.

Lynch, M. (1992) 'Extending Wittgenstein: the pivotal move from epistemology to social science', in A. Pickering (ed.), *Science as Practice and Culture*. Chicago: University of Chicago Press. pp. 215–65.

Lynch, M. (1993) *Scientific Practice and Ordinary Action: Ethnomethodology and Social Studies of Science*. Cambridge: Cambridge University Press.

MacIntyre, A. (1984) *After Virtue*, 2nd edn. London: Duckworth.

MacIntyre, A. (1988) *Whose Justice, Which Rationality?* London: Duckworth.

Nietzsche, F. (1967) *On the Genealogy of Morals*. New York: Vintage.

Okin, S.M. (1989) *Justice, Gender and the Family*. New York: Basic Books.

Pickering, A. (1984) *Constructing Quarks: A Sociological History of Particle Physics*. Edinburgh: Edinburgh University Press.

Pickering, A. (ed.) (1992) *Science as Practice and Culture*. Chicago: University of Chicago Press.

Plant, R. (1991) *Modern Political Thought*. Oxford: Blackwell.

Rawls, J. (1972) *A Theory of Justice*. Oxford: Blackwell.

Rawls, J. (1980) 'Kantian constructivism in moral theory', *Journal of Philosophy*, 88: 515–72.

Rawls, J. (1985) 'Justice as fairness: political not metaphysical', *Philosophy and Public Affairs*, 14(3): 223–51.

Rawls, J. (1989) 'The domain of the political and overlapping consensus', *New York University Law Review*, 64(2): 233–55.

Rawls, J. (1993) *Political Liberalism*. New York: Columbia University Press.

Rorty, R. (1979) *Philosophy and the Mirror of Nature*. Oxford: Blackwell.

Rorty, R. (1989) *Contingency, Irony and Solidarity*. Cambridge: Cambridge University Press.

Rorty, R. (1991a) 'Postmodernist bourgeois liberalism', in R. Rorty, *Objectivity Relativism and Truth*. Cambridge: Cambridge University Press. pp. 197–202.

Rorty, R. (1991b) 'The priority of democracy to philosophy', in *Objectivity, Relativism and Truth*. Cambridge: Cambridge University Press. pp. 175–96.

Rorty, R. (1993) 'Human rights, rationality and sentimentality', in S. Shute and S. Hurley (eds), *On Human Rights*. New York: Basic Books.

Schneewind, J.B. (1970) 'Moral knowledge and moral principles', in S. Hauerwas and A. MacIntyre (1983) (eds), *Revisions*. Notre Dame, IN: University of Notre Dame Press. pp. 113–26.

Shapin, S. and Schaffer, S. (1985) *Leviathan and the Air Pump: Hobbes, Boyle and the Experimental Life*. Princeton, NJ: Princeton University Press.

Taylor, C. (1971) 'Interpretation and the sciences of man', *Review of Metaphysics*, 25.

Taylor, C. (1992) *The Ethics of Authenticity*. Cambridge, MA: Harvard University Press.

Walzer, M. (1983) *Spheres of Justice: A Defence of Pluralism and Equality*. New York: Basic Books.

Walzer, M. (1987) *Interpretation and Social Criticism*. Cambridge, MA: Harvard University Press.

Warnke, G. (1993) *Justice and Interpretation*. Cambridge, MA: MIT Press.

Williams, B. (1985) *Ethics and the Limits of Philosophy*. London: Fontana.

Williams, B. (1993) 'A fair state', *London Review of Books*, 13 May: 7–8.

15

Constructionism, Authority and the Ethical Life

Thomas Osborne

There are many different definitions of the term 'ethics' and probably many ways of adopting what might be known as a constructionist approach to this field. The notion of ethics is sometimes held to be the science that we connect up to our moral habits. Sometimes it refers to decision procedures and particular situations (abortion, euthanasia). In each of these areas a constructionist approach might be taken; for example, one might argue in social constructionist vein that current moral issues (such as abortion) have been constructed around particular sites of more general social disturbance (the status of women in patriarchal societies) or – dropping the 'social' tag from constructionism – around certain historically specific and hence contingent procedures of rationality, persuasion and justification (medical techniques, political argument, forms of rhetoric and so forth).

In what follows, I want to take a much wider view; to be broadly dispositional not narrowly procedural about ethics. Instead of talking about ethical quandaries, sites and situations, or even specific ethical virtues as such, I want to talk about what might be called *ethical stylizations*, that is, collections of capacities attached to persons that serve the ends of ethical judgement. This means that I want to connect ethics to the issue of person-formation. Ethical styles are to ethics what styles of reasoning are to scientific truth; that is, before one can be ethical or unethical, one needs a style of ethical judgement, or rather a particular stylization of the person that is equipped to make ethical judgements (cf. Hacking, 1982). This widened notion of ethics is not original. Versions of it can be found from Aristotle to Charles Larmore. They observe that in order to follow a (moral or ethical) rule one needs to know when and how to apply the rule – one needs to become the right kind of person for the right kind of rule (Larmore, 1987).

Ethics, Rule and Authority

Obviously ethical stylizations are constructions. To press this home, ethics might be considered in distinction from morals. Moral systems are systems of interdiction; they are ideologies, codes to which individuals must relate themselves. Ethics, on the other hand, might be considered in a more positive sense, not as codes of interdiction, not as external norms to which individuals must relate themselves, but as constructed norms of 'internal consistency' (cf. Deleuze, 1988: 23; Foucault, 1984). Morality, one could say, is about doing one's duty to others or doing one's duty by some moral norm; ethics is about doing one's duty to oneself. Clearly the distinction is not absolute. On does one's duty to oneself, no doubt, by framing moral interdictions in a way that would comply with one's sense of ethical consistency. But by ethical stylisations we refer – not so much to specific ethical values or virtues – but to the act of framing forms of consistent conduct for the self; to the act of constructing the self as a subject of ethical value.

In principle, all forms of subjectification might be reduced to the rubric of ethical construction (Veyne, 1987: 9). But ethics only become really interesting when juxtaposed with the question of authority. What is interesting is not so much the construction of ethics but the ways in which ethical resources are used in the construction, expression and legitimation of forms of authority. But what is authority? It is, says E.D. Watt, more than advice yet less than command. Authority is not power, nor law, nor persuasion, rather it pertains to something like personal influence, to 'weighty counsel' (Watt, 1982: 14). Such forms of counsel clearly presuppose an element of freedom on the part of their recipients, since one – presumably – enters voluntarily into counsel and willingly submits oneself to it. So authority – in this usage at least – is something like the structuring of our willingness to shape our ethical conduct in certain ways; it is authority that seeks to determine the structuration of our ethical stylizations.

Perhaps social theorists have hitherto, as Watt says, confused authority with authoritarianism. Perhaps this is why they have not been much concerned to investigate the forms of consciousness of authority itself; and to investigate the ways in which the constitution of authority has been linked to the cultivation of ethical values. There are honourable – albeit not necessarily constructionist – exceptions, of course; Max Weber and Norbert Elias spring to mind.

One of Weber's concerns was with exploring the ethical *consequences* deriving from particular institutions of authority such as religion or science, including the ethical consequences stemming from particular religious ideologies. Weber was sensible enough to restrict himself to a workable set of interests, namely illuminating the effects of religion on specifically economic affairs, what he called 'economic ethics'. His question related to the varied ways in which religious authority affected the economic sphere. Similarly, one might take one's cue from Weber in considering the ethical consequences of the rise of science; scientific culture (cf. Schroeder, 1995). No doubt, some might want to observe that the obvious Weberian conclusion here would be that it is precisely the consequence of science that the concept of authority – and that of ethics – is eroded altogether. Hence, Arendt's question; 'what *was* authority?' (Arendt, 1961). But even this would still amount to an ethical consequence of the rise of science. After all, on one hand, the conduct of science itself clearly requires a particular ethical cultivation, and on the other, there are the ethical reactions to science to be considered, for instance under the heading of 're-enchant-ment' (Gellner, 1987); those attempts to make the world ethical again after the supposed moral depravations of scientific culture.

Aside from such consideration of the ethical consequences of authority, historical sociologists – or a few of them – have studied the relations between particular forms of ethical culture and practices of *rule*. To what extent have forms of ethical culture been connected to practices of rule? Rule is not quite the same as authority. Rule implies rationalities and means of control over populations or territories; and rule also implies a certain determination with regard to the action of subjects. Nevertheless, rule itself can still be an ethical matter; ethical stylizations of how to rule can be seen as not just an ideological veil, but an internal component of the very possi-bility of the exercise of rule (Osborne, 1994a: 289–93).

The study of ethics and rule might have two kinds of focus. One such might follow Norbert Elias and investigate ethical rationalities of rule. Elias demonstrated how the warrior aristocracy moderated its warlike propensi-ties and mutated into a social group stressing a particular economy of manners associated with etiquette and the self-monitoring of conduct (Elias, 1983). For those concerned with rationalities of rule as opposed to evolutionary sociology, *The Court Society* has to be Elias's finest work. But this kind of study has been applied in only a limited way. Above all, the ethics of rule seems habitually to be associated with aristocratic cultures (cf. e.g. Campbell, 1987: 161–72, and *passim*). J.C.D. Clark, for instance, in his plea for what he calls a 'social theory of elite hegemony' rightly argues for an understanding of ethical ideals – for example, that surrounding the ideal of 'the gentleman', which would pay close attention to the logics of *inward-ness* pertaining within social and moral codes, and for these logics to be comprehended, not as some reflection of an aberrant class interest, but as rationalities in their own right (Clark, 1985: 95).

One must have sympathy for Clark's position (regardless of its ideologi-cal starting point). But we must also be symmetrical here. For Clark, ethics of rule appear effectively to stop in Britain after 1832. For him, it seems, only aristocratic cultures possess ethical 'inwardness'. But it is surely not only aristocracies that deploy norms of ethical stylization in relation to their capabilities and justifications of rule. For instance, if it is the case that there is no specifically socialist art of government, then there are indeed socialist ethics of rule, and these are every bit as inward as their aristo-cratic counterparts. The interest in aristocracy perhaps derives from the fact that here the art of government is overlaid with the ethic of rule itself. That is, the justification for rule, the entity in whose 'name' rule is justified, is often only the continuity of the aristocratic ethical ideal itself. With socialism – one might surmise – things are different. Socialist politics, es-pecially in its more sectarian varieties, is saturated with ethical codes and veritable politics of identity; yet these ethics tend not themselves to be the rationale for desiring rule; this has to be discovered elsewhere. If ethics do not stop in 1832, then a question arises as to the specificity of ethics of rule in modernity. Perhaps – recalling Weber – we do not have ethics of rule so much as ethics of administration. But it is all too easily assumed that bureaucratic culture elides the question of ethics altogether; that the bureaucrat is not an ethical entity. This is to mistake the aims and rationale of bureaucracy for its preconditions. Bureaucracy is indeed hardly ethical in its motivations, but it is presupposed by an ethical stance on the part of the bureaucrat, and a history of the inculcation of different modes of ethical neutrality on the part of bureaucrats would certainly make interesting reading (cf. Minson, 1993: 133–9).

On the other hand, instead of focusing upon those who rule, one might investigate what could be loosely termed the political subjectivity of citizenship. By this I mean the form in which the ethical conduct of citizens is problematized and/or actualized through various mechanisms of government. What kind of subjectivity is presupposed by varying types of citizenship? The extent to which such fabrications of citizenship will be tied to wider rationalities of government will no doubt vary. For instance, there has been a certain amount of talk recently about the entrepreneurial self, and the active citizen. This domain concerns the kinds of authority we should place over ourselves when it comes to citizenship; it concerns the ways in which we program our ethical ideals in relation to our political authorities (Dean, 1994: 209–10).

Two Kinds of Ethical Authority

Forms of impersonal authority and practices of rule have been, to varying extents, subjects of sociological inquiry. On the other hand – and here we can become more properly constructionist – there are forms of authority conducted directly upon, and directly through the agency of, persons. We should not make the mistake of assuming that such forms of personal authority are necessarily of diminishing importance in the modern world. I want to consider two interrelated dimensions to these kinds of authority, and shall label these respectively the ethics of self-improvement and the aesthetics of authority.

When we study the ethics of self-improvement, we are concerned most conspicuously with various kinds of pastoral expertise; that is, with all those disciplines that are concerned with questions of how one should live, and which are concerned with such questions specifically with an eye to the cultivation and preservation of autonomy and freedom. The experience of conversion is central to ethics of improvement. Conversion requires stewardship; stewardship surrounding the conversion itself, and then the stewardship practised by converts over their own selves. The emphasis upon expertise is not important. Our ethical lives are constructed not given, and expertise is one predominant medium of that construction. We might contrast naturalistic and constructionist approaches to ethical existence in this context. Max Weber, as is well known, wrote of ethical orders of existence. These life orders, because they mutually contradictory, could be could confer a certain sense of tragedy on the odyssey of personal existence; to be caught within the logic of one life order was to find oneself necessarily excluded from meaningful action within another. Weber – in the 'Intermediate reflections' and elsewhere – wrote of religious, political, scientific, erotic life orders. But where do these distinctions, these ethical logics, come from? For Weber, no doubt, they were naturally given – if evolving – as more or less universal states of existence.

But, in fact, one can historicize such distinctions and say that political, religious and other ethical life orders are constructions. If today our ethical values are very largely mediated through the varied powers of *psychological* knowledge, this is because the ethos of the conversion of self over which psychological expertise has claimed such a monopoly has become of such import for the ways in which individual agency is governed (Rose, 1992a). Modern selfhood is predicated upon a return to a kind of perpetual stewardship of the soul, an inward accounting for ourselves, and a self-monitoring of conduct that relates not so much to finite ethical goals as to an endless rhetoric of possible capacities. Psychology has been able to lay claim to a knowledge of our identities, a knowledge of our capacities, and a motley array of practical means of intervention for getting from one to another. But psychology has not just been passive in relation to these capacities; it has constructed them.

As well as the ethic of self-improvement, there is the question of aesthetics of authority. This relates to the ethical work that authorities perform upon themselves in order, so to speak, to stabilize their status as ethical authorities. There are, perhaps, two kinds of relation involved here which might be distinguished (but not counterposed): the expressionistic and the instrumental. On the one hand, there can be an expressive relation between an ethical stylization and the actual work of ethical authority. An authority that seeks to have sway over our ethical lives and our forms of conduct will cultivate a certain kind of persona that will serve as an expression of that authority's claim to such authority. On the other hand, there can also be an instrumental relation between the ethical stylization of an authority and the ethical stylization it seeks to bring about in others; that is, authorities can use their own ethical capacities as exemplary properties for others to imitate directly.

As for the expressionistic relation, a good example would be the games of status frequently played by members of the medical profession in order to give themselves a badge of authority. That such exercises amount to more than just the expression of a certain kind of collective vanity can readily be seen. Doctors, for instance, will claim that their personae function as positive devices in treatment (Osborne, 1994b). Or, otherwise, take the example of military leadership. For John Keegan, the authority of military command rests not just upon skill, knowledge or strength, but upon what amounts to the cultivation of a particular ethical style (Keegan, 1988: esp. 1–11; cf. Veyne, 1987: 15–17). What is important about Keegan's account is that he does not reduce the question of styles of authority simply to that of ideology; the mask of command is not just an illusory gesture, but a constructive technique, a means of communication. And no mask would work without a requisite terrain, a whole environment in which it might be appropriate.

A sociological language already exists for discussing such issues; that of *charisma*. We know that charisma, even for Weber, was not a natural phenomenon; it was not because agents really did bear some objective 'gift of grace' that they achieved designation as charismatics. But nor should charisma be seen as merely the effect of some collective recognition. Charisma is an ethical technique. It is a means of aligning certain personal qualities with transcendent force such that they become properties valued by the collectivity. Alongside the technique of charisma, one might add that of *exemplarity*. This takes us already to the instrumental angle on the aesthetics of authority. Of course, in a sense, those who bear charismatic authority are necessarily exemplary in so far as they embody particular values, ideals or aspirations. Charismatics are incarnations of values. Such a value-bearing charismatic might be termed a moral exemplar in distinction – if continuity – from what might be called an ethical exemplar (cf. Scheler, 1987). An ethical exemplar would not be – or would not only be – a figure that embodies particular values, ideals or aspirations. Ethical exemplars are not just that incarnations of values, but are personae that deploy their attributes directly upon the conduct of conduct of those they deal with. Rather than being merely ideological or external to the exercise of their authority, the ethical conduct, or the ethical make-up, of ethical exemplars is internal to the deployment of their authority. Their ethical make-up is not just expressive of, but instrumental in, the deployment of their authority.

Perhaps the prototype and paradigm of the ethical exemplar in this sense is the psychoanalyst. Most sociologists appear to take the view that psychoanalysis is a generally marginal endeavour in relation to the wider exercise of authority in our societies. And so it is. But the social interest of psychoanalysis lies in its own exemplarity rather than its effectiveness, for psychoanalysis is itself exemplary of a certain stylization of authority (cf. Foucault, 1989: 64). At least with regard to the usually neglected area of technique (as opposed to doctrine), psychoanalysis has been surprisingly influential or paradigmatic as a mode of authority (cf. Miller and Rose, 1994; Osborne, 1993). The central notion here is that of transference. The psychoanalyst does not say 'follow me' or 'do as I say'. The psychoanalyst does not really have to do anything,. except *be* a psychoanalyst. It is psychoanalysis itself that is a little machine for influencing the conduct of the analysand (even unconsciously); the analysand experiences a transference relation with the analyst and takes on some of the analyst's attributes. Psychoanalysis is an assemblage for disseminating – not so much values, ideals or aspirations as such but ethical qualities: those of the psychoanalyst.

Exemplarity is an instrumental technique that works in the co-presence of persons. It need not be so; one can attain a kind of abstract exemplarity as well. Exemplarity can act at a distance. Of course, it is probably most effective in situations of co-presence. It is a basic technique of the psychotherapeutic trades, but also of current techniques of business management which use methods of exemplarity, and an abundance of educational techniques of a multitude of kinds. Nor is ethical exemplarity all that novel. In the nineteenth century, during the debate on the reorganization of the civil service, Edwin Chadwick suggested, sensibly enough, that it should be a key function of postmen to be ethical exemplars. The postman is not somebody who exactly exercises a social control of the populace; yet the postman can be exemplary in so far as he can be the embodiment of ethical attributes (modesty, good sense, propriety) that should be generally adopted by the people at large, especially – thinks Chadwick – in difficult places like Ireland (PP 1854–55:5: cf. Osborne, 1994a).

Excursus: Professional Authority

Should the discussion so far seem somewhat over-abstract, perhaps it is best to pursue a particular sociological topic. Consider the issue of professional authority. Sociologists have laboured over definitions of the profession. Sociological studies have tended to provide either functionalist accounts of professional authority in terms of the nature of the concerns with which professionals deal, or more or less Marxist accounts concerned with the supposedly malign consequences of professional 'monopoly'. More rarely asked is the question: of what state of affairs is the construction of a professional ethos an expression?

In fact, the ethical character of the profession seems to be the expression of a double articulation of concerns. Professional conduct is distinguished, on the one hand, by the fact that it concerns the regulation of persons, and, on the other, by the fact that it tends to embody particular forms of practical intelligence. Professions typically seek to embody a particular form of authority: one which preserves the ethical integrity of those who make up the constituency or target population of the profession. Doctors, lawyers and clergy are the archetypal professions because they work upon the conduct of their constituencies; not necessarily by directing their activities but through advice, succour and persuasion. This strategy of ethical respect requires, in return, that steps are taken to regulate and control the ethical integrity of professionals themselves. Professionals must embody the requisite attributes. This ethical stylization can take place partly by means of a disciplining of the professional body. But a better way to ethicalize the profession is by problematizing the work of the professional in a particular – ethical – way. That is to say, one needs to make something out of the fact that professional work embodies a particular stylization of practical intelligence; one that must take an ethical form.

In order to see how professional work itself might be described as ethical, take the well-known distinction between a profession and an occupation. One might say that in an occupation one has no ethical relation to the tasks that one performs; one is 'occupied' in a passive sense. But in a profession there is, so to speak, a symbiotic relation between the work one performs in one's occupational acts and the work one performs upon the self; and these two types of exercise will be mutually reinforcing. In other words, the ethical component of professional work is internal to that kind of work itself.

Perhaps the language of constructionism can be useful at this point. The view that I have represented of the profession is somewhat archaic in that it takes professional self-stylization almost completely at face value. But my argument is not that the profession is the embodiment of a kindly ethical necessity. Rather, the profession is a construction. It is a form of authority designed to regulate the ethical conduct of others, and to do so under the auspices of the exemplary self-regulation of the persona of the professional. The ethical valorization of the professional is integral and not coincidental to the status of the profession itself. Hence, the analysis of professional power must pay attention to the diversity of ways in which professionals construct ethical stylizations as expressions and instruments of their authority. But, taken on its own terms, the profession is neither good nor bad; it is an ingenious – if historically limited – ethical machine.

Fixation and Flotation

The language of ethics takes us, however, beyond a return to the sociology of the professions. Could one have a general history of the links between ethics and authority? Can we say something about the specificity of ethical demands in different periods? In Foucault's work, there is the trace of a dialectic between ethical injunctions and moral regulation. Or rather there is a relation to self that is derived more or less from external forces; and one which relates to an internal constitution of ethical ideas. Morals or religious ideologies are rather passive; one can be less constructionist about them. Morals come packaged in code or ideological form; they take the form of a more or less finite set of rules that are external to the individual and must be adhered to. Ethics, on the other hand, are produced through the individual; they relate to a certain amount of labour upon the self. According to the character of rule in a particular period, a ruling order will stress moral codes or ethical individualization. For instance, from the third century BC the city-state faded in relative importance to the imperial power in the Roman-Hellenistic world (Foucault, 1986a: 82). Foucault's contention is that this led, not so much – as in the eyes of some commentators – to an era of anxiety-ridden individualization on the part of the ruling orders, but to an enhanced ethical attention to one's relation to self; an intensification of the work one was to perform in order to construct oneself as an ethical being.

It is more than a little unlikely, of course, that Foucault was thinking of drawing up a general typology of ethical and moral injunctions in history. Nevertheless, it does seem as if he was prepared to draw up broad analogies between periods that were subjected to varieties of ethical intensification. It is in this vein that he compares the Roman-Hellenistic period to the contemporary era in which he sees a similar need for an autonomous ethics other than one founded upon a scientific knowledge of the self, desire or the unconscious (Foucault, 1984: 343). But then there are ethics and there are ethics. The difference between ethics and morals does not relate to an absence of norms in ethics and a preponderance of them in morals. For some regimes of manners deploy rigid systems of normalization without, for all that, being moral systems as such. In light of this, I propose a distinction that can be made from within the realms of ethics: between ethical fixation and ethical flotation.

For ethical fixation, consider the Victorian period. It is customary to think of this era – at least among the Victorian bourgeoisie – as one of moralism and a stifling, and not uncommonly hypocritical, religious fervour. It is usually said that the Victorian period entailed an enhancement of prohibitions over individual conduct. The sphere of sexuality would be an obvious case in point (Gay, 1984). No doubt there was indeed a tightening of codes defining prohibited acts. But this prohibition also related to an intensification of the relation to oneself by which one constituted oneself as the subject of one's acts (cf. Foucault, 1986a: 41). It was not just that more forms of conduct became prohibited, but that the question of one's intentions with regard to conduct became increasingly problematized as an index of the status of one's self. Perhaps what we have in the Victorian period was not so much a moralization of pleasure and sexual conduct, but an ethicalization of the self *through* the troubled problematization of pleasure and sexual conduct. So what mattered was not just moral values themselves, but the relation of such values to the constitution of the self. No doubt the status of the self was just as, or more, important than the fact of upholding the values.

We can take this a little further by considering some of the things that Stefan Collini says about the Victorian intellectual classes. Again, what we have here is an argument about the construction of an ethic of the self and its importance. What mattered, once more, was a certain steadfastness of self and not moral values as such. Take the virtue of altruism (Collini, 1991: 60–90). Surely altruism is a moral virtue in that it relates to one's conduct towards others; it is for the benefit of the other that one is altruistic. Yet the Victorian ethic of altruism can also be understood as a particular way of establishing a certain relation to self. In this sense there is not necessarily a contradiction between a society concerned with altruistic values and one known for a commitment to rational premises of self-interest (ibid.: 62). For what was at issue was not an opposition between selfishness and generosity, but a common concern for the sturdiness of the self. What mattered was to keep at bay the demons of sloth which lead to misery. Hence altruism served to motivate one towards action. Collini writes that:

> The constant, one could say, was the need for purposes – the kind of purposes which, when supported by the appropriate feelings are sufficient to motivate action. The representative Victorian intellectual, whether believer or sceptic, did not have a constant impulse to serve: he or she had a constant anxiety about apathy and infirmity of the will. . . . Thus, it was *because* altruistic aims were assumed to motivate that Victorian intellectuals found social work an antidote to doubt, and not that, already having the motivation, they 'transferred' its direction from God to man. (ibid.: 84–5)

Hence, the ethic of altruism related more to the establishment of a particular motivation towards conduct than to an overriding moral demand for altruistic virtues as such. It was the ethical work not the ideology or moral code that was important. What mattered was the relation to self established by the ethical labour of altruism.

Now, one of the many things that is interesting about such an ethic is what might be called its fixity. It could be said that the Victorians were generally fixated when it came to ethics. By this I mean that it was imperative to construct a certain constancy of the self; to make of the self a kind of irresistible material. The self had to be fixed in the face of the perturbed world. So what was important was ethical consistency or, better (to adopt Collini's term) – muscularity. This accounts for the relative ease with which it might be possible to draw up a list of Victorian ethical codes: altruism, self-interest, austerity, character, sobriety and so forth. These virtues were more or less fixed; yet they were ethical rather than moral virtues. It was an era, in short, in which ethical elaborations related to specific virtues.

The relatively high specificity of virtues is but one corollary of a regime of ethical fixation. Other such corollaries relate to what might be called the *ethical threshold*, the *demarcation of ethics from morals*, and the *demarcation of authority*. The Victorian era could be said to have been characterized by a high ethical threshold in that only the select few could be cultivated or ethically valuable. Romantic culture, and the aestheticism of the later Victorian period, were, of course, strictly elitist projects. This meant that there was a relatively firm demarcation of ethics from morals. Of course, everyone was expected to act in a moral way; but only the best could be truly ethical, since this required practices of conscience and hence a certain degree of freedom. As for the masses and the others, their destiny was to be not ethical culture but *moral* regulation (cf. Corrigan and Sawyer, 1985; Mort, 1987). Precepts of good conduct applied to all; but only the few could expect the intensity of an ethical relation to self in which, for instance, 'one is called upon to take oneself as an object of knowledge and a field of action, so as to transform, correct, and purify oneself, and find salvation' (Foucault, 1986a: 42). Lastly, the demarcation of authority took a fairly rigid form. This is not to say that the structures of authority simply overlapped with established criteria of class favouritism or elitist privilege. Authority, no doubt, required more than the blandishments of high birth as its guarantor, one had to become an authority, to work upon oneself, to become irritable. Yet, equally, being in authority clearly represented a different order of existence from not being in authority. In other words, authority took on a kind of monolithic, more or less non-negotiable form.

At the other end of the scale of ethical stylizations one might envisage a different sort of regime. One may, for instance, envisage societies where an ethical intensification is not related to specific virtues. At the other end of the scale from fixated, muscular Victorian ethics, we might consider eras – maybe such as our own – in which dominant ethics are less specific with regard to the contents of virtuous traits. Such a society might be characterized by a certain ethical flotation (cf. Donzelot, 1979: Ch. 5). Here, specific virtues are allowed to float in relation to ethical codes. It is not that virtues have no place; but rather that there is no fixed relation between a particular ethical regime and the cultivation of certain virtues. Yet the intensity of the ethical charge levied on social existence will be none the less for all that; the argument is not necessarily that our societies have witnessed a diminution of ethical or moral bonds; that the only way forward is moral disintegration. Rather, it is that we live in societies in which the constitution of subjectivity on the basis of a relation to the self is pushed to some kind of an extreme, yet in which there is a certain pluralization with regard to the substance of such ethical demands. It is not that we live in an immoral world. Rather, we live in a world that is saturated with a diversity of ethical stylizations, but which is low on specificity when it comes to ethical content.

The notion of flotation makes for a nice metaphor not just because it suggests a degree of flexibility with regard to the cultivation of specific virtues, but because of its obvious association with economic forms of rationality. The fact of flotation suggests that there is a market in ethics. And this is indeed the case. Within the general parameters of a social system that places a premium upon the cultivation of the ethical life – be it through the life of the body, the intellect, the soul, the emotions, intentionality or the erogenous zones – there is room for rival ethical values to seek their own equilibrium.

Such a regime of ethical manners would also be characterized by a low ethical threshold. Anybody can take part in the ethical life; perhaps the cultivation of self actually becomes something like an attribute of democratic citizenship. Similarly, there would be in such regimes a relatively low demarcation from the moral sphere. A regime of low ethical fixity would not set up a rigid demarcation between the ethical and the moral spheres. Hence we see that, paradoxically, ethical flotation can lead to the prevalence of a kind of low-grade moralism; think, for example, of how enlightened psychosomatic discourses, or psychological designations in general, also function as instruments of blame. Lastly, within a regime of ethical flotation there will be no monopoly on the rights of authority. Authority will take the form less of a kind of status than of a kind of practice. And, typically, authority will be relational rather than uniform. That is to say, not only does authority take the form of expertise over relations rather than identities or statuses, but the practice of authority will be relational to the circumstances in which – and the personae upon which – it is practised, and that the function of authority will be to set up a relation between the individual and the self. Another way of saying this is to point to the way in which authority frequently becomes reflexive, its own powers subjected to critical scrutiny (Miller and Rose, 1994: 59). All these might be features of an ethical flotation.

Concluding Ethical Postscript

There are two broad approaches to constructionism in social theory (cf. Velody, 1994). On one hand we have what could be called macho constructionism; this is the kind we are used to from the sociology of science. The macho constructionist likes to be iconoclastic, generating drama by saying 'Look here! You thought this or that was natural but it's not, it's constructed all along!' But I have not been macho constructionist in this chapter. It generates less drama to say that ethics are constructed than it does to say, even these days, that scientific facts are constructed. Perhaps this is ultimately down to Kant. It is certainly at the heart of the way that someone like that notable Kantian Michel Foucault thinks about ethics:

> Among the radical novelties of Kant was the notion that we *construct* our ethical position. Kant said we do this by recourse to reason, but the innovation is not reason but construction. Kant taught that the only was the moral law can be moral is if we make it. Foucault's historicism combined with that notion of constructing morality leads one away from the letter and law of Kant, but curiously preserves Kant's spirit. (Hacking, 1986: 239, as quoted in Owen, 1994: 202; cf. Foucault, 1984: 372)

This constructionism does not just relate to the fabrication of particular ethical choices, problems or virtues. It relates to the very possibility of being an ethical animal with the capability – if hardly the right – to make ethical choices in the construction of particular ethical stylizations. And here one might perhaps be deceived into envisaging a certain alignment with a second predominant approach to constructionism. This is the phenomenological constructionism that currently seems to be popular, especially in social psychology. This kind of constructionism says that the self is produced through both human interaction and various kinds of non-human mediations; that subjectivity itself is the product of construction. But, in fact, I have not wanted to take this road. It is much more interesting to consider, not the diverse forms through which subjectivity is produced, but how our subjective lives are subjected to various sorts of authority. Ethics are not constructed out of nothing. They are effects of the construction of authority. In this sense, it is more interesting to be constructionist abut authority than ethics.

There is also a contemporary reason for this preference. It is related, too, to a possible ethic for social theory itself. Ethics is interesting in relation to authority because it is through forms of ethical authority that our very freedom is governed. The question of ethics is intrinsically tied to that of freedom. It is true that the social sciences have generally preferred to work with notions of constraint rather than freedom. But freedom might be analysed in its own right. Nikolas Rose, for example, has proposed that we complement our notions of freedom as resistance with an attention to freedom as a formula of power (Rajchman, 1991: 109–21; Rose, 1992b: 3; cf. Bauman, 1988). We live in 'free societies'; that is, not so much societies that *are* free, but societies which take freedom as a principal resource for rule. In our societies, freedom is not simply an end of government but a condition of the security or integrity of government; to govern without respect for liberty would be to govern badly, that is, cumbersomely, indelicately, inefficiently (Gordon, 1991: 19–20). In any case, freedom itself is not a natural kind; freedom requires principles of production, means of technicization, and norms of realization. Sociology might concern itself with the study of such formulae of freedom. It is the perception of our ethics, and our ethical perceptions, that guide us in relation to those spaces of indetermination which constitute the condition of our freedoms. As Foucault observed: 'Freedom is the ontological condition of ethics. But ethics is the positive form given to freedom' (Foucault, 1986b: 3; translation altered). To study ethics and the relation of ethics to systems of authority might be, in this sense, to study the way that people model their own freedom and subject their freedoms to the regulation of others. It would be a move towards a critical sociology of the limits of our freedoms.

References

Arendt, H. (1961) *Between Past and Future*. London: Faber and Faber.
Bauman, Z. (1988) *Freedom*. Milton Keynes: Open University Press.
Campbell, C. (1987) *The Romantic Ethic and the Spirit of Modern Consumerism*. Oxford: Blackwell.
Clark, J.C.D. (1985) *English Society, 1688–1832*. Cambridge: Cambridge University Press.
Collini, S. (1991) *Public Moralists: Political Thought and Intellectual Life in Britain 1850–1930*. Oxford: Oxford University Press.
Corrigan, P. and Sayer, D. (1985) *The Great Arch: English State Formation as Cultural Revolution*. Oxford: Blackwell.
Dean, M. (1994) *Critical and Effective Histories*. London: Routledge.
Deleuze, G. (1988) *Spinoza, Practical Philosophy*. San Francisco: City Lights.
Donzelot, J. (1979) *The Policing of Families*. London: Macmillan.
Elias, N. (1983) *The Court Society*, trans. E. Jephcott. Oxford: Blackwell.
Foucault, M. (1984) 'On the genealogy of ethics', in P. Rabnow (ed.), *The Foucault Reader*. Harmondsworth: Penguin. pp. 340–72.
Foucault, M. (1986a) *The Care of the Self*. Harmondsworth: Penguin.
Foucault, M. (1986b) 'The ethic of the care of the self as a practice of freedom', in J. Bernauer and D. Rasmussen (eds), *The Final Foucault*. Cambridge, MA: MIT Press.
Foucault, M. (1989) *Résumé des cours*. Paris: Vuillard.
Gay, P. (1984) *The Bourgeois Experience*. Oxford: Oxford University Press.
Gellner, E. (1987) *Culture, Identity and Politics*. Cambridge: Cambridge University Press.

Gordon, C. (1991) 'Governmental rationality: an introduction', in G. Burchell, C. Gordon and P. Miller (eds), *The Foucault Effect*. Hemel Hempstead: Harvester Wheatsheaf. pp. 1–51.

Hacking, I. (1982) 'Language, truth and reason', in M. Hollis and S. Lukes (eds), *Rationality and Relativism*. Oxford: Blackwell. pp. 48–66.

Hacking, I. (1986) 'Self-improvement', in D.C. Hoy (ed.), *Foucault: A Critical Reader*. Oxford: Blackwell. pp. 235–40.

Keegan, J. (1988) *The Mask of Command*. Harmondsworth: Penguin.

Larmore, C. (1987) *Patterns of Moral Complexity*. Cambridge: Cambridge University Press.

Miller, P. and Rose, N. (1994) 'On therapeutic authority', *History of the Human Sciences*, 7(3): 29–64.

Minson, J. (1993) *Questions of Conduct*. London: Macmillan.

Mort, F. (1987) *Dangerous Sexualities*. London: Routledge & Kegan Paul.

Osborne, T. (1993) 'Mobilizing psychoanalysis: Michael Balint and the general practitioners', *Social Studies of Science*, 23(1): 175–200.

Osborne, T. (1994a) 'Bureaucracy as a vocation: governmentality and administration in nineteenth century Britain', *Journal of Historical Sociology*, 7(3): 289–313.

Osborne, T. (1994b) 'Power and persons: on ethical stylisation and person-centred medicine', *Sociology of Health and Illness*, 16(4): 515–35.

Owen, D. (1994) *Maturity and Modernity: Nietzsche, Weber, Foucault and the Ambivalence of Reason*. London: Routledge.

PP (Parliamentary Papers) 1854–55 [1870], Vol. XX (Report and Papers Relating to the Reorganization of the Civil Service).

Rajchman, J. (1991) *Truth and Eros*. London: Routledge.

Rose, N. (1992a) 'Engineering the human soul: analyzing psychological expertise', *Science in Context*, 5(2): 351–69.

Rose, N. (1992b) 'Towards a critical sociology of freedom', inaugural lecture, London, Goldsmiths' College, mimeo.

Scheler, M. (1987) 'Exemplars of persons and leaders', in M.S. Frings (ed. and trans.), *Person and Self-Value: Three Essays*. Dordrecht: Martinus Nijhoff. pp. 127–98.

Schroeder, R. (1995) 'Disenchantment and its discontents: Weberian perspectives on science and technology', *Sociological Review*, 43(2): 227–50.

Velody, I. (1994) 'Introduction', *History of the Human Sciences*, 7(2): 1–7.

Veyne, P. (1987) 'L'individu atteint au coeur par la puissance publique', in P. Veyne et al. *Sur L'Individu*, Paris: Seuil.

Watt, D.C. (1982) *Authority*. London: Croom Helm.

Index

Note: The letter n following a page number indicates a reference in the notes.